Also by Daniel F. Tortora

HELP! THIS ANIMAL IS DRIVING ME CRAZY:
Solutions to Your Dog's Behavior Problems

Choosing a Breed That Matches Your Personality, Family and Life-style

THE RIGHT DOG FOR YOU

Daniel F. Tortora, Ph.D.

A FIRESIDE BOOK
Published by Simon & Schuster
New York   London   Toronto   Sydney   Tokyo   Singapore

FIRESIDE and colophon are registered trademarks
of Simon & Schuster, Inc.

Designed by Stanley S. Drate
Manufactured in the United States of America

20   19   18   17   16   15   14   13   Pbk.

Library of Congress Cataloging in Publication Data

Tortora, Daniel F,   date.
  The right dog for you.

  Includes index.
  1. Dog breeds. 2. Dogs—Buying. I. Title.
SF426.T67   636.7′081   80-10845

ISBN 0-671-24221-0
ISBN 0-671-47247-X Pbk.

ACKNOWLEDGMENTS

This book could not have been written without the help of the numerous breeders, trainers and veterinarians who have, over the years, shared their experiences with me. Nor could it have been written without the information supplied by the researchers in canine behavior such as John Paul Scott, John L. Fuller and others who have spent a lifetime studying breed differences in dogs.

Finally, and most important, this book would not have been written without the patient help and assistance supplied by my secretary, Pat Brennan. She transformed my illegible and semiliterate draft into a readable and literate manuscript. She also helped—and this was a very tedious and time-consuming activity—to construct the numerous graphs and tables presented in this book.

DEDICATION

To my daughter and son, Dawn and Danny, who patiently and understandingly suffered the loss of a responsive father during the time it took to complete this manuscript;

and,

To my dogs, Smokey, a Miniature Schnauzer, and Captain, a Mastiff, who patiently listened to drafts of the chapters herein and provided valuable inside information on at least two breeds of dogs.

Contents

List of Tables

List of Figures

Introduction

I was recently visited by a woman I shall call Barbara Smith and her charming, quiet, petite ten-year-old daughter, Dolores. They had a beautiful chocolate-colored eight-month-old male, Labrador Retriever named Coco in tow. More accurately, *he* was towing *them*. Dolores had bruises all over her arms and legs. They told me that Dolores had been playing with Coco when suddenly he had started to treat her like a toy, dragging her around by her arms and legs. There were no puncture wounds, but it was still a serious situation, and it became my job to determine the cause for such behavior, which was most unusual for a Labrador Retriever.

The background to this story turned out to be very interesting and revealing. Barbara was a live-in cook and housekeeper for an affluent family I shall call the Johnstones. Eight months previously the Johnstones had decided to get a Lab puppy. They had had a Labrador Retriever twelve years before this and continued to have an affection for the breed. In addition Mrs. Johnstone felt that her thirteen-year-old boy, Jeff, needed a dog, and a rare, chocolate-colored Lab would be a nice show and conversation piece, its color harmonizing perfectly with the decor of her house. They had selected Coco as the largest puppy from a particularly big-boned litter of one of the largest-sized lines of Labs.

As Coco grew, so did Barbara's apprehension. It quickly became her responsibility to take complete care of the dog. The Johnstones were simply too busy. Jeff had taken the dog out three times in the last eight months. He never fed the dog consistently; that became Dolores' job. When Mr. Johnstone insisted that Coco be made controllable, his wife tried her hand at training the dog, but soon Barbara had to take over because Mrs. Johnstone's career responsibilities didn't allow her the time for training. Eventually a trainer was hired who managed to teach Coco to obey a few simple commands, but Barbara was too frail and nondominant to maintain even this minimum control, and the "puppy," who was steadily increasing in size, strength, vigor and forcefulness of behavior, soon lost what little obedience he had learned. By the time I saw him at eight months he stood almost 2 feet tall at the shoulders and weighed about 85 pounds, an inch and 10 pounds over the standard for this breed, and he still had six to ten months of growing to reach his full potential size and weight. Except for Coco's uncontrolled, vigorous puppy exuberance and his tendency to eat the furniture, both of which behaviors had gone unchecked, the Johnstones had felt their dog was developing beautifully—until the incident occurred with Dolores.

After a lengthy interview with all the members of the Johnstone family, it became clear to me that this breed of dog was totally unsuited to both the personality and the life-style of the family into which he had been thrust. Coco was not a vicious child molester, but at this point in the family's life they were not the kind of people who could exert the necessary control over this dominant and powerful dog. Mrs. Johnstone was actively involved in a new career; Mr. Johnstone's business responsibilities made him a weekend father; Jeff was far more interested in girls and baseball than in dogs. Earlier in their lives, Mr. and Mrs. Johnstone had handled this breed successfully, but their present life-style precluded this. So the dog was raised now by their rather submissive housekeeper and her small daughter, neither of whom was temperamentally or physically suited to the breed's exuberant characteristics. The dog's behavior had essentially gone unchecked for eight months, and finally Dolores, through no fault of her own, had felt the effects.

If the Johnstones had gotten any of a number of other breeds that were more suitable to their current life-style, this whole scenario would not have occurred. Maybe the Johnstones were irresponsible for not making sure that Coco was under control, but I think they could be better described as ignorant of the potential hazard.

This may seem like a rather extreme example of the potential consequences of a mismatch between the temperament of a breed of dog and its caretakers' personality and life-style. I would hope it is rare, but given the facts that there are over fifty million dogs owned in the United States and an estimated *one million five hundred thousand serious dog bites reported each year*, it may not be as rare as you might expect. This works out to be one serious bite *reported* for every thirty-three dogs owned in the United States, and most incidents like the one with Dolores go unreported. The tragic result is that over *three hundred dogs* are put to death *each day* for curable behavior problems. A "problem" is, of course, defined as such from the owner's point of view. Bowser may have great fun tearing gaping holes in his master's new, $4,000 sofa.

I don't mean to imply that all of these incidents are caused by a human–dog mismatch. Surely some are, but many are not. Nor do I mean to suggest that you are taking your life or furniture into your hands when you choose to obtain a dog. I just want to highlight the seriousness of a decision to get a dog and the importance of the choice of breed.

The best choice, leading to the most satisfactory relationship between pet and caretaker, is the one that matches the personality and unique life-style of the owners with the temperamental characteristics of the breed. Given the diversity of human personality and life-style and the difference in temperament and appearance of various breeds of dogs, it seems reasonable and is, indeed, the premise of this book that one can find a unique match between person and pet.

Unfortunately, there are just too many differences between breeds to permit a quick rational judgment. There are 123 genetically distinct breeds of dogs registered by the American Kennel Club. The species *Canis familiaris*—or common dogs— has the greatest diversity of appearance of all species of animals now or ever in existence, including *Homo sapiens*. It is understandable that you would tend to give up and select a breed on the basis of what you know, which may not be very much if you are the typical would-be pet owner. This book is designed to help you make this decision with some degree of rationality.

First, the word "temperament" will be defined and the relevant dimensions of temperament on which the breeds vary will be discussed.

Second, the temperament of all the breeds will be described using this common terminology. The information on breeds will be organized according to the American Kennel Club (AKC) functional classification—the Sporting Dogs, the Hounds, the Working Dogs, the Terriers, the Toy Dogs and the Non-Sporting Dogs. In successive chapters the breeds in each classification will be compared.

Finally, you will be given a series of do-it-yourself questionnaires that will help you decide in step-by-step fashion which breed suits you and your family for each dimension. Hopefully, at the end of this process you will have a good idea of how the breeds differ and which breeds are best suited to your personality and life-style. Armed with that information, and a considerably narrowed number of alternatives, you will be prepared to make a thoughtful choice.

An important point needs to be made. In this book I have chosen to describe characteristics of purebred dogs, that is, breeds for which the American Kennel Club has established a set of standards. Why have I chosen to ignore that most popular of pets, the mutt? The reason is that the physical and temperamental characteristics of mutts, dogs of unknown ancestry, are far less predictable than for their purebred cousins. Dog breeds were developed in the first place because dog owners saw some set of characteristics they wanted to perpetuate in the offspring. Offspring that did not have the characteristics were not bred further; offspring that did have the desired characteristics were bred with other offspring or similar dogs that also had those characteristics. Through this process pure breeds were created. If specimens of a pure breed are mated, their offspring reliably show the physical and temperamental traits of their forebears. Knowledge of the general characteristics of a pure breed can therefore be used to predict the physical and temperamental characteristics of any member of that breed. This knowledge is available only about purebred dogs. It is not available, by definition, about mutts.

Hence my decision to deal only with the 123 breeds* registered with the A.K.C.

I have assumed that you are looking for a dog that you can have fun with, that you will enjoy. Having a dog "for the fun of it" is exactly the right attitude to have. If you make a rational choice of a dog with a temperament that matches your individual personality and life-style, you will have great fun and the dog will have great fun with you.

*The 124th breed registered by the AKC, the Ibezian Hound, will not be described because it has only recently appeared in the United States and there is very little information on the breed.

1

Breed, Behavior and Temperament

What do we mean by "temperament"? We may think of terms such as loyal, congenial, affectionate, regal, aristocratic, tranquil, eager to please, shy, happy-go-lucky, attentive, alert, self-confident, energetic, obedient, sweet, rollicking, courageous, intelligent, gentle, upstanding and quiet. On the other side of the coin, we may think of words such as aggressive, mean, stupid, lazy, quarrelsome, aloof and so on.

These terms, normally used to describe a dog's behavior by everyday folk and by the American Kennel Club, are useful to the extent that they enable us to predict the behavior of a dog so labeled. For example, you would expect a shy dog to avoid strangers and novel objects, an affectionate dog to engage in a lot of nuzzling and licking, an obedient dog to train easily and retain its skills a long time. A rollicking dog would be one that does a lot of jumping and running about. A quiet dog is one that probably doesn't bark or howl very much. An attentive or alert dog is one that notices subtle changes in its environment or in its owners.

The problem, of course, is that there is no generally accepted definition for any of these potentially useful words. Even though we have just defined them my way, the average person may not agree with me or simply proceed to use the words any old way that pleases him or her at the moment.

In addition, these words have not been objectified by identifying, through a repeatable set of operations, the behaviors that go along with them. Since there is no standard set of operational definitions, we are free to use the words any way we choose, and we usually do. The result is labeling chaos.

To add to this chaos, we also use words like regal, aristocratic, congenial, courageous, upstanding, happy-go-lucky, sweet, quarrelsome and so on. These words do not reflect any definite canine behavior. I have never witnessed a quarrel among dogs, nor even a heated discussion, but I have seen a dog bark and fight with other dogs. Upstanding could mean standing erect and upright, but it is probably used in the sense of morally right and honest. You know, the kind of dog you would vote for.

There is a further problem in using such terms to describe temperament in dogs. Because all the previously mentioned terms are frequently used to describe human behavior too, we can fall into the trap of "anthropomorphizing" (i.e., attributing human characteristics to) the looks, temperament and behavior of dogs. This is an error of logic. It is best to remember that even though an English Bulldog may remind us of Winston Churchill, it would not really make an effective Prime Minister of England.

Canine Behavior

In spite of the fact that people frequently treat their pets like humans and think of their dog's behavior in human terms, dogs are canines. They are a member of the family Canidae, which includes wolves, coyotes, foxes, jackals and some obscure canids from Asia, Africa and South America. Our pets are also members of the genus *Canis* and the species *familiaris*. Table 1 provides a list of our dogs' family relatives.

Our pet dog, *Canis familiaris*, has roots that can be traced back some forty million years. It is commonly believed that the domestic dog, *Canis familiaris*, was developed from the Eurasian wolf, *Canis lupus*, beginning some twelve thousand years ago as the people who captured and domesticated wolf puppies started the practice of selective breeding. Each culture probably had a concept of what would be the most desirable behavioral and physical characteristics of the captured canines and mated those animals which exhibited these traits. Voilà! Twelve thousand years later we have 123 or more distinct breeds in the United States (500 throughout the world) varying

TABLE 1.
The Members of a Dog's Family, Canidae

Genus	Species	Common Name
Canis	familiaris	Domestic dog, also Australian dingo
Canis	lupus	Wolf. Europe, Asia *(C. lupus pallipos),* North America, Arctic
Canis	niger	Red wolf. North America, Texas Gulf region
Canis	latrans	Coyote. North & Central America
Canis	aureus	Asiatic jackal. South Asia and North Africa
Canis	mesomelus	Black-backed jackal. Africa
Canis	adustus	Side-striped jackal. Africa
Canis	simensis	Simenian jackal. Northeast Africa
Alopex	lagopus	Arctic fox. Arctic
Vulpes	velox	Swift fox. North America
Vulpes	macrotis	Kit fox. North America
Vulpes	vulpes	Red fox. North America, Asia, North Africa, Europe
Vulpes	corsac	Corsac fox. Central Asia
Vulpes	bengalensis	Bengal fox. South Asia
Vulpes	ruppelli	Sand fox. North Africa and Southwest Asia
Vulpes	pallida	Pale fox. North Africa
Vulpes	cana	Blanford's fox. South Asia
Vulpes	chama	Cape fox. South Africa
Vulpes	ferrilata	Tibetan sand fox. Central Asia
Fennecus	zerda	Fennec fox. North Africa and Southwest Asia
Urocyon	cinereo-argenteus	Gray fox. North and South America
Urocyon	littoralis	Island gray fox. Islands off North America
Nyctereutes	procyonides	Racconlike dog. East Asia
Dusicyon	culpacolus	Soriano, Uraguay
Dusicyon	culpaeus	Culpeo, more wolf- or doglike, in Bolivia and Chile, Andes of Ecuador
Dusicyon	fulvipes	Chiloe fox. Island of Chiloe (South America)
Dusicyon	griseus	Argentine gray fox. Patagonia
Dusicyon	gymmocercus	Azara's fox. Argentina
Dusicyon	inca	Southern Peru
Dusicyon	sechurae	Peru and Ecuador
Dusicyon	vetulus	Hoary fox (or small-toothed dog)
	(in subgenus *Lycalopex*)	South-central Brazil
Cerdocyon	thous	Crab-eating fox. Colombia
Atelocynus	microtis	Small-eared dog. Brazil
Chrysocyon	brachyurus	Maned wolf. Bolivia, Paraguay, Argentina
Cyon	alpinus	Asiatic wild dog
Icticyon	Speothos venaticus	South and Central American bush dog
Lycaon	pictus	African Cape hunting dog
Otocyon	megalotis	African bat-eared or Delalande fox

in size from the Chihuahua, which can be 4 to 6 inches at the shoulder and weigh less than six pounds, to the Mastiff, which can be as much as 34 inches at the shoulder and weigh over 200 pounds.

Only recently has the study of animal behavior in general, and that of *Canis familiaris* in particular, come under scientific scrutiny. Researchers in this area most frequently are interested in identifying the genetic determinants of behavior and temperament (instinctual behavior) and separating such behavior from behaviors and traits that develop as a result of reinforced practice (learned behavior).

Around 1950, Dr. John Paul Scott and Dr. John L. Fuller started what turned out to be a fifteen-year project on the genetics of canine social behavior. Some of their observations will be incorporated herein. For our purposes, the important conclusion to be drawn from this work is that canine temperament was reliably shown to vary with breeds, at least in the five breeds these researchers tested. It's a pretty safe inference that the rest of the breeds vary systematically in temperament as well.

There are certain behaviors that have developed over millions of years of evolutionary trial and error. Some of these behaviors are common to the whole family of *Canidae* and can be called *family-typical behaviors*. The set of behaviors common to the genus *Canis* are *genus-typical behaviors*. The set of behaviors common to the species *Canis familiaris* are *species-typical behaviors*. The set of behaviors common to specific breeds of dogs are *breed-typical behaviors*. Finally, each individual dog may exhibit more or less of these family, genus, species and breed typical behaviors in its *individual-typical behavior*. Thus I define temperament, in part, as the degree to which an individual dog exhibits these individual typical behaviors.

Table 2 gives some examples of family typical and genus typical facial expressions in canids.

You can see from Table 2 that some facial expressions are common to all canids. These are family-typical behaviors. For example, all canids show a submissive grin by pulling their lips way back. This facial expression seems to indicate to other canids and even to some other species, "You're the master; I

TABLE 2.
**Comparison of Facial Expressions in Canids and Primates
(after Van Hooff, 1967)**

Behavior Typical of:	Behavior	Situation/Motivation	Primate Counterpart
1. Genus: seen only in W, D and C*	Agonistic "pucker." Vertical retraction of lips.	Tendency to attack.	Tense-mouth face
2. Family: seen in all canids	Threat gape (marked in foxes)	Tendency to attack. Signals bite intention.	Open-mouth face
3. Genus: seen only in W, D and C	Threat gape with vertical and horizontal retraction of lips.	Signals bite intention with some flight tendency.	Staring bared-teeth, scream face
4. Genus: seen only in W, D and C	Above with wider gape and greater vertical lip retraction.	Defensive threat when escape is blocked.	Frowning bared-teeth scream face
5. Family: seen in all canids	Submissive grin (horizontal retraction of lips)	Low tendency to flee: ritualized appeasement.	Silent bared-teeth face: "smile"
6. Genus: seen only in W, D and C	Agonistic tooth snapping.	Tendency to flee.	Teeth-chattering
7. Genus: seen only in W, D and C	Licking intention.	Strong approach tendency and weaker flight tendency.	Lip-smacking face, tongue-smacking face
8. Genus: seen only in W, D and C	Nibbling intention.	Strong approach tendency and weaker flight tendency.	Chewing-smacking face, snarl-smacking face
9. Genus: seen only in W, D and C	Submissive rooting approach and forepaw raising.	Approach (infant–mother) intention movement to take nipple in mouth, and between adults.	Pout face
10. Family: seen in all canids	Play face: relaxed open-mouth face	During play or leads to play.	Relaxed open-mouth face

*W = Wolf.   D = Domestic Dog.   C = Coyote.

don't want to fight, and I'm not going to run away. So don't be aggressive toward me; let's be friends and I'll obey you." It's amazing what a smile can say.

A genus-typical behavior would be common only to dogs, wolves and coyotes. Submissive rooting is genus-typical. Your dog does this when he comes up to you and nuzzles his head under your hand or arm and pushes up or forward. Some people would call this a kind of cuddling behavior. It also occurs when your dog puts his paw on your hand or lap. Your dog is probably saying through this behavior, "Pay attention to me, scratch my head, pet me."

I have included another column in Table 2 labeled "Primate Counterpart." I did this to show how we as humans can sometimes understand what our dogs are trying to communicate. Human beings, *Homo sapiens,* are primates. We share some common behavioral characteristics with our simian cousins, the Great Apes, Orangutans and Chimps. Interestingly, these primate-typical behaviors are sometimes similar to our canine comrades' genus-typical behaviors. For example, smiling in people probably means about the same thing as the submissive grin in dogs. They both say, "I'm friendly; I'm not going to be a threat; in fact, I acknowledge your dominance over me."

This is probably why humans have been able to cohabit with canines for so long. We are both pack or social animals and share some social signals. This is also why humans have the unfortunate habit of anthropomorphizing canine behavior. We interpret the behavior of dogs as if it were human and give dog behavior human labels. Sometimes our interpretations are on the mark, especially when there is a congruence between human and canine social signals. This lulls us into believing that our interpretations will be always right. This conclusion, of course, is in error, because there are an equal number of social signals we don't share with dogs. For the most part, men don't define the boundaries of their territory by lifting their legs and urinating on the nearest tree or bush. Thus, it would be better for us to avoid anthropomorphizing our dog's temperamental characteristics. Rather, we need to categorize a dog's temperament along dimensions of canine genus- and species-typical behavior.

Dimensions of Temperament

Categorizing a dog's temperament along dimensions has two advantages over the use of terms like quarrelsome, congenial, loyal, etc., that I mentioned earlier. First, it provides "evolutionary validity" for our definition of temperament. That is, it connects the definition to the body of knowledge that has been accumulated on the evolutionary and genetic determinants of canine behavior. Secondly, a consideration of "dimensions" of temperament permits us to specify much more precisely what we are talking about. When our descriptions are dimensionalized, we can begin to say that some breeds show more or less of a temperamental trait than others, and we can specify how large the difference is. Defining a breed's temperament by locating its typical behavior along several dimensions will thus allow you to compare that breed's behavior with the behavior of other breeds. This in turn will provide you with information you need to match your own personality and life-style to the temperament of a particular breed.

To dimensionalize a component of temperament, we define the end points of that component and then define a series of points between those end points. By doing this, the component becomes a dimension and we can then locate any breed's behavior along that dimension. I have followed this procedure to generate sixteen dimensions that I think are the most relevant in identifying temperament differences among breeds. Those dimensions are listed in Table 3.

Several different sources were used to locate each breed on each of these dimensions of temperament. These sources included: data from surveys of veterinarians, obedience trainers, groomers and other animal service personnel; measurements taken from samples of the various breeds; breed books and dog encyclopedias; and various relevant scientific books and papers. Finally, I have drawn heavily upon data I have collected and experiences I have had while working with behavior problems in dogs.

It is also possible to infer at least some of the general behavior characteristics of each breed and breed type from the

TABLE 3

Dimensions of Temperament in Dogs and General and Specific Levels of Each Dimension

Dimension	General Levels of Dimensions				
	Very high	High	Medium	Low	Very low
	Specific Levels of Dimensions				
1. Indoor activity	Very active	Active	Moderate	Inactive	Very inactive
2. Outdoor activity	Very active	Active	Moderate	Inactive	Very inactive
3. Vigor	Very vigorous	Vigorous	Moderate	Gentle	Very gentle
4. Behavioral constancy	Very constant	Constant	Moderate	Variable	Very variable
5. Dominance—strange dogs	Very dominant	Dominant	Intermediate	Submissive	Very submissive
6. Dominance—familiar people	Very dominant	Dominant	Intermediate	Submissive	Very submissive
7. Territoriality	Extreme	High	Moderate	Low	None
8. Emotional stability	Very stable	Stable	Normal	Vacillating	Greatly vacillating
9. Sociability—within family	Any person	Open family	One family	One person	No person
10. Sociability—with children	Very sociable	Sociable	Tolerant	Bad	Dangerous
11. Sociability—with strangers	Any person	Friendly	Tolerant	Reserved	Dangerous
12. Learning—rate	Very fast	Fast	Moderate	Slow	Very slow
13. Learning—obedience	Very good	Good	Average	Poor	Very poor
14. Learning—problem solving	Very good	Good	Average	Poor	Very poor
15. Watchdog ability	Very alert	Alert	Moderate	Sluggish	Very sluggish
16. Guard-dog ability	Very aggressive	Aggressive	Moderate	Passive	Very passive

facts of average body size, shape and function, and by sifting through the mass of propaganda, hearsay and opinions commonly held by the "experts." For example, we would expect that a breed specializing in guarding would have a different temperament profile from that of a breed designed for following small animals into their burrows. There are also some general rules about behavior that relate to body size and even coat color. Very tiny breeds have trouble maintaining their body temperature, and this can have effects on temperament. Coat color is related to the amount of melanin, a skin pigment, which also can have behavioral effects.

Finally, breed devotees sometimes make some slips of the tongue or pen that may expose their animal's true nature. Sigmund Freud said that "It is impossible to keep a secret; we leak self-disclosure from every pore." Perhaps this is an over-statement, but it surely occurs on occasion. For example, the A.K.C. description of an Airedale, a terrier, is glowing until it says, "Its disposition can be molded by the patience of the master." Reading between the lines, we can assume that Airedales might tend to be difficult to get along with, and an owner will need to spend some time and energy if he or she wants a sociable, obedient pet.

Hopefully, combining the facts, results of my measurements analyses of written descriptions, opinions of professionals working with dogs, and my own experience, I will be able to approximate a hypothetical picture of the average temperament of each breed. To do this I have summarized what has been said about each breed by the breeders, handlers and trainers I have interviewed. I have combined this information with my observations of the breed and descriptions of breeds published by breed books, the *American Kennel Club Complete Dog Book* and other dog encyclopedias.

Now that you have a general idea of how I intend to differentiate the various breeds of dogs, I want to become much more specific. As you can see in Table 3, I have taken each of the dimensions of temperament and expanded it into a five-point scale. Each point represents a level on its associated dimension and is defined by a representative set of behaviors. You will note that four of the dimensions—activity, dominance, sociability and learning—are further broken down into more specific subdimensions.

Activity. Activity is defined as the rate of behaviors per unit of time. A very active dog is one that eats and drinks very fast; is easily aroused sexually or playfully; is constantly on the move outdoors, sniffing, smelling everything; is very exploratory, investigating every new thing in its environment; may pace and seem restless indoors; scratches and grooms itself a lot; solicits play from its owners or other dogs constantly. A very inactive dog does not do all the above-mentioned things, since it is spending most of its waking hours resting. Moderate activity involves about a 50–50 split between resting and moving. An active dog does more moving than resting and an inactive dog does more resting than moving. The activity dimension will be evaluated separately for indoor behavior and outdoor behavior.

	The Activity Dimension (Indoor and Outdoor)
Levels:	*Description of Typical Behavior*
Very active	Always on the go, moving continuously, "restless."
Active	On the go most of the time, moving at least 75% of the time.
Moderate	Moving and resting about equally.
Inactive	Never on the go for very long. Resting about 75% of the time.
Very inactive	Always resting, sleeping at least 90% of the time, "lazy."

Vigor. The vigor dimension relates to the force or intensity of behavior regardless of rate. A very vigorous dog eats and drinks with large gulps, pulls and pushes on objects with great force, strains on the leash, snaps food from its owner's hand, runs with great endurance over rough terrain, attempts to overcome obstacles by applying progressively more force, jumps great heights, carries heavy objects and so on. A very gentle dog does just the opposite: it takes food from the hand easily, collapses under the weight of a relatively light object, does not pull on the leash and so on. An animal classified as moderate does some things forcefully and some things gently.

Levels:	The Vigor Dimension Description of Typical Behavior
Very vigorous	Does almost everything with great force, regardless of the demands of the situation.
Vigorous	Acts with force at least 75% of the time.
Moderate	Moderates its force in accordance with the needs of the situation.
Gentle	Is gentle at least 75% of the time.
Very gentle	Does almost everything gently, even if the situation calls for vigor.

Behavioral Constancy. The behavioral constancy dimension relates to how many different behaviors a dog will engage in per unit of time. It can be considered to be independent of both activity and vigor. A constant dog engages in a few activities most of his waking hours. A variable dog goes from one behavior to another and is easily distractable.

Levels:	The Behavioral-constancy Dimension Description of Typical Behavior
Very constant	This dog would be almost impossible to distract once it started a behavioral sequence. It would chase that rabbit until exhausted, running past bitches in heat and so on, or play continuously ignoring anything else.
Constant	This type of dog would remain on a behavioral sequence about 75% of the time.
Moderate	This type of dog could be distracted about 50% of the time.
Variable	This type of dog could be distracted about 75% of the time.

Very variable	Highly distractable, going from ne behavioral sequence to another. It it was chasing a rabbit and you threw a ball, it would break off the chase and fetch the ball. As it was returning with the ball, if it caught a scent it would drop the ball and track the scent. While on the scent, if you started playing, it would start playing and lose the trail and so on.

Dominance and Territoriality. The dominance dimension relates to the probability that a dog will assume a dominant or submissive posture given another dog or person attempting to dominate it. Dominance is related to territoriality, which can be defined as the extent to which a dog will stake out, mark and guard a territory from intruding dogs and people and also by the size of the territory it claims as its own. However, it must be understood that a dog may be dominant, submissive or territorial toward other dogs and not toward people, and vice versa, so ratings in these dimensions must take into consideration the species with which the dog is interacting. Thus, the dominance dimension will be further broken down into dominance with strange dogs and with familiar people.

Levels:	*The Dominance Dimension* *Description of Typical Behavior*
Very dominant	Attempts to exert dominance over every dog and/or person with whom it interacts, regardless of the other's behavior.
Dominant	Dominates 75% of its interactions with dogs and/or people.
Intermediate	Moderates its behavior according to the behavior of the animal and/or person with whom it is interacting. Dominant behaviors would result in submissive postures, and submissive postures would result in dominance behaviors in the intermediate animal.

Submissive

Submissive in 75% of its interactions with dogs and/or people.

Very submissive

Submissive to every dog and/or person with whom it interacts regardless of the other's behavior.

Levels:

The Territoriality Dimension
Description of Typical Behavior

Extreme territoriality

Tends to guard a large territory extending beyond its home base and get progressively more aggressive the deeper an intruder dog and/or person penetrates its territory. Considerable boundary marking. Aggression may include attacks on intruders at the periphery of its territory.

High territoriality

Territory limited to the area immediately surrounding dog's home base. Aggressive about 75% of the times an intruder violates its territory. Aggression may include attacks or threats of attacks if intruder gets close enough to personal space.

Moderate territoriality

Territory includes only dog's home base, perhaps only the inside of the house. Aggressive or threatening about 50% of the times an intruder violates this territory. Aggression in most cases involves only barking and sometimes growling.

Low territoriality

Territory includes only a small personal space around dog. Aggressive only 25% of the times the space is violated. Aggression involves only threat postures.

Not territorial

Appears to have no territory. Accepts an animal and/or person on its "territory" with no signs of aggression. Little or no boundary marking. Unconcerned about violations of its personal space.

Emotional Stability. The emotional stability dimension takes into consideration the fact that emotional behavior varies over time. Some animals, characterized as high-strung or nervous, vacillate greatly over a short period of time. The owners' observations are that "At one moment he will be happy and in the next he will be aggressive." They often report that their dog is "moody" and that mood changes cannot be predicted. On the other hand, there are animals characterized as "easygoing." They seem to stay in the same mood no matter what happens. Usually easygoing implies friendly behaviors. However, an animal can be considered emotionally stable by reason of being consistently aggressive. What counts is that the mood doesn't vary over time, not the quality of the mood.

Levels:	The Emotional-stability Dimension Description of Typical Behaviors
Very stable	Stays almost perpetually in the same mood.
Stable	Stays about 75% of the time in the same mood. Changes are slow and small and may be explained by natural circadian rhythms.
Normal	Mood swings are moderate and are related to the natural circadian, seasonal and diurnal changes.
Vacillating	Changes mood about 75% of the time. The changes aren't fast but occur frequently, at least once per day.
Greatly Vacillating	Changes moods from moment to moment.

Sociability. The sociability dimension relates to the number and type of people an animal can stand to be with in an enclosed space and the number and speed of friendly bonds the animal is prepared to make.

Levels:	*The Sociability Dimension* *Description of Typical Behaviors*
Very sociable	Greets everyone as a friend. Will greet and rapidly bond with anyone showing the slightest degree of friendliness. May even bond with people who dislike dogs, thereby annoying them, and ignoring their rejections. Comfortable in large crowds with many people touching and playing with them.
Sociable	A one-family dog. All the members of its family are its friends, and their friends are also usually accepted. Usually "warms up" to someone after a few minutes of playful interaction and accepts that person's friendship from then on. Relatively comfortable in medium-sized crowds, but will learn to avoid people who reject it.
Moderate	A small-family dog. Owners tend to describe this dog as "reserved" with strangers and "slow to warm up." After many pleasant experiences it will form a bond with a few others besides its caretaker, but these bonds will be weaker. It is uncomfortable in crowds greater than five and will typically ignore strangers or sniff them and walk away.
Solitary	A small-family or one-person dog. Owners tend to describe the dog as "shy with most strangers." It will, over a relatively long period, form a permanent bond with a few persons, usually the ones who care for it. May tolerate other people but mostly stays away from them. Uncomfortable in crowds greater than two, one of them its master. Typically avoids most strangers and many children.

Very solitary   A one- or no-person dog. Its owners typi-
                         cally describe its behavior as "aloof and
                         independent," sometimes even with them.
                         Even over long periods of time it may not
                         completely accept the owner. It is uncom-
                         fortable in crowds greater than one, its
                         owner. It will typically avoid its owner's
                         friends and strangers. Will remain with
                         you as long as you feed it. May even refuse
                         food at times.

The sociability dimension is a complex one, because the dog's probable reactions to its master and the family with whom it resides, the dog's reaction to visiting adults who are strangers to the dog, and its potential behavior toward children must be considered separately. There is some overlap in the levels of the sociability dimension. For example, at the moderately sociable level there are some breeds that (1) tend to be one-person dogs, (2) may be friendly with adult strangers, but (3) may be unsuitable for small children. Because of this complexity, each of the areas of sociability will eventually be discussed individually.

Learning Rate. The learning rate dimension relates to how many experiences are necessary for an animal to learn something about its social or physical environment. This dimension along with the next two, obedience and problem-solving ability, can all be considered to fall under the general rubric of learning dimensions.

	The Learning-rate Dimension
Levels:	*Description of Typical Behavior*
Very fast	Acquires habits in one or two exposures to the learning contingencies and will retain these for long periods without the need for repetition or practice.
Fast	Acquires habits in five to fifteen exposures and retains them perfectly with the benefit of repetition or practice.

Moderate	Takes fifteen or thirty experiences to acquire a habit. At the point of learning, the animal can benefit by repetition and practice.
Slow	Requires thirty to eighty experiences to acquire a habit. The habits are weak, will benefit by repetition and needs practice to prevent forgetting.
Very slow	Requires perhaps hundreds of sessions to learn what the very fast learner acquired in one session. The session must be repeated, or forgetting occurs rapidly and sometimes in spite of practice.

Obedience. Obedience is more of a social learning variable. Thus, an animal may be a fast learner and still be disobedient by refusing to respond to the owner's commands. Owners typically say that their animals know what to do but refuse to do it for them, and frequently label their animals as "stubborn."

Levels:	*The Obedience Dimension* *Description of Typical Behavior*
Very good	Obeys all commands within seconds after they are given, whether the owner is near or distant from the animal. It will heel, come when called, stay on command with the owner out of sight.
Good	Obeys 75% of the time, responding to the owner's commands within seconds after they are given. Does most of the things the very good dog will do except less frequently. Usually there is a distant point of impunity beyond which the dog will not comply.
Fair	Obeys immediately about 50% of the time, usually when the owner is perceived to be in striking distance. Beyond a point of im-

punity the dog will almost completely ignore the owner's commands. Occasionally obeys commands when they are screamed.

Poor   Obeys only 25% of the time, "when it feels like it," and ignores the owner if at a distance. The owner usually resorts to screaming a lot at this animal or rationalizing that the animal is independent.

Very poor   "Unruly." Refuses to comply with commands and fights owner's attempts to enforce his authority.

Problem Solving. The problem-solving dimension relates to the dog's ability to get around obstacles in order to get what it wants. Very good problem solvers can learn on their own to open doors and windows, dig out of enclosures, open refrigerators, find objects, etc. The very poor problem solver has trouble in changing its behavior, even though that behavior does not produce a solution to a problem.

Levels:	*The Problem-solving Dimension* *Description of Typical Behavior*
Very good	Gets into and out of situations rapidly. Not deterred by detours, locked doors or closed windows. Learns to solve these and other problems rapidly, retains these solutions a long time and abandons them when ineffective. Owners typically call this dog intelligent.
Good	Solves about 75% of the problems encountered.
Fair or normal	Solves about 50% of the problems encountered. The solutions are usually retained, but the animal may persistently attempt to use solutions that were effective but now are ineffective.

Poor	Solves about 25% of the problems encountered.
Very poor	Barely solves any problems. If path is blocked, sits there perplexed. If it happens to stumble onto a solution, dog may not remember to use it the next time. Owners typically call this dog stupid.

Watchdog and Guard-dog Abilities. The last two dimensions we will consider are the abilities that relate to watch and guard work. A watchdog simply barks to alert its owners to a potential intruder. A guard dog will threaten intruders, hold them at bay and, in extreme cases, attack them. Many breeds can be trained to be watch, guard or attack dogs; others exhibit these qualities more or less naturally; yet others are simply too friendly or sluggish to perform any of these functions well. For a watchdog we are talking about the degree of alertness or sensitivity to strange stimuli. The guard-dog dimension involves the degree of aggressiveness once aroused.

Levels:	*The Watch Dimension* *Description of Typical Behavior*
Very alert	Barks at the slightest strange stimulus, and keeps barking some time after the stimulation is over. Sometimes hypersensitive to stimuli and barks at insignificant things.
Alert	Barks at strange noises, but stops barking as soon as the stimulus stops. Shows some discrimination regarding what is barked at.
Normal	Barks spontaneously at about 50% of the strange stimuli it perceives, ignoring the rest. May bark if confronted directly with a stranger on the premises.
Sluggish	Can be made to bark if the owner works it up first and tries to get it excited. Usually you get one or two woofs and then the dog goes back to sleep.

| Very sluggish | Sleeps through house fires and burglaries. Such a sound sleeper that the owner has to shake it awake if he suspects an intruder and it still may fall back asleep. |

Levels:	*The Guard Dimension* *Description of Typical Behavior*
Aggressive	Naturally aggressive to any strangers entering its territory. May attack if provoked, or may just hold intruders at bay.
Natural	Usually holds intruders at bay by barking and growling, but has to be trained to attack.
Average	Gets confused with intruders, barking and growling indiscriminately at anyone. Without training it would be an undependable guard dog.
Accepting	Usually greets most strangers as friends. Occasionally encounters a stranger whom it fears.
Very accepting	Everyone's friend. Would not protect owner even when he/she was being attacked. May be playful under these circumstances.

The Rest of the Book

The six main breed types designated by the American Kennel Club have been used as chapter titles for the next six chapters. These breed types are the Sporting Dogs, the Hounds, the Working Dogs, the Terriers, the Toy Dogs and the Non-Sporting Dogs. I have constructed a format of information for each breed that parallels Table 3. The levels of dimensions of temperament are indicated for an adult male specimen of each breed, followed by relevant details concerning that breed which I have obtained from owners, trainers, breeders, veterinarians, handlers, my experience and a comprehensive search of the literature. To assess the temperament for females of the breed, a few simple rules of thumb have been developed in later chapters. A series of self-administered questionnaires then are presented which will permit you to assess your own personality traits and the circumstances of your life-style which are relevant to owning a dog. Responding to these questionnaires will permit you to match the temperamental characteristics of any specific breed with your own personality and life-style.

Dogs are remarkable animals. They have, in the course of human history, been seen as gods, workers, guards, guides, best friends and pets. They have been adapted to the forests, the plains, the mountains and the polar regions, always in the company of humans. Choosing to share your life with a dog is not a frivolous decision. The choice may affect your life for the next ten to fifteen years. By using the information in this book you will be able to select from the great variety available the kind of dog that will provide you with an endless source of affection, protection, work, fun—whatever you want.

2
The Sporting Dogs

Sporting Dogs is a breed type that identifies 24 separate breeds, each of which has been adapted for hunting. The group includes three breeds of pointers, five breeds of retrievers, three breeds of setters, ten breeds of spaniels and the Vizsla, Weimaraner and Wirehaired Pointing Griffon. These dogs were selectively bred for pointing, flushing and/or retrieving game. A few of the breeds have been used as guide dogs; only two or three out of the twenty-four are natural guard dogs. Most of these dogs need a lot of exercise.

Standard Pointer

A.K.C. Popularity: 86th

Dimension of Temperament	Level of Dimension				
	Very high	High	Med.	Low	Very low
1. Indoor activity	▓				
2. Outdoor activity	▓				
3. Vigor		▓			
4. Behavioral constancy		▓			
5. Dominance to strange dogs		▓▓			
6. Dominance to familiar people			▓		
7. Territoriality				▓	
8. Emotional stability			▓		
9. Sociability – within family			▓		
10. Sociability – with children			▓		
11. Sociability – with strangers			▓▓		
12. Learning – rate				▓	
13. Learning – obedience			▓		
14. Learning – problem solving				▓	
15. Watchdog ability		▓			
16. Guard-dog ability		▓▓▓			

The Standard Pointer has a large, muscular body, and its function as a pointing dog has been maintained. Descriptions include "full of nervous energy and hunt"; "put together for speed, endurance and courage"; "can maintain a point without distraction"; has the "ability to concentrate on a job"; "a disposition adaptable to the kennel"; "dignified and possessing a competitive spirit"; "never shows timidity toward man or dog"; "tendency toward early development, with two-month-old puppies frequently barking and pointing"; "requires less personal attention"; "they will work for someone other than their master"; "every inch a gun dog" and "even-tempered, but stubborn."

Behavior problems may include restlessness indoors, a tendency to destruction and barking if left alone a lot, and possibly roaming in males.

My most common experience with pointers is with those raised in kennels without much human contact for the first six or eight months of their lives. Such isolation frequently results in the "kennel dog syndrome," wherein the pointer's negative traits such as restlessness and disobedience are exaggerated, and the dog becomes dog-oriented rather than people-oriented.

German Shorthaired Pointer

Dimension of Temperament	Level of Dimension				
	Very high	High	Med.	Low	Very low
1. Indoor activity	▨				
2. Outdoor activity	▨				
3. Vigor	▨				
4. Behavioral constancy		▨			
5. Dominance to strange dogs			▨		
6. Dominance to familiar people			▨		
7. Territoriality				▨	
8. Emotional stability			▨		
9. Sociability — within family			▨		
10. Sociability — with children				▨	
11. Sociability — with strangers			▨		
12. Learning — rate		▨			
13. Learning — obedience			▨		
14. Learning — problem solving		▨			
15. Watchdog ability	▨				
16. Guard-dog ability			▨		

The German Shorthaired Pointer, slightly smaller than the Standard Pointer, shares many of its characteristics and is described by breeders as very active and vigorous. Descriptions include: "great powers of endurance," "retrieves well in rough terrain or icy waters," "highly intelligent" and "stubborn."

Behavior problems may include indoor restlessness, destruction of furniture and barking when left alone, house soiling, roaming and stealing food.

In my experience, German Shorthairs also show the "kennel dog syndrome" if raised in a kennel from puppyhood, and the "isolation syndrome" when kept in pet shops for prolonged periods of time. The latter syndrome is certainly the worse of the two, since the restlessness, destruction, barking and insensitivity to punishment are greatly exaggerated.

German Wirehaired Pointer

A.K.C. Popularity:
66th

Dimension of Temperament	Level of Dimension				
	Very high	High	Med.	Low	Very low
1. Indoor activity	▣				
2. Outdoor activity	▣				
3. Vigor	▣				
4. Behavioral constancy		▣			
5. Dominance to strange dogs		▣			
6. Dominance to familiar people		▣			
7. Territoriality		▣			
8. Emotional stability		▣			
9. Sociability — within family			▣		
10. Sociability — with children				▣	
11. Sociability — with strangers				▣	
12. Learning — rate		▣			
13. Learning — obedience			▣		
14. Learning — problem solving			▣		
15. Watchdog ability	▣				
16. Guard-dog ability		▣			

The German Wirehaired Pointer is shorter than the Standard Pointer, but as heavy. Descriptions include "very energetic in action," "extra-rugged hunter capable of working any terrain in any weather" and "intelligent."

Behavior problems may include indoor restlessness, jumping up on visitors, dominance problems and guarding of place or property, barking at noises, roaming and stealing food.

I recently worked with an eighteen-month-old male German Wirehaired Pointer named Ralph, owned by a practicing psychologist and his college-professor wife. Ralph was completely uncontrollable. Constantly moving, running and jumping, he was a dervish twirling in progressively tighter circles the more excited he got. My hands and legs were lacerated from the rope burns inflicted by his twirling when I began working with him. It took nearly four weeks of work, twelve hours a day, to straighten out Ralph's problems. Ralph wouldn't have had these problems if he had been raised properly, in a home with plenty of human contact, instead of being kept in an isolated kennel for his first eight months of existence.

Chesapeake Bay Retriever

A.K.C. Popularity: 45th

Dimension of Temperament	Level of Dimension				
	Very high	High	Med.	Low	Very low
1. Indoor activity				▨	
2. Outdoor activity	▨				
3. Vigor			▨	▨	
4. Behavioral constancy			▨		
5. Dominance to strange dogs			▨		
6. Dominance to familiar people			▨		
7. Territoriality		▨			
8. Emotional stability		▨			
9. Sociability – within family			▨		
10. Sociability – with children	▨				
11. Sociability – with strangers				▨	
12. Learning – rate				▨	
13. Learning – obedience			▨		
14. Learning – problem solving			▨		
15. Watchdog ability	▨				
16. Guard-dog ability	▨				

The Chesapeake Bay Retriever is about the same size as the pointers, but more powerfully muscled in the chest. It is considered to have a high degree of territoriality, but surprisingly, most breeders suggest that it does not show aggression toward other dogs and is not likely to dominate familiar and/or submissive people. It is described as "easygoing, but more aggressive and stubborn than other retrievers," "a roughhouser."

Behavior problems may include dominance and unwarranted aggressions toward visitors and barking at noises.

In my practice, Chesapeakes are usually brought to me because they exhibit dominance threats toward their rather intimidated owners and aggression toward other dogs in the household. However, I think such cases are exceptions to the rule.

Curly-coated Retriever

A.K.C. Popularity:
114th

Dimension of Temperament	Level of Dimension				
	Very high	High	Med.	Low	Very low
1. Indoor activity				▨	
2. Outdoor activity	▨				
3. Vigor			▨		
4. Behavioral constancy				▨	
5. Dominance to strange dogs			▨		
6. Dominance to familiar people				▨	
7. Territoriality			▨		
8. Emotional stability				▨	
9. Sociability – within family		▨			
10. Sociability – with children	▨				
11. Sociability – with strangers				▨	
12. Learning – rate		▨			
13. Learning – obedience		▨			
14. Learning – problem solving			▨		
15. Watchdog ability		▨			
16. Guard-dog ability			▨		

The Curly-coated Retriever is a large retriever with tight curls over its entire body except its forehead and muzzle, which have very short hair, giving its forehead a peculiar, bald look. It is very rare in the United States. Descriptions include "enduring and hardy," "fondness for swimming," "affectionate" and "timid."

Behavior problems may arise from its timidity. In my experience, specimens are very susceptible to fear conditioning, and if not socialized early to many people including adults and children, it may become a fear biter. This breed should not be harshly punished.

Flat-coated Retriever

A.K.C. Popularity: 108th

Dimension of Temperament	Level of Dimension				
	Very high	High	Med.	Low	Very low
1. Indoor activity				▨	
2. Outdoor activity	▨				
3. Vigor			▨		
4. Behavioral constancy				▨	
5. Dominance to strange dogs				▨	
6. Dominance to familiar people				▨	
7. Territoriality				▨	
8. Emotional stability		▨			
9. Sociability — within family	▨				
10. Sociability — with children	▨				
11. Sociability — with strangers	▨				
12. Learning — rate	▨				
13. Learning — obedience		▨			
14. Learning — problem solving			▨		
15. Watchdog ability		▨			
16. Guard-dog ability				▨	

The Flat-coated Retriever looks like a longer-haired Labrador Retriever, with a similar body size and shape. Descriptions include "bright and active dog," "easily distractable," "untemperamental," "intelligent expression" and "very friendly."

Behavior problems may include overfriendliness, jumping up on everyone as a greeting, stealing food and rummaging through the garbage.

I have had a few cases in which these retrievers have shown excessive timidity toward people. Usually, these animals were poorly socialized or completely unsocialized.

Golden Retriever

A.K.C. Popularity: 7th

Dimension of Temperament	Level of Dimension				
	Very high	High	Med.	Low	Very low
1. Indoor activity		▬			
2. Outdoor activity			▬		
3. Vigor			▬		
4. Behavioral constancy				▬	
5. Dominance to strange dogs					▬
6. Dominance to familiar people					▬
7. Territoriality					▬
8. Emotional stability		▬			
9. Sociability — within family	▬				
10. Sociability — with children	▬				
11. Sociability — with strangers	▬				
12. Learning — rate	▬				
13. Learning — obedience		▬			
14. Learning — problem solving			▬		
15. Watchdog ability		▬			
16. Guard-dog ability				▬	

The Golden Retriever is about the same size as the Labrador and Flat-coated Retrievers, but less vigorous. Descriptions include: "active, eager, alert and self-confident"; "easily distractable"; "untemperamental"; "potential for timidity if not socialized" and "likes everyone indiscriminately."

Behavior problems may include exuberant jumping on everyone as a greeting and, possibly, uncontrolled playfulness. I have had rare cases of excessively timid and fearful Goldens, and even rarer cases of dominance guarding with Goldens. Usually these problems occur with female dogs that tend to protect their male master from his wife. The owners claim that their dogs appear "jealous." The protection takes the form of mild threats that are more bluff than anything else.

Labrador Retriever

Dimension of Temperament	Level of Dimension				
	Very high	High	Med.	Low	Very low
1. Indoor activity		▨			
2. Outdoor activity			▨		
3. Vigor			▨		
4. Behavioral constancy		▨			
5. Dominance to strange dogs			▨		
6. Dominance to familiar people			▨		
7. Territoriality			▨		
8. Emotional stability		▨			
9. Sociability — within family		▨			
10. Sociability — with children	▨				
11. Sociability — with strangers			▨		
12. Learning — rate	▨				
13. Learning — obedience		▨			
14. Learning — problem solving			▨		
15. Watchdog ability	▨				
16. Guard-dog ability		▨	▨	▨	

The Labrador Retriever is about the same size as the Golden Retriever, but appears more powerfully muscled. The yellow-coated variety may be more dominant than the black. Descriptions include "good temper," "bold" and "exceptional with children and liking everyone."

Behavior problems may include barking incessantly at noises, occasional house soiling, and occasional chewing and destruction. Some may show willful disobedience as a form of dominance challenge.

In my experience, Labs are more dominant and territorial than Goldens, and a bit more discriminating about their friendships. Some can be pretty tough cookies, and most are relatively insensitive to rough handling and have high pain thresholds. Fear conditioning is hardly ever a problem with Labs. When it does occur, it is the result of continual fear-arousing experiences over a long period of time.

English Setter

A.K.C. Popularity: 54th

Dimension of Temperament	Level of Dimension				
	Very high	High	Med.	Low	Very low
1. Indoor activity				▩	
2. Outdoor activity	▩				
3. Vigor			▩		
4. Behavioral constancy			▩		
5. Dominance to strange dogs			▩		
6. Dominance to familiar people			▩		
7. Territoriality				▩	
8. Emotional stability	▩				
9. Sociability — within family	▩				
10. Sociability — with children	▩				
11. Sociability — with strangers	▩				
12. Learning — rate				▩	
13. Learning — obedience			▩		
14. Learning — problem solving		▩			
15. Watchdog ability		▩			
16. Guard-dog ability				▩	

The English Setter is a medium-sized dog with long, silky hair that feathers on the legs and tail. Descriptions include "active rugged, outdoor dog more suited to the suburbs than the city"; "very placid" and "quiet and friendly."

Behavior problems may include roaming and house soiling.

In my experience, English Setters are the least vigorous of the setters and are located toward the variable end of the constancy dimension. They are usually playful with other dogs. Some show a "stubborn streak."

Gordon Setter

A.K.C. Popularity: 61st

Dimension of Temperament	Level of Dimension				
	Very high	High	Med.	Low	Very low
1. Indoor activity			▨		
2. Outdoor activity	▨				
3. Vigor		▨			
4. Behavioral constancy		▨			
5. Dominance to strange dogs		▨			
6. Dominance to familiar people			▨	▨	
7. Territoriality			▨		
8. Emotional stability		▨			
9. Sociability — within family		▨			
10. Sociability — with children	▨				
11. Sociability — with strangers				▨	
12. Learning — rate		▨			
13. Learning — obedience			▨		
14. Learning — problem solving			▨		
15. Watchdog ability		▨			
16. Guard-dog ability		▨	▨	▨	

The Gordon Setter has a slightly more powerful body than the English and Irish Setters, with a shorter coat than the English Setter. It is temperamentally intermediate between the English and Irish setters on many dimensions. Descriptions include "a methodically dependable birdfinder"; "tireless worker" and "may occasionally be aggressive, guarding its owner."

Behavior problems may include roaming, house soiling and perhaps being a picky eater.

Irish Setter*

A.K.C. Popularity: 10th

Dimension of Temperament	Level of Dimension				
	Very high	High	Med.	Low	Very low
1. Indoor activity	▨				
2. Outdoor activity	▨				
3. Vigor	▨				
4. Behavioral constancy					▨
5. Dominance to strange dogs				▨	
6. Dominance to familiar people				▨	
7. Territoriality				▨	
8. Emotional stability				▨	
9. Sociability — within family	▨				
10. Sociability — with children	▨				
11. Sociability — with strangers	▨				
12. Learning — rate		▨			
13. Learning — obedience		▨			
14. Learning — problem solving		▨			
15. Watchdog ability		▨			
16. Guard-dog ability					▨

The Irish Setter, with its long, glossy, chestnut-colored coat and exuberant nature, is very popular in the United States. Descriptions include "impulsive," "highly distractible," "rollicking," "gay," "has moments of sheer giddiness," "excitable," "good with energetic older children, but a bit too excitable for toddlers."

Behavior problems, which may be inferred from the above descriptions, center on overexuberance and flightiness. In my experience, these qualities may have been exacerbated by puppy-mill production resulting from the breed's great popularity. A dog of this breed may develop bad habits if left alone and/or untrained. Other problems may include roaming, house soiling, mischievous playful destruction, pulling on lead, jumping on visitors and barking.

*Watch out for puppy-mill variety.

American Water Spaniel

A.K.C. Popularity: 92nd

Dimension of Temperament	Very high	High	Med.	Low	Very low
1. Indoor activity		▨			
2. Outdoor activity	▨				
3. Vigor				▨	
4. Behavioral constancy		▨			
5. Dominance to strange dogs		▨			
6. Dominance to familiar people		▨			
7. Territoriality		▨			
8. Emotional stability		▨			
9. Sociability – within family			▨		
10. Sociability – with children				▨	
11. Sociability – with strangers			▨		
12. Learning – rate		▨			
13. Learning – obedience		▨			
14. Learning – problem solving		▨			
15. Watchdog ability		▨			
16. Guard-dog ability			▨		

The American Water Spaniel has a tightly curled coat. It is a strong swimmer, the oil content of its coat giving it a waterproof quality. Descriptions include "thorough" when retrieving birds and "eagerness may render him overanxious."

Behavior problems may include barking, whining, roaming and irritable snapping. Certain specimens may drool, snore and have a strong coat odor.

My experience has always been with specimens that are timid and phobic. In most of my cases, fear biting has been the main problem. These cases, however, are rare, and they are treatable. Usually the owners have used excessively punitive techniques in disciplining the dog.

Brittany Spaniel

A.K.C. Popularity: 18th

Dimension of Temperament	Level of Dimension				
	Very high	High	Med.	Low	Very low
1. Indoor activity		▨			
2. Outdoor activity	▨				
3. Vigor		▨			
4. Behavioral constancy				▨	
5. Dominance to strange dogs			▨		
6. Dominance to familiar people			▨		
7. Territoriality			▨		
8. Emotional stability				▨	
9. Sociability – within family	▨				
10. Sociability – with children	▨				
11. Sociability – with strangers	▨				
12. Learning – rate	▨				
13. Learning – obedience		▨			
14. Learning – problem solving		▨			
15. Watchdog ability		▨			
16. Guard-dog ability				▨	

The Brittany Spaniel is larger and has longer legs than the water spaniels, with a distinctive coat of white and dark orange. Descriptions include "capable dog, can be trained to retrieve and is strong, vigorous, energetic and quick of movement"; "less inclined to live in its master's shadow than other spaniels" and "one of the brightest spaniels."

Behavior problems may include restlessness when not exercised, possible destructiveness, excessive barking when left alone, phobias, fear in cities, roaming and stealing food. In my experience, this breed has a tendency to be distracted by novel stimuli.

Clumber Spaniel

A.K.C. Popularity:
116th

Dimension of Temperament	Level of Dimension				
	Very high	High	Med.	Low	Very low
1. Indoor activity					▓
2. Outdoor activity				▓	
3. Vigor				▓	
4. Behavioral constancy	▓				
5. Dominance to strange dogs			▓		
6. Dominance to familiar people		▓			
7. Territoriality				▓	
8. Emotional stability	▓				
9. Sociability — within family	▓				
10. Sociability — with children	▓				
11. Sociability — with strangers	▓				
12. Learning — rate				▓	
13. Learning — obedience			▓		
14. Learning — problem solving			▓		
15. Watchdog ability				▓	
16. Guard-dog ability				▓	

The Clumber Spaniel is the heaviest of all the spaniels, looking like a combination of a silky-coated spaniel and a Basset Hound with its long, low body. Descriptions include "rather dignified, slow worker and sure finder and retriever"; "sedate in movement"; "sometimes stubborn"; "rather lazy, perfering to sleep instead of move"; "a nanny with children."

Behavior problems are minimal. Some specimens may steal food and some may wheeze, snore and drool.

(American) Cocker Spaniel*

A.K.C. Popularity: 4th

Dimension of Temperament	Level of Dimension				
	Very high	High	Med.	Low	Very low
1. Indoor activity		- - -	- - -▓		
2. Outdoor activity		- -▓- -			
3. Vigor		- - -	- - -	- - -▓	
4. Behavioral constancy			- - -▓	- - -	- - -
5. Dominance to strange dogs		- - -	- - -	- - -▓	
6. Dominance to familiar people		- - -	- - -	- - -▓	
7. Territoriality		- - -	- - -▓	- - -	
8. Emotional stability		- - -	- - -	- - -▓	- - -
9. Sociability — within family	- -▓	- - -	- - -	- - -	
10. Sociability — with children	- -▓	- - -	- - -	- - -	
11. Sociability — with strangers	- -▓	- - -	- - -	- - -	
12. Learning — rate		- - -▓	- - -	- - -	
13. Learning — obedience		- - -▓	- - -	- - -	
14. Learning — problem solving		- - -▓	- - -	- - -	
15. Watchdog ability	- - -	- - -▓			
16. Guard-dog ability					- - -▓

The Cocker Spaniel is the smallest breed of all the spaniels, and its great popularity has resulted in puppy-mill production, which has produced large numbers of animals with a general degradation in quality and some bizarre temperamental changes and behavioral problems. The puppy-mill variety has been described as "shy-sharp" by breeders—connoting a combination of fear and dominance that can cause viciousness. The well-bred variety is described as "gentle" and exhibiting "playful submission."

Potential behavior problems with the puppy-mill variety include excessive whining and barking; dominance problems; submissive urinating; aggressive guarding of objects, people and places; house soiling; self-abusive hair chewing; hyperactivity; shy-sharpness; hyperphagia; pica; polydypsia; hypersexuality and roaming. The well-bred Cocker may exhibit excessive barking, stealing food and perhaps house soiling.

*Watch out for puppy-mill dogs.
- - - - - = Puppy-mill
▓▓▓▓ = well-bred

English Cocker Spaniel

A.K.C. Popularity:
64th

Dimension of Temperament	Level of Dimension				
	Very high	High	Med.	Low	Very low
1. Indoor activity		▨			
2. Outdoor activity		▨			
3. Vigor			▨		
4. Behavioral constancy			▨	▨	
5. Dominance to strange dogs				▨	
6. Dominance to familiar people				▨	
7. Territoriality				▨	
8. Emotional stability		▨			
9. Sociability — within family	▨				
10. Sociability — with children	▨				
11. Sociability — with strangers	▨				
12. Learning — rate		▨			
13. Learning — obedience		▨			
14. Learning — problem solving			▨		
15. Watchdog ability		▨			
16. Guard-dog ability				▨	

The English Cocker Spaniel is a few inches bigger than its American cousin and is from three to eleven pounds heavier. It is less popular than the American Cocker, and as a result, problems generated by puppy-mill production have been avoided. Descriptions include "alive with energy," "alert at all times" and "merry and playful."

Behavior problems may include house soiling and food stealing. The only other English Cocker Spaniel cases I have had involved excessive submission resulting in submissive and/or excitable urination. The dog owners in these cases were usually very dominant over the dog, but not necessarily punitive.

English Springer Spaniel

A.K.C. Popularity: 16th

Dimension of Temperament	Level of Dimension				
	Very high	High	Med.	Low	Very low
1. Indoor activity		▓			
2. Outdoor activity	▓				
3. Vigor			▓		
4. Behavioral constancy			▓		
5. Dominance to strange dogs				▓	
6. Dominance to familiar people			▓		
7. Territoriality				▓	
8. Emotional stability		▓			
9. Sociability — within family	▓				
10. Sociability — with children	▓				
11. Sociability — with strangers	▓				
12. Learning — rate		▓			
13. Learning — obedience			▓		
14. Learning — problem solving			▓		
15. Watchdog ability		▓			
16. Guard-dog ability				▓	

The English Springer Spaniel is a medium-sized sporting dog with a close, straight-haired coat. Descriptions include "full of high-spirited affection" and "a dog that can keep on going under difficult hunting conditions, moreover enjoying what it is doing." Other comments, however, are "no dog should behave viciously toward handlers and judges [i.e., strangers]" and "excessive timidity in the [show] ring is a fault," suggesting that some specimens show these behaviors.

Behavior problems may include destruction and barking when alone, jumping on people, playful barking easily stimulated by the barking of other dogs, timidity and phobias and, perhaps, food stealing. Some adults find Springers "a bit too persistent in their devotion to their owners."

Field Spaniel

A.K.C. Popularity: 118th

Dimension of Temperament	Level of Dimension				
	Very high	High	Med.	Low	Very low
1. Indoor activity	▰				
2. Outdoor activity	▰				
3. Vigor		▰			
4. Behavioral constancy		▰			
5. Dominance to strange dogs			▰		
6. Dominance to familiar people				▰	
7. Territoriality				▰	
8. Emotional stability		▰			
9. Sociability – within family	▰				
10. Sociability – with children	▰				
11. Sociability – with strangers	▰				
12. Learning – rate		▰			
13. Learning – obedience		▰			
14. Learning – problem solving		▰			
15. Watchdog ability	▰				
16. Guard-dog ability				▰	

The Field Spaniel has a longer body than the English Springer Spaniel, but is of about the same weight. Descriptions include "great endurance, moderate speed and agility" and "unusually docile"; it has a reputation for an "instinct" for problem solving.

Behavior problems may include excessive barking at noises, roaming and food stealing. It may also snore.

Irish Water Spaniel

A.K.C. Popularity: 113th

Dimension of Temperament	Very high	High	Med.	Low	Very low
1. Indoor activity		■			
2. Outdoor activity	■				
3. Vigor		■			
4. Behavioral constancy		■			
5. Dominance to strange dogs				■	■
6. Dominance to familiar people		■			
7. Territoriality		■	■		
8. Emotional stability				■	
9. Sociability — within family			■		
10. Sociability — with children					■
11. Sociability — with strangers				■	■
12. Learning — rate		■			
13. Learning — obedience				■	
14. Learning — problem solving			■		
15. Watchdog ability	■				
16. Guard-dog ability		■	■	■	

The Irish Water Spaniel is an unusual-looking spaniel with a curly coat, topknot of loose curls down its forehead and ratlike tail. Descriptions include "clownish appearance"; "rugged endurance"; "sometimes timid"; and "loyal to those he knows, but forbidding to strangers."

Behavior problems may include sharp-shyness as a result of excessive dominance and fear, fear biting, irritable snapping, barking at slight noises and a tendency to drool. During hot summers the Irish Water Spaniel tends to overheat and become irritable. I wouldn't recommend this breed for households with children running in and out all day.

Sussex Spaniel

A.K.C. Popularity: 122nd

Dimension of Temperament	Level of Dimension				
	Very high	High	Med.	Low	Very low
1. Indoor activity			▦		
2. Outdoor activity			▦		
3. Vigor			▦		
4. Behavioral constancy	▦				
5. Dominance to strange dogs		▦			
6. Dominance to familiar people		▦			
7. Territoriality		▦			
8. Emotional stability	▦				
9. Sociability – within family		▦			
10. Sociability – with children	▦				
11. Sociability – with strangers			▦		
12. Learning – rate				▦	
13. Learning – obedience				▦	
14. Learning – problem solving				▦	
15. Watchdog ability		▦			
16. Guard-dog ability			▦		

The Sussex Spaniel, like the Clumber, has shorter legs and a longer body than most of the other spaniels, which make it slow but sturdy in the field. Descriptions include "slow mover and not too difficult to train," "sometimes bold," "passively stubborn in obedience," "not indiscriminately friendly."

Behavior problems may include house soiling and howling and a slight possibility of a sudden but short-lived aggressive outburst usually leading to a growl and snap, but not a bite, if the dog is pushed or annoyed too much.

Welsh Springer Spaniel

A.K.C. Popularity: 109th

Dimension of Temperament	Level of Dimension				
	Very high	High	Med.	Low	Very low
1. Indoor activity		▓			
2. Outdoor activity	▓				
3. Vigor			▓		
4. Behavioral constancy		▓			
5. Dominance to strange dogs			▓		
6. Dominance to familiar people				▓	
7. Territoriality		▓			
8. Emotional stability		▓			
9. Sociability — within family			▓		
10. Sociability — with children		▓			
11. Sociability — with strangers				▓	
12. Learning — rate		▓			
13. Learning — obedience			▓		
14. Learning — problem solving			▓		
15. Watchdog ability		▓			
16. Guard-dog ability			▓	▓	

The Welsh Springer Spaniel is another breed rarely seen in the United States. It is intermediate in size and strength between the English Cocker and the English Springer spaniels and has a rich, silky coat of white and dark red. Descriptions include "able to withstand extremes of heat and cold," "less exuberant than the English Springer," "a hardworking dog—no day is too long and no country too rough . . . a faithful and willing worker" and "shows its devotion more quietly than the English Springer."

Behavior problems may include barking in a city apartment and occasional aggressiveness. The A.K.C. stresses the need for training and says, "Welsh Springer Spaniels rarely forget lessons," from which we may infer that occasionally they do.

Vizsla

A.K.C. Popularity: 50th

Dimension of Temperament	Level of Dimension				
	Very high	High	Med.	Low	Very low
1. Indoor activity				▨	
2. Outdoor activity		▨			
3. Vigor		▨			
4. Behavioral constancy		▨			
5. Dominance to strange dogs			▨		
6. Dominance to familiar people				▨	
7. Territoriality				▨	
8. Emotional stability				▨	
9. Sociability — within family	▨				
10. Sociability — with children	▨				
11. Sociability — with strangers	▨				
12. Learning — rate		▨			
13. Learning — obedience		▨			
14. Learning — problem solving			▨		
15. Watchdog ability		▨			
16. Guard-dog ability				▨	

The Vizsla, or Hungarian Pointer, is a medium-sized sporting dog with a short, dark gold-colored coat. The breed all but disappeared in Hungary during the crises between the world wars, but survived and has become rather popular elsewhere in Europe and in the United States. Descriptions include "friendly" and "likes everyone indiscriminately."

Behavior problems may stem from its sociability, since when left alone it may chew the furniture as an anxiety response. It may also be startled easily by sudden city noises, and there is a trend toward timidity.

Weimaraner

A.K.C. Popularity: 43rd

Dimension of Temperament	Level of Dimension				
	Very high	High	Med.	Low	Very low
1. Indoor activity	▨				
2. Outdoor activity	▨				
3. Vigor	▨				
4. Behavioral constancy		▨			
5. Dominance to strange dogs		▨			
6. Dominance to familiar people		▨			
7. Territoriality		▨			
8. Emotional stability		▨			
9. Sociability – within family			▨		
10. Sociability – with children			▨		
11. Sociability – with strangers				▨	
12. Learning – rate		▨			
13. Learning – obedience				▨	
14. Learning – problem solving		▨			
15. Watchdog ability	▨				
16. Guard-dog ability	▨				

The Weimaraner (pronounced Vy-mah-rah-ner) has a distinctive metallic-gray coat which, with its violet or amber eyes, creates an impression that led to its being called the Gray Ghost. Descriptions include "a real handful," "stubborn," "bold," "too impetuous for younger children."

Behavior problems may include indoor restlessness, destructiveness when left alone, excessive barking and, perhaps, house soiling.

Wirehaired Pointing Griffon

A.K.C. Popularity: 104th

Dimension of Temperament	Level of Dimension				
	Very high	High	Med.	Low	Very low
1. Indoor activity	▨				
2. Outdoor activity		▨			
3. Vigor		▨			
4. Behavioral constancy				▨	
5. Dominance to strange dogs			▨		
6. Dominance to familiar people				▨	
7. Territoriality			▨		
8. Emotional stability				▨	
9. Sociability — within family			▨		
10. Sociability — with children				▨	
11. Sociability — with strangers			▨		
12. Learning — rate		▨			
13. Learning — obedience		▨			
14. Learning — problem solving			▨		
15. Watchdog ability	▨				
16. Guard-dog ability			▨		

The Wirehaired Pointing Griffon, a medium-sized dog, has a stiff, bristly coat and a square muzzle. Descriptions include "strong and vigorous"; "high-strung"; "terrierlike"; "nervous with strangers, strange situations, loud city noises and alarms"; "timid."

Behavior problems may occur as a result of excessive fears or phobias and may include house soiling, barking at novel stimuli and being a picky eater.

3
The Hounds

This group of dogs comprises 19 breeds more or less adapted for hunting or tracking game by sight or smell. The group includes the Afghan, Basenji, Basset Hound, Beagle, Black and Tan Coonhound, Bloodhound, Borzoi, Dachshund, American and English Foxhounds, Greyhound, Harrier, Irish Wolfhound, Norwegian Elkhound, Otterhound, Rhodesian Ridgeback, Saluki, Scottish Deerhound and Whippet. The group varies greatly in size. The hot dog–shaped Dachshund may be as small as 5 inches at the shoulder and weigh less than 10 pounds; the Irish Wolfhound, probably the tallest breed, can measure 3 feet tall at the shoulder, weigh over 160 pounds and stand up to 7 feet tall on its hind legs.

Afghan Hound

A.K.C. Popularity: 31st

Dimension of Temperament	Level of Dimension				
	Very high	High	Med.	Low	Very low
1. Indoor activity				X	
2. Outdoor activity	X				
3. Vigor				X	
4. Behavioral constancy		X			
5. Dominance to strange dogs		X			
6. Dominance to familiar people			X		
7. Territoriality			X		
8. Emotional stability		X	X	X	
9. Sociability — within family				X	X
10. Sociability — with children			X	X	
11. Sociability — with strangers				X	
12. Learning — rate				X	
13. Learning — obedience				X	
14. Learning — problem solving			X	X	
15. Watchdog ability		X			
16. Guard-dog ability				X	

The Afghan Hound was developed to hunt gazelles, leopards and rabbits. It is a medium-to-large-sized coursing dog easily recognizable by its very long, silky, flowing hair and aristocratic appearance. Descriptions include "aloof and dignified, yet gay"; "generally stubborn"; "easygoing"; "timid and high-strung"; "able to withstand extremes of temperature."

Behavior problems may include sharp-shyness that leads to fear biting and irritable snapping, house soiling, picky eating and stubbornness. The owner of an Afghan should also expect to spend considerable time grooming this dog.

My professional experience with this breed has been with very timid or shy-sharp specimens usually owned by people who get great satisfaction from grooming and showing off the dog's luxurious coat. Such dogs are usually pampered, over-protected and undersocialized, all of which increase the potential for timidity.

Basenji

A.K.C. Popularity: 55th

Dimension of Temperament	Level of Dimension				
	Very high	High	Med.	Low	Very low
1. Indoor activity	▩				
2. Outdoor activity		▩			
3. Vigor				▩	
4. Behavioral constancy				▩	
5. Dominance to strange dogs	▩				
6. Dominance to familiar people			▩		
7. Territoriality		▩			
8. Emotional stability		▩			
9. Sociability — within family			▩		
10. Sociability — with children			▩		
11. Sociability — with strangers			▩		
12. Learning — rate		▩			
13. Learning — obedience			▩		
14. Learning — problem solving	▩				
15. Watchdog ability	▩				
16. Guard-dog ability				▩	

The Basenji (pronounced Buh-SEN-jee) is an African hunting dog about the size of a Fox Terrier. It has the unique properties of not barking (it makes a low, liquid ululation instead) and of cleaning itself like a cat. Descriptions include "speedy, frisky, tireless at play and teasing the owner into play"; "dainty, fastidious habits"; "loves children"; "tractable and anxious to please and, by nature, an obedient dog"; "a sprightly, alert manner"; "stubborn."

Behavior problems may stem from the breed's unquenchable desire to play, which may tax the owner's patience and may also lead to destructiveness if the dog is left alone. Some individuals may be unpredictable with children.

My Basenji cases usually involve a mismatch between owner and pet. The owners mistake the adjective "quiet" to mean inactive instead of noiseless; thus, they become harassed by an active, though relatively silent, dog.

Basset Hound

A.K.C. Popularity: 23rd

Dimension of Temperament	Level of Dimension				
	Very high	High	Med.	Low	Very low
1. Indoor activity				▓	
2. Outdoor activity			▓		
3. Vigor			▓		
4. Behavioral constancy			▓		
5. Dominance to strange dogs			▓		
6. Dominance to familiar people			▓		
7. Territoriality				▓	
8. Emotional stability		▓			
9. Sociability — within family		▓			
10. Sociability — with children	▓				
11. Sociability — with strangers			▓		
12. Learning — rate				▓	
13. Learning — obedience			▓		
14. Learning — problem solving				▓	
15. Watchdog ability		▓			
16. Guard-dog ability				▓	

The Basset Hound is a medium-sized hound in weight, but its short, stocky legs give it a low-slung, heavy-boned appearance that is heightened by its "sad" and droopy expression. Descriptions include "great endurance in the field"; "hardy"; "able to follow a trail over and through difficult terrain"; "steady"; "can hunt in packs"; "docile, placid, easygoing, having a mild temperament, never sharp or timid"; "stubborn, but can be controlled if treated with kindness and affection"; "this dog works better for obtaining rewards than avoiding punishment."

Behavior problems may include house soiling if not broken early before bad habits set in, food stealing, howling if left alone and picky eating. Most Basset Hounds seem to snore loudly. Bassets should *not* be harshly punished.

In my experience, if it is trained and handled exclusively by its master, a Basset can become a "one-person dog" that ignores strangers and cannot be coaxed away by them.

Beagle*

A.K.C. Popularity: 6th

Dimension of Temperament	Level of Dimension				
	Very high	High	Med.	Low	Very low
1. Indoor activity	▨				
2. Outdoor activity			▨		
3. Vigor				▨	
4. Behavioral constancy			▨		
5. Dominance to strange dogs				▨	
6. Dominance to familiar people				▨	
7. Territoriality					▨
8. Emotional stability		▨			
9. Sociability — within family	▨				
10. Sociability — with children	▨				
11. Sociability — with strangers	▨				
12. Learning — rate		▨			
13. Learning — obedience				▨	
14. Learning — problem solving		▨			
15. Watchdog ability		▨			
16. Guard-dog ability				▨	

The Beagle is a small, pack-oriented hunting hound that is very popular in the United States. This popularity has led to puppy-mill production of large numbers without control of temperament, so the potential owner should be particularly careful in choosing a Beagle. I have found some puppy-mill Beagles to be irritable and snappy. Descriptions include "work together gaily and cheerfully"; "lively"; "hardy"; "very clever at following a scent"; "requires firm, patient training"; "stubborn and bold."

Behavior problems may include roaming, baying and howling when left alone, house soiling if not broken early and food stealing. Some individuals may be timid; they need firm and patient training.

My experience with Beagles usually involves specimens that exhibit a unique combination of timidity, shyness and sociability. They seem to fear being left alone. Bosco was a case in point. She was destructive and incontinent and howled when alone. These problems were caused by the animal's agoraphobia and exacerbated by her owner's punishment and isolation techniques. Bosco became claustrophobic and refused to ride the elevator the twenty stories to the street after her owner began locking her in the bathroom to prevent destruction and muffle the noise. The claustrophobia further irritated her owners, since they had to carry her up and down twenty stories to go for a walk. Bosco's problems were solved not by punishment, but by a cure of her basic phobia.

*Watch out for puppy-mill varieties.

Black and Tan Coonhound

A.K.C. Popularity: 90th

Dimension of Temperament	Level of Dimension				
	Very high	High	Med.	Low	Very low
1. Indoor activity				▦	
2. Outdoor activity		▦			
3. Vigor		▦			
4. Behavioral constancy		▦			
5. Dominance to strange dogs		▦			
6. Dominance to familiar people			▦		
7. Territoriality			▦		
8. Emotional stability		▦			
9. Sociability — within family			▦		
10. Sociability — with children		▦			
11. Sociability — with strangers			▦		
12. Learning — rate				▦	
13. Learning — obedience				▦	
14. Learning — problem solving				▦	
15. Watchdog ability		▦			
16. Guard-dog ability		▦			

The Black and Tan Coonhound is a large dog used for scent-hunting everything from racoons to bears. It trails a scent slowly and then gives a characteristic howl the moment its quarry is treed or cornered, holding the quarry at bay until the hunter arrives. Descriptions include "alert, friendly, eager and at the same time aggressive and slow"; capable of "withstanding rigorous winters and hot summers and difficult terrain"; "consummate skill and determination while scenting and keeping its quarry at bay"; "easygoing"; "amiable, even temper"; "gentle with people"; "stubborn and bold, needing firm, patient training."

Behavior problems may include food stealing and howling if left alone.

The only Coonhound cases I have had involved hunter-owned specimens that wouldn't perform their function—i.e. treeing raccoons, opossums and other wild critters. For example, Spike refused to hunt after he was hit by a car while chasing a raccoon. Spike's owner, a macho type, considered Spike's refusal to be cowardice and shocked the dog for his "yellow streak." Spike got worse and was cured only after his owner divested himself of his "cowardice" concept and began coaxing and rewarding Spike's hunting habits.

Bloodhound

A.K.C. Popularity: 52nd

Dimension of Temperament	Level of Dimension				
	Very high	High	Med.	Low	Very low
1. Indoor activity				▨	
2. Outdoor activity		▨			
3. Vigor	▨				
4. Behavioral constancy	▨				
5. Dominance to strange dogs		▨			
6. Dominance to familiar people			▨		
7. Territoriality			▨		
8. Emotional stability	▨				
9. Sociability – within family	▨				
10. Sociability – with children	▨				
11. Sociability – with strangers	▨				
12. Learning – rate				▨	
13. Learning – obedience			▨		
14. Learning – problem solving			▨		
15. Watchdog ability		▨			
16. Guard-dog ability				▨	

The Bloodhound is considered the best scent tracker of all the 123 breeds. The name is derived from the fact that the breed has been kept pure-blooded and has nothing to do with liking blood. Descriptions include "tracks, but never attacks"; "strong"; "possessing stamina and determination ... some specimens following human quarry up to 138 miles with success and being able to follow trails 100 hours old"; "no sparkler, easygoing and the most docile of all breeds, lovable, patient and kindly"; "gentle with people"; "somewhat stubborn."

Behavior problems stemming from the purpose for which the breed was developed may include excessive sniffing of embarrassing locations, roaming and baying when left alone. Bloodhounds may also steal food occasionally, snore and drool.

Borzoi (Russian Wolfhound)

A.K.C. Popularity:
56th

Dimension of Temperament	Level of Dimension				
	Very high	High	Med.	Low	Very low
1. Indoor activity				■	
2. Outdoor activity	■				
3. Vigor				■	
4. Behavioral constancy		■			
5. Dominance to strange dogs			■		
6. Dominance to familiar people			■		
7. Territoriality				■	
8. Emotional stability				■	
9. Sociability – within family				■	
10. Sociability – with children				■	■
11. Sociability – with strangers				■	
12. Learning – rate		■			
13. Learning – obedience			■	■	
14. Learning – problem solving				■	
15. Watchdog ability			■		
16. Guard-dog ability				■	

The Borzoi (pronounced BAWR-zoy), once known as the Russian Wolfhound, is a very large, long and lean dog that was developed to course in packs by sight. Descriptions include "undemanding of its owner"; "extremely well-tempered up to a point, then may suddenly bite if annoyed"; "somewhat stubborn."

Behavior problems may include roaming, irritable snapping, touch shyness and, perhaps, picky eating.

Dachshund*

A.K.C. Popularity: 8th

Dimension of Temperament	Very high	High	Med.	Low	Very low
1. Indoor activity	▦				
2. Outdoor activity	▦				
3. Vigor		▦			
4. Behavioral constancy					▦
5. Dominance to strange dogs			▦		
6. Dominance to familiar people			▦		
7. Territoriality			▦		
8. Emotional stability				▦	
9. Sociability — within family				▦	
10. Sociability — with children				▦	
11. Sociability — with strangers				▦	▦
12. Learning — rate		▦			
13. Learning — obedience				▦	
14. Learning — problem solving	▦				
15. Watchdog ability	▦				
16. Guard-dog ability					▦

Dachshund (pronounced DOCKS-Hoond) is a general name for six separate varieties, each of which exhibits the very short legs and long body characteristic of these dogs. The six varieties are the result of the combination of two sizes (small and miniature) and three coat types (short, long and wiry). They were developed to hunt badgers into their holes and to dig them out or go in after them. Descriptions include "always clowning around, jumping, romping and digging a lot, hilarious at play"; "lively and courageous to the point of rashness"; "going from resting to play in seconds"; "stubborn and bold."

Behavior problems may include excessive barking, snapping when irritated, house soiling and food stealing.

My most peculiar problem with Dachshunds was with Terrence, a four-year-old male owned by a woman in her seventies. Terrence developed an elevator phobia and could be walked only if carried down and up seven flights of stairs. As it turned out, Terrence's phobia was related to his proximity to the ground. He feared the crack between the elevator and the floor, in which he had repeatedly caught his nails. I eliminated this phobia by teaching him to jump into and out of the elevator, hurdling the crack.

*Watch out for puppy-mill variety.

American Foxhound/English Foxhound

A.K.C. Popularity: 117th, 123rd

Dimension of Temperament	Level of Dimension				
	Very high	High	Med.	Low	Very low
1. Indoor activity	▓				
2. Outdoor activity	▓				
3. Vigor		▓			
4. Behavioral constancy				▓	
5. Dominance to strange dogs				▓	
6. Dominance to familiar people				▓	
7. Territoriality					▓
8. Emotional stability		▓			
9. Sociability — within family	▓				
10. Sociability — with children	▓				
11. Sociability — with strangers	▓				
12. Learning — rate				▓	
13. Learning — obedience			▓		
14. Learning — problem solving			▓		
15. Watchdog ability		▓			
16. Guard-dog ability				▓	

Foxhounds were bred for four different functions, and there are therefore four different varieties: trail field hounds, lone fox hunters, drag hounds and pack hunting dogs. The pack hunter makes the best pet and is, therefore, the variety represented on the dimensions of temperament above.

The English Foxhound is a little stouter than its American cousin, but its appearance and temperament are almost identical. The pack hunting Foxhound is a large dog, developed to hunt in packs of 15 or 20 dogs. This essentially social activity has resulted in a very vigorous but submissive dog.

Behavior problems may include roaming, baying when a member of the breed hears other dogs barking, and house soiling.

In my experience, the "kennel dog syndrome" has been the most common complaint with this breed.

Greyhound

A.K.C. Popularity: 105th

Dimension of Temperament	Level of Dimension				
	Very high	High	Med.	Low	Very low
1. Indoor activity				▦	
2. Outdoor activity	▦				
3. Vigor				▦	
4. Behavioral constancy				▦	
5. Dominance to strange dogs			▦		
6. Dominance to familiar people			▦		
7. Territoriality			▦		
8. Emotional stability				▦	
9. Sociability — within family			▦		
10. Sociability — with children				▦	▦
11. Sociability — with strangers				▦	
12. Learning — rate		▦			
13. Learning — obedience				▦	▦
14. Learning — problem solving				▦	
15. Watchdog ability		▦			
16. Guard-dog ability				▦	

The Greyhound is another dog whose function is clearly observable from its build. Greyhounds are built to run fast, to course after deer and, more recently, to race. Descriptions include "lovable and tractable"; "high-strung, easily upset by sudden movements, starting readily"; "stubborn, and trainaable only while calm." There is a divided opinion on the temperament of the Greyhound, some sources praising its friendliness and gentleness, others focusing on its potential for being high-strung and nervous. Because of its willowy build, it is prone to tremble in cold weather.

Behavior problems may include fear biting, phobias and timidity, touch shyness, irritable snapping and house soiling.

Harrier

A.K.C. Popularity:
119th

Dimension of Temperament	Level of Dimension				
	Very high	High	Med.	Low	Very low
1. Indoor activity	▰				
2. Outdoor activity	▰				
3. Vigor		▰			
4. Behavioral constancy				▰	
5. Dominance to strange dogs			▰		
6. Dominance to familiar people				▰	
7. Territoriality					▰
8. Emotional stability		▰			
9. Sociability — within family			▰		
10. Sociability — with children	▰				
11. Sociability — with strangers				▰	
12. Learning — rate		▰			
13. Learning — obedience				▰	
14. Learning — problem solving			▰		
15. Watchdog ability	▰				
16. Guard-dog ability				▰	

The Harrier looks like a smaller version of the English Foxhound and is used for a similar purpose, hunting by scent in a pack. The Harrier's quarry was, appropriately enough, the hare. Descriptions include "easygoing"; "solidly built, handy in size, well constructed and muscular, and both hardy and active"; "gentle with people"; "stubborn and bold"; "too restless for the city."

Behavior problems may include indoor restlessness, excessive barking, roaming and house soiling.

Irish Wolfhound

A.K.C. Popularity: 62nd

Dimension of Temperament	Level of Dimension				
	Very high	High	Med.	Low	Very low
1. Indoor activity				▒	
2. Outdoor activity			▒		
3. Vigor				▒	
4. Behavioral constancy		▒			
5. Dominance to strange dogs		▒	▒		
6. Dominance to familiar people			▒		
7. Territoriality			▒		
8. Emotional stability		▒			
9. Sociability – within family		▒	▒		
10. Sociability – with children	▒				
11. Sociability – with strangers				▒	
12. Learning – rate		▒			
13. Learning – obedience			▒		
14. Learning – problem solving			▒		
15. Watchdog ability			▒	▒	
16. Guard-dog ability			▒	▒	

The Irish Wolfhound is an enormous animal, probably the tallest breed of dog in existence—up to 36 inches at the shoulder and reaching up to over 7 feet when standing on its hind legs. In the past it was used for hunting wolves in Ireland and for bringing down the six-foot-tall Irish elk. Today, given the conspicuous scarcity of Irish wolves and elk, the breed is perpetuated primarily as a pet. Descriptions include "quiet-mannered and dignified . . . beneath the fierce-looking exterior there beats a gentle heart"; "it treats most other dogs as insignificant"; "commands are slowly executed"; "sluggish."

Behavior problems may include clumsiness, an occasional dominant animal's challenging its owner's authority and other dominance-related problems.

Norwegian Elkhound

A.K.C. Popularity: 38th

Dimension of Temperament	Level of Dimension				
	Very high	High	Med.	Low	Very low
1. Indoor activity		▩			
2. Outdoor activity			▩		
3. Vigor	▩				
4. Behavioral constancy		▩			
5. Dominance to strange dogs		▩	▩		
6. Dominance to familiar people		▩	▩		
7. Territoriality		▩			
8. Emotional stability		▩			
9. Sociability — within family		▩	▩	▩	
10. Sociability — with children			▩	▩	
11. Sociability — with strangers		▩	▩	▩	
12. Learning — rate	▩				
13. Learning — obedience				▩	
14. Learning — problem solving		▩			
15. Watchdog ability	▩				
16. Guard-dog ability		▩			

The Norwegian Elkhound is a medium-sized, thick-coated, powerfully built dog adapted to the severe Scandinavian winters. Originially used to hunt the huge Scandinavian elk, this breed is strong, compact and extremely hardy. Descriptions include "willingness to hunt day after day and all day long in rugged country, where stamina rather than extreme speed is called for"; "being able to bounce like a rubber ball when struck by elk hooves"; absolutely dependable and trustworthy"; "may start bullying in an attempt to have its own way"; "easygoing"; "reliability and quickness to learn"; "stubborn and bold"; "intelligence and eagerness for praise"; "staunchness, dignity and independence." The contradictions stem from the dog's potential for dominance. It may be obedient to dominant owners but disobey submissive ones. Its tendency to hold its quarry at bay makes it a potentially effective guard dog.

Behavior problems may include excessive barking, roaming, dominance problems and stealing and guarding food.

81

Otter Hound

A.K.C. Popularity:
120th

Dimension of Temperament	Level of Dimension				
	Very high	High	Med.	Low	Very low
1. Indoor activity				▨	
2. Outdoor activity		▨			
3. Vigor				▨	
4. Behavioral constancy			▨		
5. Dominance to strange dogs			▨		
6. Dominance to familiar people			▨		
7. Territoriality				▨	
8. Emotional stability		▨			
9. Sociability — within family	▨				
10. Sociability — with children	▨				
11. Sociability — with strangers	▨				
12. Learning — rate				▨	
13. Learning — obedience			▨		
14. Learning — problem solving				▨	
15. Watchdog ability		▨			
16. Guard-dog ability				▨	

The Otter Hound is an unusual-looking hound with its rough, shaggy coat. The coat is waterproof, and this breed can track its quarry by scent through rough, wet terrain, running and swimming tenaciously to the end of the hunt. Descriptions include "sagacity and unfailing devotion," "amiable and boisterous," "extremely sensitive nose, inquisitive and persevering in investigating scents," "easygoing," "occasionally stubborn."

Behavior problems may include house soiling, roaming, food stealing, clumsiness and tenacious sniffing.

Rhodesian Ridgeback

A.K.C. Popularity: 69th

Dimension of Temperament	Level of Dimension				
	Very high	High	Med.	Low	Very low
1. Indoor activity				▓	
2. Outdoor activity	▓				
3. Vigor	▓				
4. Behavioral constancy		▓			
5. Dominance to strange dogs	▓				
6. Dominance to familiar people		▓			
7. Territoriality		▓			
8. Emotional stability		▓			
9. Sociability — within family			▓		
10. Sociability — with children				▓	
11. Sociability — with strangers				▓	
12. Learning — rate		▓			
13. Learning — obedience				▓	
14. Learning — problem solving		▓			
15. Watchdog ability	▓				
16. Guard-dog ability	▓				

The Rhodesian Ridgeback is a large dog bred in Africa as a guard, scent hunter and big-game hunter. It is characterized by a ridge of hair growing in the opposite direction to the rest of its coat along the length of its spine. It is a powerful, agile dog that can pull down a wounded buck or worry a cornered lion until the hunters arrive. Descriptions include "strong, muscular and active dog . . . capable of great endurance and a fair amount of speed"; "stubborn and boldly disobedient to submissive people."

Behavior problems may include dominance-related problems, challenging family members, aggression and house soiling.

Saluki

A.K.C. Popularity: 75th

Dimension of Temperament	Level of Dimension				
	Very high	High	Med.	Low	Very low
1. Indoor activity				▨	
2. Outdoor activity	▨				
3. Vigor				▨	
4. Behavioral constancy				▨	
5. Dominance to strange dogs			▨		
6. Dominance to familiar people				▨	
7. Territoriality				▨	
8. Emotional stability					▨
9. Sociability — within family					▨
10. Sociability — with children					▨
11. Sociability — with strangers					▨
12. Learning — rate				▨	
13. Learning — obedience			▨		
14. Learning — problem solving				▨	
15. Watchdog ability		▨			
16. Guard-dog ability				▨	

The Saluki, the royal dog of Egypt, is considered by some authorities to be the oldest known breed. It has a Greyhound body with feathered ears, tail and legs. Like the Greyhound, it is a sight hound capable of tremendous speed and agility, but is hardier, able to withstand climatic changes and cold that the Greyhound cannot. Its temperament is like that of the Afghan, but a little less emotional and snappy. Dogs of this breed are "easily distracted while training," "skittish," "standoffish even with their masters," "not very playful and demonstrative."

Behavior problems may include phobias, irritable snapping, roaming and house soiling.

Scottish Deerhound

A.K.C. Popularity: 107th

Dimension of Temperament	Level of Dimension				
	Very high	High	Med.	Low	Very low
1. Indoor activity				▨	
2. Outdoor activity		▨			
3. Vigor				▨	
4. Behavioral constancy		▨			
5. Dominance to strange dogs			▨		
6. Dominance to familiar people				▨	
7. Territoriality				▨	
8. Emotional stability	▨				
9. Sociability — within family		▨			
10. Sociability — with children	▨				
11. Sociability — with strangers		▨			
12. Learning — rate				▨	
13. Learning — obedience			▨		
14. Learning — problem solving				▨	
15. Watchdog ability				▨	
16. Guard-dog ability				▨	

The Scottish Deerhound is a large dog reminiscent of, but smaller and slimmer than, the Irish Wolfhound. Its long legs and Greyhound build, slightly obscured by its shaggy coat, are designed for high speed and endurance. Descriptions include "tremendous courage, gentle dignity, quiet, keen scent, not aggressive, great persistence"; "not a sparkler"; "somewhat timid"; "not very quick to obey"; "devoted and loyal to its masters."

No potential behavior problems were mentioned in the literature or by breeders, and I have never encountered a Deerhound behavior problem.

Whippet

A.K.C. Popularity: 63rd

Dimension of Temperament	Level of Dimension				
	Very high	High	Med.	Low	Very low
1. Indoor activity				▨	
2. Outdoor activity	▨				
3. Vigor					▨
4. Behavioral constancy				▨	
5. Dominance to strange dogs				▨	
6. Dominance to familiar people				▨	
7. Territoriality				▨	
8. Emotional stability					
9. Sociability — within family			▨		
10. Sociability — with children					▨
11. Sociability — with strangers				▨	
12. Learning — rate		▨			
13. Learning — obedience			▨		
14. Learning — problem solving			▨		
15. Watchdog ability		▨			
16. Guard-dog ability				▨	

The Whippet is a small dog that looks like a miniature Greyhound. It is a small sight hound used for racing, coursing rabbits and killing rats. Descriptions include "high-strung and timid"; "not very demonstrative or playful and poorly padded for roughhousing and the cold"; "should be trained gently, never bullied or harshly punished."

Behavior problems may include phobias, house soiling, timidity and irritable snapping.

4

The Working Dogs

This group contains 30 breeds that are used mostly for herding and guarding, a few being used as guide and rescue dogs. The group includes the Akita, Alaskan Malamute, Belgian Malinois, Belgian Sheepdog, Belgian Tervueren, Bernese Mountain Dog, Bouvier des Flandres, Boxer, Briard, Bullmastiff, Collie, Doberman Pinscher, German Shepherd, Giant Schnauzer, Great Dane, Great Pyrenees, Komondor, Kuvasz, Mastiff, Newfoundland, Old English Sheepdog, Puli, Rottweiler, St. Bernard, Samoyed, Siberian Husky, Standard Schnauzer, Cardigan Welsh Corgi and the Pembroke Welsh Corgi. This group, for the most part, is made up of large to enormous breeds. There are only three breeds that could be considered small.

Akita

A.K.C. Popularity: 53rd

Dimension of Temperament	Level of Dimension				
	Very high	High	Med.	Low	Very low
1. Indoor activity				▓	
2. Outdoor activity		▓			
3. Vigor		▓			
4. Behavioral constancy		▓			
5. Dominance to strange dogs	▓	▓			
6. Dominance to familiar people			▓		
7. Territoriality		▓			
8. Emotional stability		▓			
9. Sociability — within family			▓		
10. Sociability — with children			▓	▓	
11. Sociability — with strangers				▓	▓
12. Learning — rate		▓			
13. Learning — obedience				▓	
14. Learning — problem solving			▓		
15. Watchdog ability	▓				
16. Guard-dog ability	▓				

The Akita (pronounced a-KEE-ta), the official dog of Japan, varies in size from large to very large and is characterized by a large, curled tail, erect ears and broad head. Descriptions include "dignified, good-natured, alert, bold, courageous, docile and loyal"; "fearless, and having a never-give-in attitude"; "very stubborn and needing firm training from puppyhood, especially in not attacking strange dogs and in holding intruders at bay but not biting."

Behavior problems may include dominance challenges, territorial aggression and house soiling.

*Alaskan Malamute**

A.K.C. Popularity:
32nd

Dimension of Temperament	Level of Dimension				
	Very high	High	Med.	Low	Very low
1. Indoor activity	■				
2. Outdoor activity	■				
3. Vigor	■				
4. Behavioral constancy				■	
5. Dominance to strange dogs		■	■		
6. Dominance to familiar people			■		
7. Territoriality		■			
8. Emotional stability		■			
9. Sociability – within family	■	■			
10. Sociability – with children			■		
11. Sociability – with strangers		■			
12. Learning – rate				■	
13. Learning – obedience				■	■
14. Learning – problem solving	■				
15. Watchdog ability			■		
16. Guard-dog ability				■	

The Malamute (pronounced MAH-la-myoot) is a large dog used by native Alaskans to pull sleds. Owing to its cold-weather heritage, the Malamute has a very heavy coat that sheds heavily after the winter. Descriptions include "affectionate, friendly, easygoing"; "high-spirited and bold, not a one-man dog, loyal, devoted, playful on invitation but impressive in its own dignity"; "lifelong puppy"; needing "firm, patient training, not interrupted by periods of indulgence."

Behavior problems may include pulling on the leash, roaming, howling, jumping on people, house soiling and mischievous destruction. Females may attempt to dig a den in the cushions of a sofa. Recently, owing to puppy-mill production, some Malamutes have been showing excessive destructiveness when left alone, dominance aggression, challenging owners, and guarding food, property and places from owners. Don't underestimate the puppy-mill variety's potential for destruction. In a recent case of mine, a male Malamute managed to destroy all my client's living-room furniture in a single afternoon spree. It amounted to $15,000 worth of damage in three hours. That's $83.33 per minute.

*Watch out for puppy-mill variety.

Belgians* Sheepdog
Belgians* Tervuren
Belgians* Malinois

A.K.C. Popularity:
76th, 84th, 121st

Dimension of Temperament	Level of Dimension				
	Very high	High	Med.	Low	Very low
1. Indoor activity		▨			
2. Outdoor activity		▨			
3. Vigor				▨	
4. Behavioral constancy				▨	
5. Dominance to strange dogs			▨		
6. Dominance to familiar people				▨	
7. Territoriality			▨		
8. Emotional stability				▨	
9. Sociability — within family				▨	
10. Sociability — with children		▨▨▨▨	▨	▨	
11. Sociability — with strangers				▨	
12. Learning — rate	▨				
13. Learning — obedience	▨				
14. Learning — problem solving			▨		
15. Watchdog ability	▨				
16. Guard-dog ability	▨	▨			

Belgian is actually a category for three large breeds that are very similar in body shape and temperament: the Sheepdog, Malinois and Tervuren. The primary differences in these breeds are in coat length and color. The Malinois has a short, dense coat which looks like a German Shepherd's, but is a bit shorter. The Tervuren is a longer-haired breed, similar in color to the Malinois. The Sheepdog has a long-haired black coat. Each has the erect ears and full tail reminiscent of the German Shepherd. Descriptions of all three breeds include "natural tendency to move in a circle rather than a straight line," "always in motion," "watchful and attentive," "observant and vigilant toward strangers but not apprehensive."

Behavior problems for these breeds may include fear biting, timidity, indoor restlessness, destructiveness when left alone, and sometimes "shy-sharpness."

*Some kennels are breeding timid, highly excitable, volatile animals that are difficult pets.

Bernese Mountain Dog

A.K.C. Popularity: 96th

Dimension of Temperament	Level of Dimension				
	Very high	High	Med.	Low	Very low
1. Indoor activity				▨	
2. Outdoor activity		▨			
3. Vigor				▨	
4. Behavioral constancy		▨			
5. Dominance to strange dogs			▨		
6. Dominance to familiar people				▨	
7. Territoriality			▨		
8. Emotional stability		▨			
9. Sociability – within family				▨	
10. Sociability – with children	▨				
11. Sociability – with strangers				▨	
12. Learning – rate	▨				
13. Learning – obedience		▨			
14. Learning – problem solving		▨			
15. Watchdog ability		▨			
16. Guard-dog ability		▨	▨		

The Bernese Mountain Dog is a large draft dog. Descriptions include "extremely hardy, thriving in an unheated kennel in all weather ... exceptionally faithful: once having centered its affection on an individual, it does not fawn upon or make friends with strangers."

Behavior problems may include excessive timidity, food stealing, occasional destructiveness when left alone, tendency to fear strangers, leaning against and constant attendance on its favorite family member.

My most common cases with Bernese Mountain Dogs involve a people phobia. This appears to be more prevalent in the female of the breed and could be a natural exaggeration of the breed's basic temperament. It is when the dog has not been socialized by exposure to many friendly people from puppyhood that this most often occurs. Sometimes a people phobia develops despite socialization, and then special desensitization techniques must be employed.

Bouvier des Flandres

A.K.C. Popularity: 60th

Dimension of Temperament	Level of Dimension				
	Very high	High	Med.	Low	Very low
1. Indoor activity				▨	
2. Outdoor activity		▨			
3. Vigor				▨	
4. Behavioral constancy	▨				
5. Dominance to strange dogs			▨		
6. Dominance to familiar people			▨		
7. Territoriality			▨		
8. Emotional stability	▨				
9. Sociability — within family			▨		
10. Sociability — with children	▨				
11. Sociability — with strangers			▨		
12. Learning — rate	▨				
13. Learning — obedience		▨			
14. Learning — problem solving		▨			
15. Watchdog ability	▨				
16. Guard-dog ability	▨				

The Bouvier des Flandres (pronounced BOO-vyay-day-FLAHN-dre) varies in size from large to very large. It has been variously used for cattle herding and police work and as a messenger dog, guard dog and ambulance dog in World War I. Descriptions include "very alert watchdog and a natural guard dog, being more vicious than the Bernese."

Behavior problems may include dominance.

The most unusual case I have had with a Bouvier I have called "the Case of the California Dog." The owners came to me complaining that their male Bouvier wouldn't allow them to make love. At first, only the act itself was verboten, but eventually the dog forbade any display of intimacy. A casual hug became a signal for growling threats. Since the only way my clients could enjoy any intimacy was on the sly, the motel bills started piling up, and it was at this point that they came to see me. I discovered that this dog's peculiar behavior originated from its former California owners' habit of involving the dog in their connubial recreation.

Boxer*

A.K.C. Popularity: 24th

Dimension of Temperament	Level of Dimension				
	Very high	High	Med.	Low	Very low
1. Indoor activity		▧			
2. Outdoor activity		▧			
3. Vigor		▧			
4. Behavioral constancy				▧	
5. Dominance to strange dogs		▧	▧		
6. Dominance to familiar people			▧	▧	
7. Territoriality			▧		
8. Emotional stability	▧				
9. Sociability — within family	▧				
10. Sociability — with children	▧				
11. Sociability — with strangers				▧	▧
12. Learning — rate		▧			
13. Learning — obedience				▧	
14. Learning — problem solving				▧	
15. Watchdog ability		▧			
16. Guard-dog ability	▧	▧	▧	▧	

The Boxer is a medium-sized dog that gets its name from the characteristic way it begins to fight—by rising up on its hind legs and striking out with its front paws. It was used for pit fighting and bull and bear baiting, but now it is most frequently a companion. Its popularity has given rise to a puppy-mill variety which is much less emotionally stable and may cause many problems including excessive timidity or dominance, aggression, disobedience and restlessness. Descriptions include "gentle with familiar people," "not faulted for belligerence toward other dogs," "playful and animated," "responds promptly to playful overtures," "stubborn and bold," "must be taught to obey before it becomes too dominant," "patient and stoical," "a hearing guard," "responding promptly to friendly overtures when given honestly," "deliberate and wary with strangers, exhibiting curiosity but fearless courage and tenacity if threatened."

Behavior problems for the puppy-mill variety have been mentioned above. For the well-bred variety, there are few behavior problems except perhaps for timidity, dominance, willful disobedience and food stealing, expecially if the dog has not been trained properly as a puppy. Boxers tend to drool and snore.

*Watch out for puppy-mill variety.

Briard

A.K.C. Popularity: 97th

Dimension of Temperament	Very high	High	Med.	Low	Very low
1. Indoor activity	X				
2. Outdoor activity	X				
3. Vigor		X			
4. Behavioral constancy		X			
5. Dominance to strange dogs		X			
6. Dominance to familiar people		X	X		
7. Territoriality		X			
8. Emotional stability			X	X	
9. Sociability — within family		X			
10. Sociability — with children	X	X	X		
11. Sociability — with strangers				X	
12. Learning — rate				X	
13. Learning — obedience					X
14. Learning — problem solving			X		
15. Watchdog ability	X				
16. Guard-dog ability	X				

The Briard (pronounced bree-ARD) is a large, shaggy-looking French shepherd and guard dog. Descriptions include "possesses spirit and initiative," "has a retentive memory," "some will display a certain independence," "stubborn and fairly bold," "headstrong and difficult unless taught early to obey," "possessing a protective instinct."

Behavior problems may include indoor restlessness, disobedience, dominance problems and challenging their owners.

Bullmastiff

A.K.C. Popularity:
71st

Dimension of Temperament	Level of Dimension				
	Very high	High	Med.	Low	Very low
1. Indoor activity				▨	
2. Outdoor activity		▨			
3. Vigor	▨				
4. Behavioral constancy		▨			
5. Dominance to strange dogs		▨			
6. Dominance to familiar people		▨			
7. Territoriality		▨			
8. Emotional stability		▨			
9. Sociability — within family			▨		
10. Sociability — with children	▨				
11. Sociability — with strangers				▨	
12. Learning — rate		▨			
13. Learning — obedience				▨	
14. Learning — problem solving			▨		
15. Watchdog ability	▨				
16. Guard-dog ability	▨				

The Bullmastiff is a very large breed with a genetic foundation that was 60% Mastiff and 40% Bulldog. The result was the "gamekeeper's night dog," used exclusively to pursue, knock down and hold intruding poachers. This was the dog that became Sylvester Stallone's companion in the film *Rocky*. Descriptions include "showing great strength, powerfully built but active . . . fearless yet docile, having endurance and alertness"; "stubborn."

Behavior problems may involve excessive dominance exhibited toward people the dog considers submissive, possible dominance-motivated aggression, and pulling on the leash (and this breed can have 130 pounds of muscle to pull with).

Collies (Rough- and Smooth-coated)*

A.K.C. Popularity: 13th

Dimension of Temperament	Level of Dimension				
	Very high	High	Med.	Low	Very low
1. Indoor activity				▨	
2. Outdoor activity		▨			
3. Vigor			▨	▨	
4. Behavioral constancy			▨		
5. Dominance to strange dogs			▨	▨	
6. Dominance to familiar people			▨	▨	
7. Territoriality				▨	
8. Emotional stability		▨	▨	▨	
9. Sociability – within family		▨	▨		
10. Sociability – with children	▨	▨			
11. Sociability – with strangers		▨	▨		
12. Learning – rate		▨			
13. Learning – obedience	▨				
14. Learning – problem solving		▨			
15. Watchdog ability	▨	▨			
16. Guard-dog ability	▨	▨	▨		

Anyone who has seen Lassie knows what a Rough-coated Collie looks like and has an expectation about its behavior. I call this the Lassie syndrome, since most Collies cannot match the spectacularly staged feats and humanlike qualities of which this acting dog is depicted as capable. So some naive owners find themselves disappointed. The Rough Collie is ninth in popularity in the United States, and some lines have been subject to the effects of puppy-milling. The Smooth-coated Collie looks like a Rough Collie with a crew cut and is also high in American popularity. The only difference in temperament between the two is that the Smooth Collie tends to be more aggressive. Descriptions include "lithe, strong, active, speedy and graceful" and "easy to train."

Behavior problems for some lines may include timidity, restlessness, irritable snapping and roaming.

*Watch out for puppy-mill dogs.

Doberman Pinscher*

A.K.C. Popularity: 2nd

Dimension of Temperament	Level of Dimension				
	Very high	High	Med.	Low	Very low
1. Indoor activity	▨	▨	▨		
2. Outdoor activity	▨				
3. Vigor	▨	▨	▨	▨	
4. Behavioral constancy			▨	▨	
5. Dominance to strange dogs		▨			
6. Dominance to familiar people	▨	▨	▨	▨	▨
7. Territoriality		▨			
8. Emotional stability			▨	▨	▨
9. Sociability — within family			▨	▨	▨
10. Sociability — with children				▨	▨
11. Sociability — with strangers				▨	▨
12. Learning — rate	▨	▨	▨	▨	▨
13. Learning — obedience	▨	▨	▨	▨	▨
14. Learning — problem solving	▨				
15. Watchdog ability	▨				
16. Guard-dog ability	▨				

The Doberman Pinscher suffers from a bad reputation. The Doberman is characterized as an aggressive, sometimes vicious large dog that may even turn on its master. I believe that this reputation is partly deserved. There are some members of this breed that exhibit these traits, but the breed as a whole is not as aggressive as most people think. The A.K.C. describes the Doberman as "energetic, watchful, determined, alert, fearless, loyal and obedient." It goes on to say that "if properly bred and trained, a specimen has a sane mind and sound body." This implies that if improperly bred and trained, an animal may not show these traits. Most breeders defend this breed, saying that its bad reputation is undeserved and is simply a biased judgment from the few bad specimens. They are probably correct. What this breed seems to show is variability. There are exceptions to every generalization. Breeders say that Dobies are somewhat active indoors. Some are indeed very active and tend to be restless indoors. Most can be very active outdoors and need a lot of exercise. The breed varies behaviorally from moderate to very vigorous and from normal to very variable. Most are high in territoriality, being dominant and aggressive toward

98

strange dogs. The A.K.C. says that this aggression is acceptable and "shall not be deemed as viciousness." With familiar people the breed also varies from very submissive to very dominant, with everything in between. Emotionally, individuals are normal to vacillating. Some are considered "bold"; others are not. Some are very timid. In fact, shyness is a fault, according to the A.K.C., which means that its exists, at least in some dogs. The problem with excessive timidity in Dobies is that these dogs are prime candidates for shy-sharpness, which may result in viciousness toward people, including the owners. Learning rate also varies: some dogs learn very fast, while others are somewhat slow. Obedience may vary from very good, in the dogs designated as intermediate in dominance toward people, to very poor, with very dominant animals. When training a Doberman it's best not to use punishment or have an impatient, angry attitude. A Dobie trained out of fear is not safe around anyone. It is best to use positive reinforcement and praise. In general, Dobies are very good problem solvers. They are usually very alert watchdogs and can be very aggressive guard dogs.

The breed ranks from solitary to very solitary on the sociability dimension. As pets, individuals vary from a one-family to a one-person dog. Some Dobies are bad around children and some may be tolerant if they were raised from puppyhood with children. They are either reserved or aggressive toward strangers.

Some behavior problems may include indoor restlessness, phobias and timidity, irritable snapping, dominance challenges toward master, fear biting and touch shyness. Note: Some kennels breed for "sharpness," which means quick-tempered aggression, so choose your breeder carefully—and never buy a Dobie from a pet shop.

*Watch out for puppy-mill dogs.

German Shepherd*

A.K.C. Popularity: 3rd

Dimension of Temperament	Level of Dimension				
	Very high	High	Med.	Low	Very low
1. Indoor activity	▓	▓	▓		
2. Outdoor activity	▓	▓			
3. Vigor		▓	▓		
4. Behavioral constancy		▓	▓	▓	
5. Dominance to strange dogs	▓	▓	▓	▓	▓
6. Dominance to familiar people	▓	▓	▓	▓	▓
7. Territoriality	▓	▓			
8. Emotional stability		▓	▓	▓	
9. Sociability — within family			▓	▓	▓
10. Sociability — with children	▓	▓	▓	▓	▓
11. Sociability — with strangers			▓	▓	
12. Learning — rate	▓				
13. Learning — obedience	▓	▓	▓	▓	
14. Learning — problem solving	▓	▓	▓		
15. Watchdog ability	▓				
16. Guard-dog ability	▓	▓			

The German Shepherd is another breed that suffers from media hype and puppy-mill production. Puppy-mill Shepherds obtained from pet shops may be timid, nervous, emotionally vacillating and fear biters. Shepherds bred for sharpness may be very territorial, dominant over everyone including the owners, very aggressive and poor in obedience (guarding their food and resting place from their owners). "Shy-sharp" Shepherds can be vicious.

Well-bred Shepherds have been described as follows: "loyal, courageous, able to assimilate and retain training, poised, stable, unexcitable and with well-controlled nerves," and in their capacity as guide dogs, "exhibiting a high order of intelligence and discrimination involving the qualities of observation, patience, faithful watchfulness and . . . a degree of judgment necessary for the task."

The potential in this breed for behavior problems varies with the type of breeding. Some specimens are mischievously or angrily destructive when left alone, especially the one-person dogs. Some show indoor restlessness, nervousness and fear biting, especially the puppy-mill variety. Some may challenge their owners, especially those bred for attack work, and some show no problems at all.

My most unusual case involving a German Shepherd was Sammy, a four-year-old behemoth, who had developed the disconcerting habit of nipping young ladies in the buttocks. The nip wasn't serious, sort of a dog pinch. At first the owner, a young man in his mid-twenties, found it amusing and perhaps valued the behavior, since Sammy's taste in women was similar to his. Also, the pinch was a handy ice-breaker, since abject apologies could usually be turned into dates. The young man came to see me when his bride, introduced to him by Sammy's pinch, decided the behavior should be discontinued.

- - - - - = puppy-mill
▬▬▬▬▬ = well-bred
*Watch out for puppy-mill dogs.

Giant Schnauzer

A.K.C. Popularity: 83rd

Dimension of Temperament	Level of Dimension				
	Very high	High	Med.	Low	Very low
1. Indoor activity		▨			
2. Outdoor activity		▨			
3. Vigor	▨				
4. Behavioral constancy			▨		
5. Dominance to strange dogs	▨				
6. Dominance to familiar people	▨				
7. Territoriality	▨				
8. Emotional stability		▨			
9. Sociability — within family				▨	
10. Sociability — with children				▨	
11. Sociability — with strangers				▨	
12. Learning — rate		▨			
13. Learning — obedience			▨	▨	
14. Learning — problem solving	▨				
15. Watchdog ability	▨				
16. Guard-dog ability	▨				

The Giant Schnauzer is about the size of a German Shepherd and may be considerably more aggressive. In the past it has been used for driving cattle and for guard and police work. Descriptions include "bold"; "spirited, fun-loving and playful" and "highly adaptable."

Behavior problems may include dominance challenges to the owner and indoor restlessness.

My most difficult case with this breed was Satan, an aptly named black Schnauzer. Satan ruled the household with an iron jaw. Not only did his rules define when he was to be walked and who could interact with whom, but he was the first case I had of a dog that actually enacted a curfew. No one was allowed out of his or her room after 10 P.M. To avoid Satan's wrath, the teen-age son had to sneak into his room after a late date by climbing in the window. The problem was caused by a mismatch between the rather submissive character of the family and the dominant temperament of this breed. The most difficult part of the case was persuading the family to dominate their dog.

Great Dane

A.K.C. Popularity: 19th

Dimension of Temperament	Level of Dimension				
	Very high	High	Med.	Low	Very low
1. Indoor activity				▨	
2. Outdoor activity			▨		
3. Vigor				▨	
4. Behavioral constancy	▨				
5. Dominance to strange dogs		▨			
6. Dominance to familiar people				▨	
7. Territoriality			▨		
8. Emotional stability	▨				
9. Sociability – within family		▨			
10. Sociability – with children	▨				
11. Sociability – with strangers		▨			
12. Learning – rate				▨	
13. Learning – obedience			▨		
14. Learning – problem solving				▨	
15. Watchdog ability	▨				
16. Guard-dog ability				▨	

The Great Dane is an enormous breed used at one time for boar hunting in Germany. The breed is popular in the United States, and the puppy-mill variety may look sickly, with a knobby, weak-looking back. Descriptions of the well-bred variety include "easygoing, lovable and good-tempered"; "retentive"; "must be taught not to lean against, sit on or bump into people."

Behavior problems may include, in rare instances, dominance problems and challenges to the owner's authority. Unfortunately, these instances are becoming less rare as the breed becomes more popular and puppy-mill production increases. Buy only from a recognized breeded because, owing to their great size, puppy-mill Great Danes can be extremely dangerous.

Don Chichio, a four-year-old male Dane of enormous proportions, sits beside me as I write this. His owners, a young couple, brought him to me with one of the most unusual complaints I have ever heard. It seems Don Chichio is a furniture mover in their absence. They will return home and actu-

103

ally find the living-room furniture pushed into the dining room. Once when they tied him on a six-foot lead, two feet out of reach of the nearest furniture, he turned and used his hind legs to drag the furniture to him. I am still trying to figure out why he does it.

Great Pyrenees Mountain Dog

A.K.C. Popularity: 57th

Dimension of Temperament	Level of Dimension				
	Very high	High	Med.	Low	Very low
1. Indoor activity				▨	
2. Outdoor activity			▨		
3. Vigor			▨		
4. Behavioral constancy	▨				
5. Dominance to strange dogs			▨		
6. Dominance to familiar people			▨		
7. Territoriality			▨		
8. Emotional stability	▨				
9. Sociability – within family			▨		
10. Sociability – with children				▨	
11. Sociability – with strangers	▨	▨			
12. Learning – rate				▨	
13. Learning – obedience			▨	▨	
14. Learning – problem solving			▨		
15. Watchdog ability	▨				
16. Guard-dog ability		▨			

The Great Pyrenees Mountain Dog, as the name implies, is an enormous breed developed in the Pyrenees Mountains as a shepherd and guardian. It was also used as a guard dog by the French nobility and as a draft dog by the peasants. Its coat is white and long. Descriptions include "devotion, fidelity, a sense of guardsmanship and intelligence"; "serious in play as he is in work"; the breed shows "gentleness and docility with those it knows"; "molds itself to the moods and desires of its human companions"; "loyal and protective, and less overbearing than most other enormous breeds"; "stubborn, and without firm, patient and consistent training may become very willful."

Behavior problems may include roaming. A rare, but potential, behavior problem may involve excessive dominance toward familiar people like family members, coupled with an excessive attachment to one member. This may result in serious dominance aggression if the conditions are right. At the very least it could lead to willful disobedience toward the people it considers submissive.

105

Rhumba, a six-year-old female, is a case in point. She is lovingly attached to and protective of her family, but treats joggers as both a threat and perhaps a toy, since she chases and retrieves them. Once when she got loose Rhumba's owners were startled to find six nervous joggers neatly lined up in their backyard.

Komondor

A.K.C. Popularity:
112th

Dimension of Temperament	Level of Dimension				
	Very high	High	Med.	Low	Very low
1. Indoor activity	▓▓▓	▓▓			
2. Outdoor activity	▓▓				
3. Vigor	▓▓				
4. Behavioral constancy				▓▓	
5. Dominance to strange dogs		▓▓			
6. Dominance to familiar people		▓▓			
7. Territoriality		▓▓			
8. Emotional stability		▓▓			
9. Sociability — within family				▓▓	
10. Sociability — with children					▓▓
11. Sociability — with strangers					▓▓
12. Learning — rate				▓▓	
13. Learning — obedience					▓▓
14. Learning — problem solving		▓▓			
15. Watchdog ability	▓▓				
16. Guard-dog ability	▓▓				

The Komondor is a large shepherd and guard dog developed in Hungary. It presents a most peculiar appearance. Its coat is very long and corded, giving the dog the appearance of an enormous walking dust mop of thick white yarn. Descriptions include "commanding, likely to create fear—and for good reason—and a guardian ready at any moment to fight all manner of vicious predators"; "initially living in the open throughout all weather"; "imposing strength and courageous demeanor"; "easygoing"; "playful"; "very protective of home and master"; "owner must assert dominance early on"; "stubborn and bold and, unless well trained from the start, very willful."

Behavior problems may include house soiling; possibly dominance challenges toward the owner and/or other family members, especially in the larger specimens; willful disobedience and aggression.

Kuvasz

A.K.C. Popularity: 99th

Dimension of Temperament	Level of Dimension				
	Very high	High	Med.	Low	Very low
1. Indoor activity	▪				
2. Outdoor activity	▪				
3. Vigor	▪				
4. Behavioral constancy				▪	
5. Dominance to strange dogs	▪	▪			
6. Dominance to familiar people		▪			
7. Territoriality	▪				
8. Emotional stability		▪			
9. Sociability — within family					▪
10. Sociability — with children					▪
11. Sociability — with strangers					▪
12. Learning — rate		▪			
13. Learning — obedience					▪
14. Learning — problem solving		▪			
15. Watchdog ability	▪				
16. Guard-dog ability	▪				

The Kuvasz is a large white dog with a longish, slightly wavy coat. It was developed in Hungary as a guard and later as a shepherd. It resembles the Great Pyrenees breed in appearance. Descriptions include "untiring ability to work over rough terrain and for long periods"; "bold, courageous and fearless"; "unexcelled guard able to act on its own initiative at the right moment without instruction"; "very stubborn and very independent." I would add that this dog should not be owned by anyone who has the slightest fear or submissiveness and that the whole family should be trained in how to control the dog.

Behavior problems may include restlessness, overprotectiveness and dominance challenges to the owner and family members as the dog matures.

Mastiff

A.K.C. Popularity: 68th

Dimension of Temperament	Level of Dimension				
	Very high	High	Med.	Low	Very low
1. Indoor activity				▩	
2. Outdoor activity			▩		
3. Vigor				▩	
4. Behavioral constancy	▩				
5. Dominance to strange dogs		▩			
6. Dominance to familiar people				▩	
7. Territoriality			▩		
8. Emotional stability	▩				
9. Sociability — within family		▩			
10. Sociability — with children	▩				
11. Sociability — with strangers				▩	
12. Learning — rate				▩	
13. Learning — obedience			▩		
14. Learning — problem solving				▩	
15. Watchdog ability	▩				
16. Guard-dog ability		▩			

I must confess a bit of bias, since I own a Mastiff and personally like the breed. The Mastiff is an enormous animal, a giant short-haired dog with heavy head and a relatively short muzzle. It is one of the heaviest of all breeds. Some male Mastiffs can exceed 200 pounds of solid muscle. To give you an idea of their strength, Captain, my two-year-old Mastiff, is only 180 pounds but still gets great pleasure from playing with 25-pound boulders as if they were beach balls.

Mastiffs were bred in England for two thousand years as a watchdog. The Romans used to use them as gladiator, bull, bear, lion and tiger combatants. Up to 100 years ago, they were the heavyweight pit fighting dogs featured in the "Westminster Pit," England's Madison Square Garden of dogfights. Mastiffs were also used as "tie dogs," being tied by day and left free to roam and guard the premises by night. The A.K.C. says only that this breed is powerful, agile and courageous. Powerful and courageous? Yes. Agile? That depends on the individual dog. Some enormous ones look and move like ponderous bulls;

others are agile despite their size. Descriptions include "relatively gentle, and very good-natured" and "easygoing." A 200-pound dog doesn't really have to obey anyone, but dogs of this breed usually do, given time, consistent patience and warm, rewarding and *nonpunitive* training. Never hit a Mastiff for any reason.

Behavior problems are negligible. Mastiffs may steal food if uncorrected, but respond readily to mild rebukes. Some may drool and/or wheeze, and all snore, sounding very like a chain saw.

Newfoundland

A.K.C. Popularity: 49th

Dimension of Temperament	Level of Dimension				
	Very high	High	Med.	Low	Very low
1. Indoor activity				▓	
2. Outdoor activity		▓			
3. Vigor					▓
4. Behavioral constancy	▓				
5. Dominance to strange dogs			▓		
6. Dominance to familiar people			▓	▓	
7. Territoriality				▓	
8. Emotional stability	▓				
9. Sociability — within family	▓				
10. Sociability — with children	▓				
11. Sociability — with strangers	▓				
12. Learning — rate		▓			
13. Learning — obedience		▓			
14. Learning — problem solving		▓			
15. Watchdog ability		▓			
16. Guard-dog ability				▓	

The Newfoundland is an enormous breed with a flat, dense coat of longish hair, usually black, and completely webbed feet. Newfs love the water, and puppies may sleep with their heads immersed in the water bowl. The breed has been used for water rescue and as guardians for children. Newfoundlands have a bearlike appearance and a body roll when they trot. Descriptions include "easygoing"; "able and willing to help their masters on command and acting with initiative when necessary"; "a traditional children protector"; "a careful playmate, not easily hurt by small fingers, seems to undertake the duties of nursemaid naturally without training" and "a loyal, mobile, calm and trusting breed."

Behavior problems are negligible except that a Newf may not obey rapidly when told to get out of the water. Dogs of this breed are sensitive to summer heat and need a lot of water. Many have the disconcerting habit of immersing themselves in any available body of water, like their own water bowl, and then dripping all over the house. Newfs also drool.

Old English Sheepdog*

A.K.C. Popularity: 25th

Dimension of Temperament	Level of Dimension				
	Very high	High	Med.	Low	Very low
1. Indoor activity	▓	▓			
2. Outdoor activity	▓				
3. Vigor			—	—	▓
4. Behavioral constancy			—	▓	
5. Dominance to strange dogs	—	—	—	—	▓
6. Dominance to familiar people	—	—	—	—	▓
7. Territoriality		▓	—	▓	
8. Emotional stability			—	—	▓
9. Sociability — within family	▓	—	—	—	—
10. Sociability — with children	▓	—	—	▓	
11. Sociability — with strangers	—	—	—	▓	
12. Learning — rate		▓	—	▓	
13. Learning — obedience				▓	—
14. Learning — problem solving	—	—	▓		
15. Watchdog ability	▓	—	▓		
16. Guard-dog ability				▓	

The Old English Sheepdog is familiar to anyone who has seen the Disney movie *The Shaggy D.A.* It is a large breed with a long, shaggy, profuse coat. With its film stardom came a fad popularity and the predictable puppy-mill production, so I will try to categorize both the puppy-mill and the well-bred varieties. Both have a tendency to herd their owners, pushing them and directing their movements. Descriptions of the well-bred variety include "a home-loving breed, not given to roaming or fighting; extremely agile, intelligent, affectionate animal, lacking boisterousness and having a tender mouth and a gait like that of a shuffling bear."

Some potential behavior problems for the puppy-mill animals that I have seen include stealing and guarding food and objects, guarding places, touch shyness, fear biting, indoor restlessness, willful disobedience, timidity, phobias, hyperactivity, excessive barking under mild stimulation, destructiveness when left alone, dominance challenge to submissive members of family, low snapping threshold when irritated or

112

pushed. It must be pointed out that most of these problems can be prevented and/or solved by the right training technique and can be exacerbated with the wrong one. Puppy-mill animals can be as good as the well bred. There's just more of a chance that they won't be. Moral? Buy from a careful breeder who has a good reputation and then select your puppy carefully. If you get stuck with a lemon, seek help immediately and start changing behaviors and socializing from early puppyhood.

----- = puppy-mill
■■■■■■ = well-bred
*Watch out for puppy-mill dogs.

Puli

A.K.C. Popularity: 85th

Dimension of Temperament	Level of Dimension				
	Very high	High	Med.	Low	Very low
1. Indoor activity	▨				
2. Outdoor activity	▨				
3. Vigor		▨			
4. Behavioral constancy				▨	
5. Dominance to strange dogs	▨				
6. Dominance to familiar people		▨			
7. Territoriality		▨			
8. Emotional stability				▨	
9. Sociability — within family			▨	▨	
10. Sociability — with children					▨
11. Sociability — with strangers				▨	▨
12. Learning — rate	▨				
13. Learning — obedience				▨	▨
14. Learning — problem solving	▨				
15. Watchdog ability	▨				
16. Guard-dog ability	▨				

The Puli (pronounced POO-lee) is a small- to medium-sized dog developed in Hungary for sheep herding and now used as a compact guard dog. The Puli looks like a smaller, dark-colored version of the Komondor and has the same corded coat and moplike appearance. Descriptions include "springing gait like a bouncing ball"; "lively and high-spirited, quick-tempered and bold"; "intelligent, brazenly stubborn and willful"; "versatile" and sometimes "overly protective of both master and property." In its sheep-driving days it used to jump on and run over the backs of a tightly packed flock to turn them.

Behavior problems may stem from the breed's tenacious and sharp temperament and may include excessive barking, indoor restlessness, demanding behavior, willful disobedience, overprotectiveness and dominance challenges to selected family members.

Rottweiler

A.K.C. Popularity: 47th

Dimension of Temperament	Level of Dimension				
	Very high	High	Med.	Low	Very low
1. Indoor activity				▨	
2. Outdoor activity		▨			
3. Vigor	▨				
4. Behavioral constancy		▨			
5. Dominance to strange dogs	▨				
6. Dominance to familiar people	▨				
7. Territoriality	▨				
8. Emotional stability		▨			
9. Sociability — within family			▨	▨	
10. Sociability — with children				▨	▨
11. Sociability — with strangers				▨	▨
12. Learning — rate				▨	
13. Learning — obedience				▨	▨
14. Learning — problem solving			▨		
15. Watchdog ability	▨				
16. Guard-dog ability	▨				

The Rottweiler (pronounced ROTT-why-lurr) is a very large breed originally used for cattle driving and eventually developed for guard and police work. The coat is similar to the Doberman's. Specimens recently were used as the "devil dogs" that attacked Gregory Peck in the film *The Omen,* and it is not surprising that some guard-dog trainers refer to the Rottweiler as "the Cadillac of attack dogs." Descriptions include "diligent"; "more solid and predictable than Dobermans"; "not quarrelsome"; "bold but easygoing and not easily excited"; "responsive to firm, careful training" and "easily trained to work, and naturally obedient and extremely faithful."

Behavior problems may include food stealing; guarding food, objects and places from family members; overprotectiveness; demanding behavior; willful disobedience and excessive aggression. They may snore.

St. Bernard*

A.K.C. Popularity: 28th

Dimension of Temperament	Very high	High	Med.	Low	Very low
1. Indoor activity				X	
2. Outdoor activity			X		
3. Vigor				X	
4. Behavioral constancy	X				
5. Dominance to strange dogs			X		
6. Dominance to familiar people			X		
7. Territoriality				X	
8. Emotional stability	X				
9. Sociability — within family				X	
10. Sociability — with children	X				
11. Sociability — with strangers		X			
12. Learning — rate		X			
13. Learning — obedience			X		
14. Learning — problem solving		X			
15. Watchdog ability	X				
16. Guard-dog ability				X	

(Level of Dimension)

The St. Bernard is a very popular breed and, if well bred, deserves its reputation as an Alpine rescue dog. But puppy mills have been in operation for a while, and some specimens bred this way may be quite dangerous to humans because of the puppy-mill change in this breed's temperament toward dominance, combined with its enormous size. The A.K.C. says of well-bred dogs that "they require no training for rescue work, having a natural rescuing instinct." This, of course, is absurd. The Saints of the Swiss Alps required no *human* training, but got their skill because young dogs were allowed to run with the rescue-patrol packs of three or four experienced animals. So don't expect a well-bred Saint to go out and rescue someone lost in the snow if it hasn't had this early experience. Saints are also reputed to have the uncanny sense of anticipating avalanches. This may be so. They may do it by hearing infrasounds—the very low-pitched sounds inaudible to humans—that would accompany the beginning of an avalanche. I have treated well-bred Saints with pronounced thunderstorm phobias. The dogs seemed to get uncomfortable hours before thunderstorms, perhaps because they could hear infrasounds accompanying the approaching storm.

All Saints drool, snore, wheeze, overheat and drink and shed a lot. Please note that some puppy-mill Saints may be just as nice as their well-bred cousins. However, you can check out the lineage of the well-bred variety, while with puppy-mill products you take your chances.

Behavior problems with well-bred Saints may include food stealing and, sometimes, willful disobedience. St. Bernard owners should be prepared to exert dominance over even the well-bred variety. With the puppy-mill variety, problems of one area center on excessive dominance (usually in males) which causes dominance challenges, demanding behavior, willful disobedience and, rarely, direct aggressive confrontation with the owner. On the other hand, some puppy-mill varieties may be very timid and fearful and thus prone to phobias, overprotection and fear biting. Most dangerous is the dog that vacillates between fear and dominance, because its unpredictable aggression can cause bodily harm to unsuspecting bystanders.

----- = puppy-mill
▒▒▒ = well-bred
*Watch out for puppy-mill dogs.

Samoyed

A.K.C. Popularity: 30th

Dimension of Temperament	Level of Dimension				
	Very high	High	Med.	Low	Very low
1. Indoor activity	▨				
2. Outdoor activity	▨				
3. Vigor			▨		
4. Behavioral constancy				▨	
5. Dominance to strange dogs		▨			
6. Dominance to familiar people			▨		
7. Territoriality			▨		
8. Emotional stability			▨		
9. Sociability — within family			▨		
10. Sociability — with children	▨				
11. Sociability — with strangers				▨	
12. Learning — rate		▨			
13. Learning — obedience				▨	
14. Learning — problem solving	▨				
15. Watchdog ability	▨				
16. Guard-dog ability				▨	

The Samoyed (pronounced SAM-aw-yed) is a medium-sized sled and draft dog with a longish, thick coat, usually all white or light tan, and a mane, or "ruff," around its neck. Descriptions include "intelligent, gentle, loyal, adaptable, alert, full of action, eager to serve, friendly but conservative, but not distrustful or shy or overly aggressive"; "stubborn to very obstinate, but gentle and eventually responsive to patient training."

Behavior problems may include roaming, house soiling and sometimes mischievous destruction and restlessness if left alone and not exercised. Samoyed shed heavily.

Shetland Sheepdog

A.K.C. Popularity: 11th

Dimension of Temperament	Level of Dimension				
	Very high	High	Med.	Low	Very low
1. Indoor activity		▨			
2. Outdoor activity	▨				
3. Vigor			▨		
4. Behavioral constancy			▨		
5. Dominance to strange dogs			▨		
6. Dominance to familiar people			▨		
7. Territoriality			▨		
8. Emotional stability				▨	
9. Sociability – within family		▨			
10. Sociability – with children		▨			
11. Sociability – with strangers				▨	
12. Learning – rate	▨				
13. Learning – obedience	▨				
14. Learning – problem solving	▨				
15. Watchdog ability	▨				
16. Guard-dog ability					▨

   The Shetland Sheepdog looks like a miniature Rough Collie and is the lightest of the working breeds. Shelties, as they are informally called, are rather popular in the United States and were used by Scott and Fuller in their study of genetics and canine behavior. Descriptions include "willing to obey naturally, with a few or no lessons needed" and "intensely loyal, devoted and affectionate." Breeders tend to agree that the Sheltie may be high-strung and timid, but the A.K.C. description of "desirably calm and docile" would indicate that the former emotional disposition is being and should be bred out as the temperament of this relatively new breed is refined.

   Behavior problems may include excessive, continuous barking; food stealing; timidity; phobias; touch shyness; fear biting and possibly irritable snapping. A Sheltie should be highly socialized and introduced early and exposed continuously to the strange sounds of city life to minimize timidity and barking in that environment.

Siberian Husky

A.K.C. Popularity: 15th

Dimension of Temperament	Level of Dimension				
	Very high	High	Med.	Low	Very low
1. Indoor activity	▓				
2. Outdoor activity	▓				
3. Vigor			▓		
4. Behavioral constancy		▓			
5. Dominance to strange dogs			▓		
6. Dominance to familiar people				▓	
7. Territoriality				▓	
8. Emotional stability		▓			
9. Sociability — within family	▓				
10. Sociability — with children	▓				
11. Sociability — with strangers	▓				
12. Learning — rate		▓			
13. Learning — obedience				▓	
14. Learning — problem solving	▓				
15. Watchdog ability			▓		
16. Guard-dog ability				▓	

The Siberian Husky is a medium-sized sled dog. It is smaller, more distinctly marked and friendlier than the Malamute, with which it is frequently confused. Descriptions include "a lifelong puppy," "undistractably playful," "mischievous," "shows great endurance by pulling sleds at fast or moderate speeds over long distances," "amiable and friendly" and "alert and intelligent." Training requires firmness and patience, praise and rewards and many play breaks, contingent on good performance. If the dog is indulged, mischievous and bad habits become rapidly fixed.

Behavior problems may include roaming, house soiling, playful disobedience, howling at sirens, jumping on visitors and destructiveness when left alone. Females may try to build a nest in the owner's couch during heats by digging at the cushions and removing the stuffing.

Standard Schnauzer

A.K.C. Popularity: 73rd

Dimension of Temperament	Level of Dimension				
	Very high	High	Med.	Low	Very low
1. Indoor activity	▨				
2. Outdoor activity	▨				
3. Vigor	▨				
4. Behavioral constancy	▨				
5. Dominance to strange dogs	▨▨				
6. Dominance to familiar people		▨			
7. Territoriality	▨	▨			
8. Emotional stability		▨			
9. Sociability — within family			▨	▨	
10. Sociability — with children			▨	▨	
11. Sociability — with strangers				▨	
12. Learning — rate		▨			
13. Learning — obedience			▨	▨	
14. Learning — problem solving		▨			
15. Watchdog ability	▨				
16. Guard-dog ability	▨				

The Standard Schnauzer is a powerful medium-sized dog which exhibits terrier tenacity when confronting a foe. It has been used as a ratcatcher, as a yard and guard dog and for police work. In Germany, Schnauzer clubs periodically hold ratting trials in which the dogs compete for the largest number of rats killed in the fastest period of time. Descriptions include "high-spirited"; "robust, sturdy and completely reliable"; showing "stamina and virility"; and "stubborn, bold and fearless."

Behavior problems may include dominance challenges, excessive protectiveness and guarding objects, places and people from other people. All children in the owner's family should participate in supervised training of a Schnauzer so that they may gain control over it. Also, the dog should be socialized early to prevent overprotectiveness. Finally, I strongly recommend the discouragement of roughhouse play and tug-of-war games with this breed.

Cardigan Welsh Corgi/Pembroke Welsh Corgi

A.K.C. Popularity: 89th, 48th

Dimension of Temperament	Level of Dimension				
	Very high	High	Med.	Low	Very low
1. Indoor activity	▬				
2. Outdoor activity		▬			
3. Vigor		▬	▬		
4. Behavioral constancy		▬	▬		
5. Dominance to strange dogs	▬				
6. Dominance to familiar people			▬	▬	
7. Territoriality		▬			
8. Emotional stability		▬			
9. Sociability — within family		▬	▬		
10. Sociability — with children		▬	▬		
11. Sociability — with strangers			▬	▬	
12. Learning — rate	▬				
13. Learning — obedience	▬	▬			
14. Learning — problem solving		▬	▬		
15. Watchdog ability	▬				
16. Guard-dog ability		▬			

The Cardigan Welsh Corgi and the Pembroke Welsh Corgi are very similar in appearance; both breeds have erect ears, a foxy head and the low, Dachshund-type body. The Cardigan is a bit taller and more heavily boned, has rounded ears and has bowed legs that point out. Until World War I the two breeds were mated together frequently. Both were used by Welsh farmers as "reverse" herding dogs with the responsibility of driving off neighboring cattle from the owner's crops. Their build and agility permitted them to harass the cows by darting quickly back and forth, barking and snapping as they dodged kicking hooves; this is how Corgis would probably greet any "intruder," friend or foe, unless properly trained to stop on command. Both can be good apartment-sized guard dogs.

Behavior problems for both breeds may include incessant barking and snapping at the heels of visitors if the dogs are not trained and socialized properly.

- - - - - = Cardigan
▬▬▬ = Pembroke

5

The Terriers

The American Kennel Club recognizes 22 breeds of Terriers. In size and shape they show less variety than the Working Dogs, ranging from the miniature Norwich Terrier, which measures about 10 inches and 10 pounds, to the largest Terriers—the lean Airedale at about 23 inches and 55 pounds and the stocky, fighting American Staffordshire, about 18 inches and up to 70 pounds. Terriers have been used for a variety of purposes including guarding; pit fighting; hunting small but vicious predators like foxes, badgers and other small prey animals like rabbits; and finally as ratters. All these activities involve tenacity and a well-developed rage and attack reaction to threat and punishment. Terriers were not supposed to back down no matter how painful their wounds. As far back as 1560, Dr. John Caius wrote that the Terriers were "quarrelsome and snappy animals, and to be tolerated only in the stables." Terriers have been modified since that time, so they may not all show this tenacious streak. The Terrier group includes the Airedale, American Staffordshire, Australian, Bedlington, Border, Bull, Cairn, Dandie Dinmont, Fox, Irish, Kerry Blue, Lakeland, Manchester, Miniature Schnauzer, Norwich, Scottish, Sealyham, Skye, Staffordshire Bull, Welsh, West Highland White and Wheaten.

Airedale

Dimension of Temperament	Level of Dimension				
	Very high	High	Med.	Low	Very low
1. Indoor activity	▓				
2. Outdoor activity	▓				
3. Vigor		▓			
4. Behavioral constancy		▓			
5. Dominance to strange dogs		▓			
6. Dominance to familiar people			▓		
7. Territoriality			▓		
8. Emotional stability		▓			
9. Sociability — within family			▓		
10. Sociability — with children				▓	
11. Sociability — with strangers			▓		
12. Learning — rate		▓			
13. Learning — obedience				▓	
14. Learning — problem solving		▓			
15. Watchdog ability		▓			
16. Guard-dog ability		▓			

The Airedale is a medium-sized, square-shaped dog with a short, wiry coat, whiskers and a goatee. It was used for hunting a variety of predators including foxes, badgers, weasels, otters and water rats as well as for police work, guard work and the carrying of war dispatches. Descriptions include "untiring courage, faithful attachment and the ability to suffer wounds without faltering"; "rowdy"; "protective"; "stubborn and bold"; "fun-loving and spirited"; as a puppy showing "discretion with people they meet and when mature a certain dignified aloofness with strangers and their own kind."

Behavior problems may include indoor restlessness, excessive barking especially as a puppy, jumping up on visitors and, possibly, dominance challenges toward family members. Most of my cases with Airedales involve willful disobedience, usually toward people the dog considers submissive.

American Staffordshire / Staffordshire Bull

A.K.C. Popularity: 67th, 94th

Dimension of Temperament	Level of Dimension				
	Very high	High	Med.	Low	Very low
1. Indoor activity	▨				
2. Outdoor activity		▨			
3. Vigor	▨	▨	▨	▨	
4. Behavioral constancy		▨			
5. Dominance to strange dogs	▨				
6. Dominance to familiar people		▨	▨		
7. Territoriality	▨				
8. Emotional stability		▨			
9. Sociability — within family				▨	
10. Sociability — with children				▨	
11. Sociability — with strangers				▨	
12. Learning — rate		▨			
13. Learning — obedience				▨	
14. Learning — problem solving				▨	
15. Watchdog ability	▨				
16. Guard-dog ability	▨				

The American Staffordshire is about 18 inches at the shoulder, but owing to its powerfully muscular and stocky build, it may weigh more than 50 pounds. Some specimens reach 70 pounds. The general appearance is that of a straight-legged Bulldog with a rounded muzzle. The Staffordshire Bull, the English version of the breed, is smaller and lighter than the American, but has essentially the same temperament. In the past these breeds were used for pit fighting. Descriptions include "combines the speed and agility of a Terrier with the courage and tenacity of a Bulldog," "gentle and easygoing with the family," "okay with strangers if a dominant family member is present but a menace to them when encountered alone," "very bold," docile, needing "firm, progressive and continuous training not to attack other dogs"; "can accept a new master rapidly."

Behavior problems may include indoor restlessness, domi-

125

nance challenges to submissive people, potential danger to visitors if the dog is untrained and house soiling. These breeds can be good with children with whom they have been raised from puppyhood, but I would never leave a strange child alone with these dogs.

My most spectacular case with Staffordshires involved a breeder who insisted that all four of her males live in happy harmony under the same roof. The fighting scenes were incredible displays of ferocity, for the dogs had paired off into teams, making the ensuing battles look like some insane, no-holds-barred tag-team grudge match. After unsuccessfully attempting to persuade the owner to abandon her goal and to keep the dogs separated, I took the case as a challenge. It took four months and many battles, but I won the war. The dogs no longer fight each other, for I made them into a single team against the world. Heaven help any other dog that enters that house.

Australian Terrier

A.K.C. Popularity: 70th

Dimension of Temperament	Level of Dimension				
	Very high	High	Med.	Low	Very low
1. Indoor activity		▩			
2. Outdoor activity		▩			
3. Vigor			▩		
4. Behavioral constancy				▩	
5. Dominance to strange dogs			▩		
6. Dominance to familiar people				▩	
7. Territoriality			▩		
8. Emotional stability		▩			
9. Sociability — within family			▩		
10. Sociability — with children				▩	
11. Sociability — with strangers				▩	
12. Learning — rate		▩			
13. Learning — obedience		▩			
14. Learning — problem solving	▩				
15. Watchdog ability	▩				
16. Guard-dog ability				▩	

The Australian Terrier, one of the smallest of the working Terriers, was used to tend sheep and guard the mines, although I just can't picture a 10-inch-tall, 12-pound dog guarding anything. It looks like a cute, alert, sharp-eyed, plucky little beast. Descriptions include "natural ratter and hedge hunter but is friendly, affectionate and biddable as a companion"; "not so gentle with people"; "always on the move"; "vocally quiet for a terrier"; "courage, spirit and a constant air of assurance" and "eager to please and easygoing."

The only behavior problem may be irritable snapping if the dog is teased or provoked.

Bedlington Terrier

A.K.C. Popularity: 88th

Dimension of Temperament	Level of Dimension				
	Very high	High	Med.	Low	Very low
1. Indoor activity		▓			
2. Outdoor activity		▓			
3. Vigor			▓		
4. Behavioral constancy		▓			
5. Dominance to strange dogs			▓		
6. Dominance to familiar people				▓	
7. Territoriality			▓		
8. Emotional stability				▓	
9. Sociability — within family			▓		
10. Sociability — with children			▓		
11. Sociability — with strangers			▓		
12. Learning — rate		▓			
13. Learning — obedience			▓		
14. Learning — problem solving			▓		
15. Watchdog ability	▓				
16. Guard-dog ability					▓

The Bedlington Terrier is a small, graceful, fast-running dog. The way it is usually trimmed gives it the appearance of a little lamb with a body shape suggesting a curly-coated Whippet. Descriptions include "it's full of immense energy, courage and endurance"; "high-strung"; "it fights to the death"; "jealous nature."

Behavior problems may include excessive barking, house soiling and irritable snapping.

Border Terrier

A.K.C. Popularity: 106th

Dimension of Temperament	Level of Dimension				
	Very high	High	Med.	Low	Very low
1. Indoor activity		▨			
2. Outdoor activity		▨			
3. Vigor				▨	
4. Behavioral constancy	▨				
5. Dominance to strange dogs			▨		
6. Dominance to familiar people				▨	
7. Territoriality				▨	
8. Emotional stability	▨				
9. Sociability — within family		▨			
10. Sociability — with children	▨				
11. Sociability — with strangers			▨		
12. Learning — rate		▨			
13. Learning — obedience		▨			
14. Learning — problem solving		▨			
15. Watchdog ability		▨			
16. Guard-dog ability				▨	

The Border Terrier is a small breed with a broad, otterlike head and a short muzzle. It was used to hunt, bolt and kill foxes. Descriptions include "strong, tireless hard worker and full of pluck, rapidly traversing any kind of terrain"; "good-tempered and affectionate"; "easily trained" and "the most mild-mannered and least quick-tempered of all the Terriers."

Behavior problems may center on excessive timidity if the dog is not socialized and exposed to varying stimuli early.

Bull Terrier

A.K.C. Popularity: 65th

Dimension of Temperament	Level of Dimension				
	Very high	High	Med.	Low	Very low
1. Indoor activity		▨			
2. Outdoor activity		▨			
3. Vigor	▨				
4. Behavioral constancy		▨			
5. Dominance to strange dogs		▨			
6. Dominance to familiar people			▨		
7. Territoriality		▨			
8. Emotional stability		▨			
9. Sociability — within family			▨		
10. Sociability — with children				▨	
11. Sociability — with strangers				▨	
12. Learning — rate				▨	
13. Learning — obedience				▨	
14. Learning — problem solving				▨	
15. Watchdog ability	▨				
16. Guard-dog ability		▨			

Bull Terriers may look beautiful to their owners and to other Bull Terriers, but to me this medium-sized fighting dog looks like a little pig with a short rat tail. The breed was developed for pit fighting. Descriptions include "full of fire but of sweet disposition"; "always ready for a fight or a frolic"; can be "taught to defend itself and master courageously but not necessarily seeking to provoke fights"; "thriving on affection" and "wayward and stubborn and needing firm, patient training from the start."

Behavior problems may include willful disobedience, dominance challenges, dog fighting and pulling on the leash. The breed is known to snore. Most commonly, my cases with this breed involve trying to persuade a specimen not to fight with other dogs. Surprisingly, I have been generally successful, which suggests that this breed's tenacious nature can be altered.

Cairn Terrier

A.K.C. Popularity: 37th

Dimension of Temperament	Level of Dimension				
	Very high	High	Med.	Low	Very low
1. Indoor activity	▨				
2. Outdoor activity			▨		
3. Vigor			▨		
4. Behavioral constancy			▨		
5. Dominance to strange dogs			▨		
6. Dominance to familiar people			▨		
7. Territoriality			▨		
8. Emotional stability		▨			
9. Sociability — within family		▨			
10. Sociability — with children				▨	
11. Sociability — with strangers				▨	
12. Learning — rate		▨			
13. Learning — obedience			▨		
14. Learning — problem solving	▨				
15. Watchdog ability	▨				
16. Guard-dog ability				▨	

The Cairn Terrier is a cute little dog used for hunting, its job being to drive otters, foxes and other "vermin" out of their hiding places in the rocks, cliffs and ledges of Scotland. Descriptions include "a feisty and tenacious fighter"; "an active, hardy and game working terrier"; "alert and energetic"; "bold and stubborn" and "not particularly gentle with people."

Behavior problems may center on dominance challenges, and sometimes this little Terrier will guard objects from family members.

132

Dandie Dinmont Terrier

A.K.C. Popularity: 98th

Dimension of Temperament	Level of Dimension				
	Very high	High	Med.	Low	Very low
1. Indoor activity		▨			
2. Outdoor activity			▨		
3. Vigor			▨		
4. Behavioral constancy			▨		
5. Dominance to strange dogs			▨		
6. Dominance to familiar people			▨		
7. Territoriality			▨		
8. Emotional stability		▨			
9. Sociability — within family			▨		
10. Sociability — with children				▨	
11. Sociability — with strangers				▨	
12. Learning — rate	▨				
13. Learning — obedience			▨	▨	
14. Learning — problem solving	▨				
15. Watchdog ability		▨			
16. Guard-dog ability				▨	

The Dandie Dinmont Terrier has short legs and a long body with a rough, longish coat and a silky topknot. It looks like a toy manufacturer's dream of a dog doll—the face, with its large, expressive eyes, topknot and whiskers, gives the appearance of Gabby Hayes with a pompadour. Descriptions include "filled with pluck," "rough-and-tumble," "one of the brightest Terriers," "seldom nasty," "having a will of its own and obeying reluctantly" and "a trickster."

Behavior problems may include dominance challenges, which may seem ridiculous given the breed's size, but these dogs can be formidable in their Terrier tenacity. These challenges take the form of willful disobedience and guarding of objects. Some specimens may be hard to housebreak. Some snore.

Fox Terrier

A.K.C. Popularity: 44th

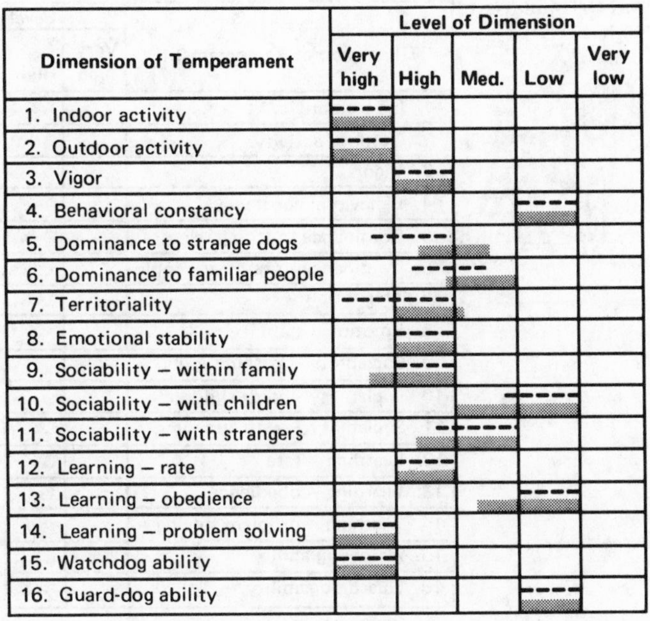

Dimension of Temperament	Level of Dimension				
	Very high	High	Med.	Low	Very low
1. Indoor activity	�				
2. Outdoor activity	■				
3. Vigor		■			
4. Behavioral constancy				▭	
5. Dominance to strange dogs	▭	■			
6. Dominance to familiar people		▭	■		
7. Territoriality	▭	■			
8. Emotional stability		▭			
9. Sociability — within family	■				
10. Sociability — with children				▭	
11. Sociability — with strangers		■	▭		
12. Learning — rate		■			
13. Learning — obedience				▭	
14. Learning — problem solving	▭				
15. Watchdog ability	▭				
16. Guard-dog ability				■	

The Fox Terrier is a small dog. There are two varieties, one with a smooth coat and the other with a wirehaired coat. As the name implies, these dogs were developed to harass a fox out of its hiding place by lunging, snapping and growling with unrelenting tenacity until the fox bolted. The fox would then be chased by the Foxhounds and followed by so-called English "gentlemen" on horseback who considered it sporting to chase a little fox over hill and dale with up to 35 hounds in fierce pursuit. Descriptions include "strong and gay, brave and wise, full of pride, lively and active, having speed and endurance"; "a scrappy, impulsive, extraverted, lovable dynamo"; "generally sociable"; "excellent at learning tricks" and "disobedient when excited."

Behavior problems may include dominance challenges, especially with meek owners; guarding objects, places and their own food from the owner, and excessive barking.

- - - - - = Shorthair
■■■■■ = Longhair

Irish Terrier

A.K.C. Popularity: 95th

Dimension of Temperament	Level of Dimension				
	Very high	High	Med.	Low	Very low
1. Indoor activity		▨			
2. Outdoor activity		▨			
3. Vigor		▨			
4. Behavioral constancy		▨			
5. Dominance to strange dogs	▨	▨			
6. Dominance to familiar people		▨			
7. Territoriality		▨			
8. Emotional stability				▨	
9. Sociability — within family			▨	▨	
10. Sociability — with children				▨	
11. Sociability — with strangers				▨	
12. Learning — rate		▨			
13. Learning — obedience				▨	
14. Learning — problem solving		▨			
15. Watchdog ability	▨				
16. Guard-dog ability		▨			

The Irish Terrier looks like a small, reddish miniature of an Irish Wolfhound. It has earned the name "red devil" or "daredevil" from its fearless tenacity in a fight. The breed was developed to catch and kill vermin and to hunt small predators and prey. Irish Terriers have a rather racy appearance. Descriptions include "loyal and unyielding protector, faithful, having heedless and reckless pluck, dashing headlong and blind to all consequences"; "highly sensitive and hot-tempered scrapper, spirited, game and eager to join the fun and frolic" and "grim and challenging to adversaries, guarding family members without fear."

Behavior problems may include dominance challenges, guarding objects and places from family members and house soiling. The owner should not hit this dog, because pain simply makes it more ferocious.

Kerry Blue Terrier

A.K.C. Popularity: 80th

Dimension of Temperament	Level of Dimension				
	Very high	High	Med.	Low	Very low
1. Indoor activity		▨			
2. Outdoor activity		▨			
3. Vigor		▨			
4. Behavioral constancy		▨			
5. Dominance to strange dogs		▨			
6. Dominance to familiar people		▨			
7. Territoriality		▨			
8. Emotional stability			▨		
9. Sociability – within family			▨		
10. Sociability – with children				▨	
11. Sociability – with strangers				▨	
12. Learning – rate		▨			
13. Learning – obedience				▨	
14. Learning – problem solving	▨				
15. Watchdog ability	▨				
16. Guard-dog ability		▨			

The Kerry Blue is large for a Terrier, but is a medium-sized dog in relation to other breeds. It was used for hunting, retrieving, herding and guarding. The soft, wavy coat takes on a blue-gray cast as the dog matures. Descriptions include "usually retains its activeness to the end" and "hardy, tireless, roughhousing."

Behavior problems may include dominance challenges, especially the guarding of objects, places and family members from other family members. Also, some specimens may be touch-shy, may steal and guard food, may eat pickily and may bark excessively.

My most common cases with this breed involve a mismatch between the submissive owner's personality and this dog's tendency to dominate, the result being a dog that runs the household.

Lakeland Terrier / Welsh Terrier

A.K.C. Popularity: 101st, 74th

Dimension of Temperament	Level of Dimension				
	Very high	High	Med.	Low	Very low
1. Indoor activity	▦				
2. Outdoor activity	▦				
3. Vigor			▦		
4. Behavioral constancy			▦		
5. Dominance to strange dogs		▦	▦		
6. Dominance to familiar people			▦		
7. Territoriality		▦	▦		
8. Emotional stability		▦	▦		
9. Sociability — within family			▦		
10. Sociability — with children		▦	▦		
11. Sociability — with strangers				▦	
12. Learning — rate		▦			
13. Learning — obedience				▦	▦
14. Learning — problem solving			▦		
15. Watchdog ability	▦				
16. Guard-dog ability				▦	

The Lakeland is a small dog with a short, wiry coat. In England it was used to bolt, catch and kill foxes that preyed upon farmers' livestock, doing this by following the fox, sometimes for great distances, deep into its underground lair. The Welsh Terrier is a bit larger than the Lakeland, but has a similar appearance. Descriptions of the Lakeland include "self-confident, with a cock-of-the-walk attitude" and "bold and feisty," while Welsh Terriers are described as having a slightly milder temperament.

Behavior problems in both breeds may include dominance challenges, especially in the guarding of objects, places and family members from other family members; touch shyness; stealing and guarding food; picky eating and excessive barking.

----- = Lakeland
▦▦▦ = Welsh

Manchester Terrier

A.K.C. Popularity: 81st

Dimension of Temperament	Level of Dimension				
	Very high	High	Med.	Low	Very low
1. Indoor activity	▩				
2. Outdoor activity	▩				
3. Vigor			▩		
4. Behavioral constancy				▩	
5. Dominance to strange dogs			▩		
6. Dominance to familiar people			▩		
7. Territoriality			▩		
8. Emotional stability				▩	
9. Sociability – within family				▩	▩
10. Sociability – with children				▩	▩
11. Sociability – with strangers				▩	
12. Learning – rate		▩			
13. Learning – obedience				▩	
14. Learning – problem solving			▩		
15. Watchdog ability	▩				
16. Guard-dog ability				▩	

The Manchester Terrier is a small dog with a short, glossy black-and-tan coat. It looks like a small Doberman Pinscher, but is not related; it is probably the product of a cross between a smooth-coated black-and-tan rat-killing Terrier and a Whippet. The Manchester was used for rat killing and for coursing rabbits.

Descriptions include "alternating between timidity and boldness"; "doesn't readily get into dogfights"; "stubborn" and needing "careful training, early introduction into the home and much socialization to prevent potential aggression."

Behavior problems may include irritable snapping, dominance challenges and stealing or guarding food from the owner.

Miniature Schnauzer*

Dimension of Temperament	Level of Dimension				
	Very high	High	Med.	Low	Very low
1. Indoor activity	-----	-----	--▓		
2. Outdoor activity	-----	-----	--▓		
3. Vigor			----		
4. Behavioral constancy		-----	▓----	----	
5. Dominance to strange dogs			----		
6. Dominance to familiar people		--			
7. Territoriality		--	----		
8. Emotional stability		-----	▓		
9. Sociability – within family			▓----		
10. Sociability – with children			▓	-----	-----
11. Sociability – with strangers			▓	-----	-----
12. Learning – rate		----			
13. Learning – obedience			-----	----	
14. Learning – problem solving			----		
15. Watchdog ability	---- ▓				
16. Guard-dog ability				▓----	

   The Miniature Schnauzer and the Australian Terrier are the only Terriers which do not come from the British Isles. The Miniature Schnauzer was developed in Germany to patrol the yard or stable for vermin and intruders. It is a very popular breed in the United States and, as always seems to be the case, has suffered from puppy-mill production. Because of this, I have indicated the temperamental levels for both the well-bred and the puppy-mill varieties. As a breed, Mini Schnausers are temperamentally diverse. Some descriptions are "active, quiet and calm"; "quarrelsome"; "timid, high-strung, gentle and stubborn"; "yappy, friendly and reserved"; "suspicious" and "accepting, good and bad with kids."

   Behavior problems may include excessive barking, dominance challenges, and stealing and guarding food.

   Smokey, my puppy-mill Mini Schnauzer, exhibited all the Schnauzer's bad qualities. He was a yappy, snappy little seven-week-old beast. Now, at five years, he is docile, quiet, gentle, calm and inactive indoors. Magic? No, just the Power of Positive Reinforcement. Reward the positive and ignore or mildly punish the negative.

----- = puppy-mill
▓▓▓▓ = well-bred
*Watch out for puppy-mill dogs.

Norwich Terrier

A.K.C. Popularity:
91st

Dimension of Temperament	Level of Dimension				
	Very high	High	Med.	Low	Very low
1. Indoor activity	▓				
2. Outdoor activity	▓				
3. Vigor			▓		
4. Behavioral constancy		▓			
5. Dominance to strange dogs			▓		
6. Dominance to familiar people			▓		
7. Territoriality			▓		
8. Emotional stability		▓			
9. Sociability – within family				▓	
10. Sociability – with children			▓		
11. Sociability – with strangers			▓		
12. Learning – rate		▓			
13. Learning – obedience				▓	
14. Learning – problem solving		▓			
15. Watchdog ability	▓				
16. Guard-dog ability				▓	

The Norwich Terrier is tiny, with erect, pointed ears and bright eyes. It was once used for the same job the Fox Terrier does, driving foxes out of their hiding places for the hounds and the hunt. Descriptions include "game to the core and loyal," "scrappy with other dogs," "bold," "stubborn and obstinate and a one-person dog," "its loyalty, once given, never swerves."

Behavior problems may include excessive barking.

Scottish Terrier

A.K.C. Popularity: 35th

Dimension of Temperament	Level of Dimension				
	Very high	High	Med.	Low	Very low
1. Indoor activity	▨				
2. Outdoor activity	▨				
3. Vigor			▨		
4. Behavioral constancy					▨
5. Dominance to strange dogs		▨			
6. Dominance to familiar people			▨		
7. Territoriality		▨			
8. Emotional stability		▨			
9. Sociability — within family				▨	
10. Sociability — with children				▨	
11. Sociability — with strangers				▨	
12. Learning — rate		▨			
13. Learning — obedience				▨	
14. Learning — problem solving			▨		
15. Watchdog ability	▨				
16. Guard-dog ability				▨	

The Scottish Terrier is a well-knit small dog with short legs, strong bones and a compact, muscular body. It is the most behaviorally variable of all the Terriers—in any one day a member of this breed can be playful, irritable, loving, aggressive, obedient, dominant, stubborn, submissive, sullen, snappish, quiet and noisy. It has been described as "bold" and as "crusty and independent."

Behavior problems may include excessive barking and dominance challenges. Some people find its behavioral variability a problem.

Sealyham Terrier

A.K.C. Popularity: 111th

Dimension of Temperament	Level of Dimension				
	Very high	High	Med.	Low	Very low
1. Indoor activity				▨	
2. Outdoor activity			▨		
3. Vigor		▨			
4. Behavioral constancy		▨			
5. Dominance to strange dogs			▨		
6. Dominance to familiar people			▨		
7. Territoriality			▨		
8. Emotional stability	▨				
9. Sociability — within family			▨		
10. Sociability — with children				▨	
11. Sociability — with strangers				▨	
12. Learning — rate		▨			
13. Learning — obedience				▨	
14. Learning — problem solving				▨	
15. Watchdog ability		▨			
16. Guard-dog ability				▨	

The Sealyham Terrier has a longish coat, usually white. The breed was developed to quarry badgers, otters and foxes and has the short, powerful forelegs of a master digger. Descriptions include "extreme gameness, and endurance enough to dig and battle background"; "bold but easygoing"; "not likely to be mischievous." It is one of the few Terriers considered to be inactive indoors.

Behavior problems may include dominance challenges and inappropriate guarding.

Skye Terrier

A.K.C. Popularity: 102nd

Dimension of Temperament	Level of Dimension				
	Very high	High	Med.	Low	Very low
1. Indoor activity				▪	
2. Outdoor activity			▪		
3. Vigor			▪		
4. Behavioral constancy			▪		
5. Dominance to strange dogs			▪		
6. Dominance to familiar people			▪		
7. Territoriality			▪		
8. Emotional stability				▪	
9. Sociability — within family				▪	
10. Sociability — with children					▪
11. Sociability — with strangers			▪		
12. Learning — rate		▪			
13. Learning — obedience			▪		
14. Learning — problem solving				▪	
15. Watchdog ability	▪				
16. Guard-dog ability				▪	

The Skye Terrier is a long, low animal with a long, profuse coat that falls straight down either side of its head and body, forming an apron of hair all around it and obscuring the legs—a look that I find very peculiar. Descriptions include "extremely sensitive to owner's approval, disapproval and moods" and "loyal and protective."

Behavior problems may include overprotectiveness and irritable snapping if manhandled. Some may be picky eaters. Some specimens may develop a peculiar mixture of timidity and dominance that makes them very cautious but exploratory and "shy-sharp."

West Highland White Terrier

A.K.C. Popularity: 39th

Dimension of Temperament	Level of Dimension				
	Very high	High	Med.	Low	Very low
1. Indoor activity	▨				
2. Outdoor activity	▨				
3. Vigor			▨		
4. Behavioral constancy		▨			
5. Dominance to strange dogs			▨		
6. Dominance to familiar people			▨		
7. Territoriality				▨	
8. Emotional stability				▨	
9. Sociability — within family	▨				
10. Sociability — with children			▨		
11. Sociability — with strangers	▨				
12. Learning — rate		▨			
13. Learning — obedience		▨			
14. Learning — problem solving	▨				
15. Watchdog ability		▨			
16. Guard-dog ability				▨	

The West Highland White Terrier is a small white dog with bright, button eyes, shaggy eyebrows and a black nose. Descriptions include "alert, gay, courageous and self-reliant, but friendly"; "hardy and needs no pampering, loving to romp and play in the snow"; showing "only occasional aggressive and snappy outbursts, timid and tenacious, a little bit stubborn" and "speedy, understanding and cunning."

Behavior problems may include irritable snapping and hyperexcitability that may lead to biting.

Wilbur was an interesting case I had involving this breed. He would attack the mother in the family whenever she yelled at her teen-age daughter. This aggression had gotten progressively worse over the years, resulting in the mother's complete inability to even admonish her child. It turned out that the daughter was rewarding Wilbur for his protection by soothing and calming him down after each attack or threat to her mother. Thus, the daughter was perceived as helping her mother by preventing further assaults when in fact she was helping herself.

Soft-coated Wheaten Terrier

A.K.C. Popularity: 72nd

Dimension of Temperament	Level of Dimension				
	Very high	High	Med.	Low	Very low
1. Indoor activity		▨			
2. Outdoor activity		▨			
3. Vigor		▨			
4. Behavioral constancy		▨			
5. Dominance to strange dogs			▨		
6. Dominance to familiar people			▨		
7. Territoriality				▨	
8. Emotional stability		▨			
9. Sociability — within family	▨				
10. Sociability — with children	▨				
11. Sociability — with strangers	▨				
12. Learning — rate		▨			
13. Learning — obedience			▨		
14. Learning — problem solving		▨			
15. Watchdog ability		▨			
16. Guard-dog ability			▨		

The Soft-coated Wheaten Terrier is a medium-sized dog with a longish, silky and wavy coat the color of wheat. Descriptions include "good-natured, spirited and game, but exhibits less aggressiveness than is sometimes encouraged in Terriers"; "steadiness and discrimination while preserving the joy of living and the stamina of a Terrier"; "easygoing, far less quick-tempered than all other Terriers"; "not prone to dogfights."

Behavior problems may occur with an occasional dominant animal that will tend to pick on the members of the family who are lowest in dominance.

6

The Toy Dogs

The Toys as a group are extremely tiny dogs ranging in weight from 1 to 18 pounds and averaging about 8 pounds. Have you ever seen a 1-pound dog? If not, try to imagine how small it might be. Some Toys are so small that they can stand on all fours in the palm of a large man's hand or ride comfortably in a woman's handbag. Can you imagine what it would be like for a dog to live in a world where everything towers over it and it may be in grave danger of being crushed by a toddler?

Most guinea pigs can exceed 1 pound in weight. The difference is that these animals are kept in a cage and don't form much of a social attachment to their keepers. Tiny Toy Dogs can run at large and form powerful attachments to their owners. Many have to be pampered and protected because of their size. Essentially, they were bred for this purpose. Many Toys are very sensitive to extremes of temperature, and the smaller the breed the more sensitive it is. It is simply a law of physics that the lower the mass, the more rapidly the body cools or heats. All mammals must maintain a constant temperature. Thus some tiny Toy Dogs may shiver in the summer when a cloud obscures the sun's rays or a gentle breeze blows over their body.

As other small mammals, like rodents, evolved and became progressively smaller, mechanisms to maintain their body heat and metabolic constancy were also evolved. However, tiny dogs did not evolve naturally. They were created in a mere second on the evolutionary time scale to suit human whims and fancies through selective breeding for diminutive size without regard to the other behavioral and physical mechanisms necessary to maintain such a tiny animal. They are totally artificial and unnatural as a subspecies and would perish if left to their own devices. Thus it is not a criticism for an owner to pamper these animals, because most of them have to be pampered to survive. But it may be a criticism of us as humans that we have created such a dependent animal. Paradoxically, it is also a compliment to humans that we are willing to accept the responsibility of our dependent creations.

There are 17 breeds classified as Toy Dogs: the Affenpinscher, Brussels Griffon, Chihuahua, English Toy Spaniel, Italian Greyhound, Japanese Spaniel, Maltese, Toy Manchester Terrier, Miniature Pinscher, Papillon, Pekingese, Pomeranian, Toy Poodle, Pug, Shih Tzu, Silky Terrier and Yorkshire Terrier.

Affenpinscher

A.K.C. Popularity: 110th

Dimension of Temperament	Level of Dimension				
	Very high	High	Med.	Low	Very low
1. Indoor activity	▦				
2. Outdoor activity	▦				
3. Vigor				▦	
4. Behavioral constancy			▦	▦	
5. Dominance to strange dogs			▦		
6. Dominance to familiar people		▦	▦		
7. Territoriality			▦		
8. Emotional stability				▦	
9. Sociability — within family		▦			
10. Sociability — with children					▦
11. Sociability — with strangers		▦			
12. Learning — rate		▦			
13. Learning — obedience			▦		
14. Learning — problem solving		▦			
15. Watchdog ability	▦				
16. Guard-dog ability					▦

The Affenpinscher, progenitor to the Griffon, is a frail dog weighing between 7 and 8 pounds. It is called the "Monkey Dog" because the prominent chin, hair tufts on its forehead and face, and large, round, bright eyes give it a "monkeyish expression." Descriptions include "game, alert, intelligent, sturdy, little 'terrier type' "; "very demanding of attention"; "high-strung, nervous, timid and yappy"; can get "vehemently excited"; "usually runs the household" and "when attacked it can be foolishly fearless toward an aggressor but usually doesn't pick fights."

Behavior problems may include house soiling, excessive barking, irritable snapping, excessively demanding behavior, aggressiveness when a threat is perceived and (ridiculous as it may seem) dominance challenges to people the dog sees as submissive. Some specimens may nervously guard small objects, toys or food. The breed is sensitive to cold and trembles a lot.

Brussels Griffon

A.K.C. Popularity: 100th

Dimension of Temperament	Level of Dimension				
	Very high	High	Med.	Low	Very low
1. Indoor activity	■				
2. Outdoor activity	■				
3. Vigor			■		
4. Behavioral constancy				■	
5. Dominance to strange dogs			■		
6. Dominance to familiar people		■	■		
7. Territoriality			■		
8. Emotional stability				■	
9. Sociability — within family		■			
10. Sociability — with children			■	■	
11. Sociability — with strangers			■	■	
12. Learning — rate		■			
13. Learning — obedience				■	
14. Learning — problem solving	■				
15. Watchdog ability	■				
16. Guard-dog ability					■

The Brussels Griffon weighs about 8 to 10 pounds and can be rough-coated or smooth-coated. It has large, round eyes and a short, flat muzzle. Descriptions include "teeming with personality and a bundle of jaunty good nature, spunky"; "not gentle with people"; "pulls hard and refuses to heel or follow"; "doesn't start fights"; high-strung but bold"; "very demanding pet that will heckle its owners into spoiling it if allowed" and its "super intelligence causes it to be sensitive in the presence of strangers."

Behavior problems may include house soiling, excessive yappy barking, stubbornness on the leash and possibly guarding "stolen" objects and food. The breed wheezes and snores, and some specimens may be picky eaters.

In my experience, Brussels Griffons may be very sensitive to social signals like facial expressions and body postures. If they sense a threat, they may threaten back even if a stranger doesn't consciously mean to be threatening. The short-coated variety shows marked stubbornness, refusing to break to the lead, more so than the rough-coated variety.

Chihuahua

A.K.C. Popularity: 21st

Dimension of Temperament	Level of Dimension				
	Very high	High	Med.	Low	Very low
1. Indoor activity	▤				
2. Outdoor activity	▤				
3. Vigor			▤		
4. Behavioral constancy			▤		
5. Dominance to strange dogs		▤	▤		
6. Dominance to familiar people			▤		
7. Territoriality	▤				
8. Emotional stability				▤	
9. Sociability — within family				▤	▤
10. Sociability — with children					▤
11. Sociability — with strangers				▤	▤
12. Learning — rate		▤			
13. Learning — obedience	▤	▤	▤	▤	
14. Learning — problem solving	▤				
15. Watchdog ability	▤				
16. Guard-dog ability					▤

The Chihuahua (pronounced chih-WHA-wha), developed in Mexico, is the smallest of all breeds. At one time its larger, barkless progenitors were used in religious ceremonies by the Toltecs and Aztecs as a sacrificial vehicle to expunge the sins of the dead and lead their souls to their ultimate destination. Descriptions include "swift-moving, saucy, with Terrier-like qualities," "bold and timid" and "clannish."

Behavior problems may include house soiling, yapping, fear snapping and the guarding of food, objects or toys.

In my experience, Chihuahuas' aggression toward strange dogs has no relation to their opponent's size but is a direct reaction to their opponent's proximity. They do seem to recognize their own kind, and are clearly more comfortable with members of their own breed than with other breeds. Their antisocial attitude and clannishness may be encouraged by owners who get them young and usually in pairs, causing exclusive imprinting of their owners and their canine companion. Not socializing them with other dogs or people out of protectiveness also encourages antisocial behavior. These dogs make a racket disproportionate to their size. There are some Chihuahuas, called "Teacup Chihuahuas," that are so minuscule as to weigh less than a pound and are able to stand on all fours in the palm of a person's hand. These specimens are fragile, high-strung and timorous. Anyone desiring this variety of dog would be better off with a hamster.

English Toy Spaniel

A.K.C. Popularity: 115th

Dimension of Temperament	Level of Dimension				
	Very high	High	Med.	Low	Very low
1. Indoor activity				▦	
2. Outdoor activity			▦		
3. Vigor				▦	
4. Behavioral constancy		▦			
5. Dominance to strange dogs				▦	
6. Dominance to familiar people				▦	
7. Territoriality				▦	
8. Emotional stability			▦		
9. Sociability – within family			▦		
10. Sociability – with children			▦		
11. Sociability – with strangers			▦		
12. Learning – rate		▦			
13. Learning – obedience			▦		
14. Learning – problem solving				▦	
15. Watchdog ability		▦			
16. Guard-dog ability					▦

The English Toy Spaniel weighs about 10 pounds and looks like a little spaniel with a short, pug nose. Descriptions include "an affectionate, intelligent little dog," "a bit stubborn." Unlike most other Toys, this breed is generally inactive indoors.

Behavior problems may include picky eating, and some specimens may wheeze and snore. Basically, however, it is a quiet, amiable, undemanding animal.

Italian Greyhound

A.K.C. Popularity: 77th

Dimension of Temperament	Level of Dimension				
	Very high	High	Med.	Low	Very low
1. Indoor activity		■			
2. Outdoor activity	■				
3. Vigor					■
4. Behavioral constancy			■		
5. Dominance to strange dogs				■	
6. Dominance to familiar people				■	
7. Territoriality				■	
8. Emotional stability					■
9. Sociability — within family			■		
10. Sociability — with children				■	■
11. Sociability — with strangers			■	■	
12. Learning — rate		■			
13. Learning — obedience		■			
14. Learning — problem solving				■	
15. Watchdog ability		■			
16. Guard-dog ability					■

The Italian Greyhound looks very much like a Greyhound, but it is only about 14 inches tall and weighs about 9 pounds. The A.K.C. suggests that the breed has looked pretty much the same for the last 2,000 years. The Romans bred Italian Greyhounds for pets, and the Latin motto *Cave canem,* or "Beware of the dog," could easily have meant "Don't step on the tiny dog." It has no function other than as a pet, not having been used for racing or other sporting activities. Because of its skinny body and short coat, this breed is particularly sensitive to the cold. Some descriptions include "prefers to run rather than fight," "high-strung."

Behavior problems may include house soiling and fear snapping.

Japanese Spaniel

A.K.C. Popularity: 86th

Dimension of Temperament	Level of Dimension				
	Very high	High	Med.	Low	Very low
1. Indoor activity		▨			
2. Outdoor activity				▨	
3. Vigor					▨
4. Behavioral constancy			▨		
5. Dominance to strange dogs				▨	
6. Dominance to familiar people				▨	
7. Territoriality					▨
8. Emotional stability		▨			
9. Sociability — within family	▨				
10. Sociability — with children			▨		
11. Sociability — with strangers	▨				
12. Learning — rate		▨			
13. Learning — obedience	▨				
14. Learning — problem solving	▨				
15. Watchdog ability	▨				
16. Guard-dog ability					▨

The Japanese Spaniel is about 9 inches tall and weighs about 7 pounds, with large, dark eyes, a short, wide muzzle and long, silky coat. Descriptions include "a good companion, bright and alert, naturally clean and game, sensitive, with definite likes and dislikes, and never forgets a friend or foe"; "quiet and easygoing"; "less temperamental than most Toys"; "don't have to spend much time training—they learn all kinds of tricks on their own and perform them on request."

Behavior problems may include sensitivity to extremes of temperature. Some specimens may wheeze and snore.

Maltese

A.K.C. Popularity: 34th

Dimension of Temperament	Level of Dimension				
	Very high	High	Med.	Low	Very low
1. Indoor activity	▪				
2. Outdoor activity			▪		
3. Vigor					▪
4. Behavioral constancy				▪	
5. Dominance to strange dogs			▪		
6. Dominance to familiar people					▪
7. Territoriality			▪		
8. Emotional stability			▪		
9. Sociability — within family			▪		
10. Sociability — with children				▪	
11. Sociability — with strangers				▪	
12. Learning — rate		▪			
13. Learning — obedience		▪			
14. Learning — problem solving		▪			
15. Watchdog ability	▪				
16. Guard-dog ability					▪

The Maltese is another Toy spaniel weighing less than 7 pounds and measuring about 5 inches tall. It has an extremely long, silky white coat that requires regular bathing and combing. It is the classic lady's lapdog. Descriptions include "fearless, trusting, affectionate, among the gentlest-mannered, lively and playful as well as vigorous"; "lively and spirited but not very robust"; "not high-strung or timid, but bold for its size"; "able to learn many cute tricks."

Behavior problems may include house soiling, irritable snapping and excessive barking.

My most common problem with this breed is not with the dog, but with its owner, usually female. The owners are solicitous and overprotective, and dote on their pampered pets to the extent that the animal becomes completely dependent on them for almost everything. I had one Maltese overprotected to the point where he had his own lavishly furnished room, in which he had lived his entire life. He would become rigid and paralyzed when taken out of his room. The problem surfaced when his owner had to move and discovered the dog had become literally catatonic.

154

Toy Manchester Terrier

A.K.C. Popularity:
81st

Dimension of Temperament	Level of Dimension				
	Very high	High	Med.	Low	Very low
1. Indoor activity	▨				
2. Outdoor activity	▨				
3. Vigor			▨		
4. Behavioral constancy				▨	
5. Dominance to strange dogs		▨			
6. Dominance to familiar people			▨		
7. Territoriality		▨			
8. Emotional stability				▨	
9. Sociability — within family				▨	
10. Sociability — with children				▨	
11. Sociability — with strangers					▨
12. Learning — rate		▨			
13. Learning — obedience				▨	
14. Learning — problem solving		▨			
15. Watchdog ability	▨				
16. Guard-dog ability					▨

The Toy Manchester Terrier looks like a small version of its Terrier cousins or a tiny Doberman. There are two varieties, one under 7 pounds and one weighing from 7 to 12 pounds. In my experience the smaller the specimen, the more dominant, aggressive, solitary, noisy, high-strung and poor in obedience it becomes. This breed is described as "a devoted companion," "gentle with people," "high-strung," "timid and bold" and "demanding."

Behavior problems may include house soiling, irritable snapping, demanding attention and excessive barking.

Miniature Pinscher

Dimension of Temperament	Level of Dimension				
	Very high	High	Med.	Low	Very low
1. Indoor activity	▦				
2. Outdoor activity	▦				
3. Vigor			▦		
4. Behavioral constancy				▦	
5. Dominance to strange dogs	▦				
6. Dominance to familiar people		▦			
7. Territoriality		▦			
8. Emotional stability				▦	
9. Sociability — within family				▦	
10. Sociability — with children			▦		
11. Sociability — with strangers					▦
12. Learning — rate		▦			
13. Learning — obedience					▦
14. Learning — problem solving		▦			
15. Watchdog ability	▦				
16. Guard-dog ability					▦

The Miniature Pinscher is a bit smaller than the Toy Manchester Terrier, but looks very similar to it and to its large cousin, the Doberman Pinscher. Descriptions include "lively temperament and is intelligent, with style, smartness and pep, being proud, vigorous, alert, completely self-possessed and having a spirited presence"; "not very gentle"; "one of the hardiest of the toys"; "the most demanding and headstrong of all Toys; a real little Napoleon"; "high-strung, both belligerent and bold"; "the kind of dog that one is constantly aware of but doesn't have to pamper." Some breeders and the A.K.C. warn of temperamental flaws such as "lethargy, timidity, shyness and viciousness."

Behavior problems may include excessive barking, irritable snapping and dominance struggles when the dog guards objects, places or food from family members. This breed is sensitive to the cold.

Papillon

A.K.C. Popularity: 78th

Dimension of Temperament	Level of Dimension				
	Very high	High	Med.	Low	Very low
1. Indoor activity		▨			
2. Outdoor activity			▨		
3. Vigor					▨
4. Behavioral constancy				▨	
5. Dominance to strange dogs				▨	
6. Dominance to familiar people				▨	
7. Territoriality				▨	
8. Emotional stability				▨	
9. Sociability – within family	▨				
10. Sociability – with children			▨		
11. Sociability – with strangers		▨			
12. Learning – rate		▨			
13. Learning – obedience	▨				
14. Learning – problem solving		▨			
15. Watchdog ability		▨			
16. Guard-dog ability					▨

The Papillon (pronounced pah-pee-YOWN) is fine-boned, light, dainty in appearance, with large, erect ears like butterfly wings, whence it gets its name. Another variety has drooping ears. Descriptions include "hardy and not particularly sensitive to heat or cold"; "high-strung and timid"; "they are an amiable, loving, nervous, dependent and easy-to-pamper breed"; "likely to develop little quirky habits and tricks"; "useful ratters, too small to actually kill one directly, but able to worry it to exhaustion and then dispatch it quickly." I sincerely doubt this last comment.

Behavior problems may include house soiling and fear snapping. Breeders have indicated to me that the breed is rather more fragile and sensitive to the cold than the literature would indicate.

Pekingese

A.K.C. Popularity: 17th

Dimension of Temperament	Level of Dimension				
	Very high	High	Med.	Low	Very low
1. Indoor activity				▨	
2. Outdoor activity				▨	
3. Vigor			▨		
4. Behavioral constancy		▨			
5. Dominance to strange dogs			▨		
6. Dominance to familiar people			▨		
7. Territoriality			▨		
8. Emotional stability		▨			
9. Sociability – within family				▨	
10. Sociability – with children				▨	
11. Sociability – with strangers					▨
12. Learning – rate		▨			
13. Learning – obedience					▨
14. Learning – problem solving				▨	
15. Watchdog ability	▨				
16. Guard-dog ability					▨

The Pekingese is a surprisingly solid little dog, only 8 inches tall, but weighing up to 14 pounds. It has a long, smooth, profuse coat and a ruff, or mane, around the neck. It has bulging eyes and a pug nose. Descriptions include "marked dignity and an exasperating stubbornness"; "independent willful and regal, calm and good-natured and condescendingly cordial"; "not a fighter or especially gentle."

Behavior problems may include irritable snapping, excessive barking, picky eating and demanding behavior. Some Pekes have been known to bite to get attention. At times a Peke will guard objects. It may wheeze and snore.

In my experience, this breed also suffers from overprotection, making it susceptible to phobias and fearful of novelty.

Pomeranian

A.K.C. Popularity: 20th

Dimension of Temperament	Level of Dimension				
	Very high	High	Med.	Low	Very low
1. Indoor activity	▦				
2. Outdoor activity			▦		
3. Vigor			▦		
4. Behavioral constancy				▦	
5. Dominance to strange dogs		▦			
6. Dominance to familiar people		▦			
7. Territoriality		▦			
8. Emotional stability		▦			
9. Sociability — within family				▦	
10. Sociability — with children					▦
11. Sociability — with strangers					▦
12. Learning — rate		▦			
13. Learning — obedience					▦
14. Learning — problem solving		▦			
15. Watchdog ability	▦				
16. Guard-dog ability					▦

The Pomeranian, about 6 inches tall and 5 pounds, is descended from the "Spitz" line of Arctic dogs and has a long coat that puffs out from its body and creates a mane. Descriptions include "docile temper and a vivacious spirit"; "not particularly gentle"; "bold, very plucky and independent and sharptempered"; "responsive to training if it knows the trainer is boss" and "acts toward intruders as if it didn't know it is tiny."

Behavior problems may include irritable snapping and, silly as it seems in a tiny dog, dominance guarding and willful disobedience.

Toy Poodle*

A.K.C. Popularity: 1st

Dimension of Temperament	Level of Dimension				
	Very high	High	Med.	Low	Very low
1. Indoor activity	▨				
2. Outdoor activity	▨				
3. Vigor			— — —	▨ —	
4. Behavioral constancy				— — —	— — —
5. Dominance to strange dogs		— — —	▨ —		
6. Dominance to familiar people		— — —	▨ —		
7. Territoriality		— —	— —	▨ —	
8. Emotional stability				— — —	— — —
9. Sociability — within family				— — —	— — —
10. Sociability — with children				— ▨ —	— —
11. Sociability — with strangers				— — —	— — —
12. Learning — rate	▨ —				
13. Learning — obedience	▨	— — —	— — —	— — —	— —
14. Learning — problem solving	▨ —				
15. Watchdog ability	▨ —				
16. Guard-dog ability					▨ —

The Toy Poodle is the most popular of all the Toy breeds, and we thus have the problem of puppy-mill strains, which I distinguish from well-bred varieties. Descriptions include "sulking and nagging and demanding its owner's continuous attention"; "brightest of all the Toys."

Behavior problems with the well-bred variety may include excessive barking, irritable snapping and dominance guarding. Behavior problems I have encountered with the puppy-mill variety would fill the rest of this book and include, for example: enuresis, encopresis, pica, hyperphagia, anorexia, polydipsia, alcoholism (by owner's initiative), hypersexuality, asexuality, impotence, excessive masturbation, dominance guarding, phobias, excessive barking, demandingness, aggression, destructiveness, etc., etc., etc. I have treated some puppy-mill specimens that vacillated so extremely their owners erroneously called them "schizophrenic." Luckily, most can be treated, and will calm down if the correct procedures are applied.

----- = puppy-mill
▨▨▨ = well-bred
*Watch out for puppy-mill dogs.

Pug

A.K.C. Popularity:
42nd

Dimension of Temperament	Level of Dimension				
	Very high	High	Med.	Low	Very low
1. Indoor activity				▒	
2. Outdoor activity				▒	
3. Vigor				▒	
4. Behavioral constancy		▒			
5. Dominance to strange dogs		▒	▒		
6. Dominance to familiar people			▒	▒	
7. Territoriality			▒		
8. Emotional stability		▒			
9. Sociability — within family			▒	▒	
10. Sociability — with children	▒				
11. Sociability — with strangers				▒	
12. Learning — rate		▒			
13. Learning — obedience			▒		
14. Learning — problem solving				▒	
15. Watchdog ability	▒				
16. Guard-dog ability					▒

The Pug is a little, snub-nosed dog with a short coat and a curly tail, developed in China. To me it looks like a cute little pig. Descriptions include "compact, alert, clean, tractable, companionable, needing minimum care and not requiring coddling"; "stubborn but easygoing" and "sturdier and more stable than most toys."

Behavior problems are minimal. Individual dogs may wheeze and snore, but they are considered easy to live with and to care for.

Shih Tzu

Dimension of Temperament	Level of Dimension				
	Very high	High	Med.	Low	Very low
1. Indoor activity		▨			
2. Outdoor activity				▨	
3. Vigor			▨		
4. Behavioral constancy		▨			
5. Dominance to strange dogs		▨			
6. Dominance to familiar people		▨			
7. Territoriality				▨	
8. Emotional stability	▨				
9. Sociability – within family		▨			
10. Sociability – with children		▨			
11. Sociability – with strangers			▨		
12. Learning – rate		▨			
13. Learning – obedience			▨		
14. Learning – problem solving				▨	
15. Watchdog ability	▨				
16. Guard-dog ability					▨

The Shih Tzu (pronounced Sheed-zoo) has a long, dense, wavy coat that completely hides its legs. Its name means "little lion" in Chinese. Descriptions include "very active, lively and alert, with a distinctly arrogant carriage"; "gentle to people and not a fighter"; "stubborn but quiet." Because of its coat, this little dog is particularly sensitive to hot weather.

Behavior problems may include irritable snapping and touch-shyness, especially when hot. A Shih Tzu may be hard to housebreak. As the breed's popularity increases, puppy-mill specimens are being produced that are considerably more aggressive than well-bred ones, tend to get into dogfights and bite their owners.

Silky Terrier

A.K.C. Popularity:
46th

Dimension of Temperament	Level of Dimension				
	Very high	High	Med.	Low	Very low
1. Indoor activity		▨			
2. Outdoor activity		▨			
3. Vigor			▨		
4. Behavioral constancy		▨			
5. Dominance to strange dogs			▨	▨	
6. Dominance to familiar people				▨	
7. Territoriality				▨	
8. Emotional stability		▨			
9. Sociability – within family			▨		
10. Sociability – with children			▨		
11. Sociability – with strangers			▨		
12. Learning – rate		▨			
13. Learning – obedience			▨		
14. Learning – problem solving		▨			
15. Watchdog ability	▨				
16. Guard-dog ability					▨

The Silky Terrier originated in Australia as a cross between
the Australian and Yorkshire terriers. It weighs about 8 pounds
and was used as a rat and snake killer. Descriptions include
"keen air of a terrier, quick, friendly and responsive"; "bold,
spirited, spunky and loving"; "one of the hardiest of the toys";
"fights only if attacked, but can battle with typical Terrier
tenacity"; "occasionally stubborn and yappy."

Behavior problems may include irritable snapping, house
soiling and excessive barking.

Yorkshire Terrier

A.K.C. Popularity: 14th

Dimension of Temperament	Level of Dimension				
	Very high	High	Med.	Low	Very low
1. Indoor activity	▦				
2. Outdoor activity	▦				
3. Vigor				▦	
4. Behavioral constancy			▦	▦	
5. Dominance to strange dogs		▦			
6. Dominance to familiar people			▦		
7. Territoriality		▦			
8. Emotional stability				▦	
9. Sociability – within family			▦		
10. Sociability – with children			▦		
11. Sociability – with strangers			▦		
12. Learning – rate		▦			
13. Learning – obedience			▦	▦	
14. Learning – problem solving		▦			
15. Watchdog ability	▦				
16. Guard-dog ability					▦

The Yorkshire Terrier weighs about 7 pounds and stands about 7 inches tall. It has long, straight, silky hair parted down the back from head to tail, forming a draping coat that hangs like a skirt over each side of its body. Some owners of this breed seem more interested in the dog's appearance than in its temperament and actually put stockings and boots on the dog's feet and keep its coat wrapped in paper to prevent damage between shows. Personally I think this is a ridiculous practice and that such owners should trade in their dog for a dress-up doll, which is clearly what they want. Descriptions include "stubborn and willful"; "spirited Terrier personality." In my experience, the smaller specimens and the puppy-mill varieties are more likely to be behaviorly variable and emotionally vacillating, both timid and bold, solitary, bad with children, suspicious, often aggressive with strangers, yappy, irritable and snappy.

Behavior problems may include house soiling, incessant barking, irritable snapping, unpredictable aggression, dominance and fear biting, touch shyness and the guarding of objects, places and people from other family members.

Of all the breeds the Yorky's problems make up my most frequent cases from New York apartment dwellers. I believe the problems stem from breeding for ridiculously small size and from owners' overprotection and permissiveness.

7

The Non-Sporting Dogs

As the name implies, this is essentially a miscellaneous category and does not mean that these dogs are not good sports. It includes dogs that have not been classified as Toys, Sporting Dogs, Working Dogs, Hounds, and Terriers. The functions of the Non-Sporting Dog group have in the past varied from being a companion to the possibility of guard work and retrieving. However, since they do not currently serve these working functions and since it is insulting for fanciers to have their breeds classified as miscellaneous, the Non-Sporting class was created.

The Non-Sporting Class is a most varied group, comprising the Bichon Frise, Boston Terrier, English Bulldog, Chow Chow, Dalmatian, French Bulldog, Keeshond, Lhasa Apso, Miniature and Standard Poodles, Schipperke and Tibetan Terrier.

Bichon Frise

A.K.C. Popularity: 51st

Dimension of Temperament	Level of Dimension				
	Very high	High	Med.	Low	Very low
1. Indoor activity	▨				
2. Outdoor activity			▨		
3. Vigor				▨	
4. Behavioral constancy			▨		
5. Dominance to strange dogs				▨	
6. Dominance to familiar people				▨	
7. Territoriality				▨	
8. Emotional stability		▨			
9. Sociability — within family	▨				
10. Sociability — with children	▨				
11. Sociability — with strangers	▨				
12. Learning — rate	▨	▨			
13. Learning — obedience	▨				
14. Learning — problem solving	▨				
15. Watchdog ability		▨			
16. Guard-dog ability					▨

The Bichon Frise (pronounced bee-SHOW free-ZAY) was developed in the Canary Islands. The breed is the size of a Toy Dog; the coat is white to apricot in color and is profuse, silky and loosely curled. The Bichon Frise resembles an unclipped Miniature or Toy Poodle with a smoother and silkier coat. Like the poodles, it is a minimal shedder and requires frequent professional grooming. When well groomed, this breed reminds me of an animated little Kewpie dog used to decorate a young girl's bedroom. Descriptions include "easygoing and amiable"; "a great trick dog." Only recently (in 1972) was the breed officially recognized by the A.K.C.

Behavior problems may include house soiling and touch-shyness, especially if the dog has been groomed roughly and painfully. Some specimens have exhibited self-abusive hair chewing as a result of skin ailments.

Boston Terrier*

A.K.C. Popularity: 27th

Dimension of Temperament	Level of Dimension				
	Very high	High	Med.	Low	Very low
1. Indoor activity				X	
2. Outdoor activity			X		
3. Vigor				X	
4. Behavioral constancy			X		
5. Dominance to strange dogs			X		
6. Dominance to familiar people			X	X	
7. Territoriality				X	
8. Emotional stability				X	
9. Sociability — within family		X	X		
10. Sociability — with children	X		X	X	
11. Sociability — with strangers		X	X		
12. Learning — rate		X			X
13. Learning — obedience		X			X
14. Learning — problem solving			X		
15. Watchdog ability	X				
16. Guard-dog ability				X	

The Boston Terrier is the result of a cross between the English Bulldog and the English Terrier. It is small and short-coated, with a Terrier-shaped body and a round head, short muzzle, erect ears and bulging eyes. Puppy-mill specimens of the breed are occasionally subject to a curious kind of anomaly, the result of early fusing of the bone plates in the skull that prevents normal growth of the brain. This can produce, as I have seen in my practice, dogs that appear to have the intelligence of a sea slug. Descriptions of normal examples of the breed include "gentle disposition and while not a fighter, can take care of itself" and "responsive, devoted and adaptable."

Behavior problems with normal specimens are minimal. The small-brained variety is socially similar to a warm "pet rock," but may exhibit excessive barking and other antisocial behavior. It is not that such specimens are willfully antisocial; it's simply that they don't have the brains to be sociable.

I have recently come across a string of cases of well-bred Bostons that fight ferociously. Usually two males, while living together, get into a dominance struggle. This starts an escalating sequence of attack and counterattack until the fight frequency may exceed four or five bloody battles per day. Moral: Don't have more than one male Boston at a time.

----- = puppy-mill
▨▨▨▨▨ = well-bred
*Watch out for puppy-mill dogs.

English Bulldog

A.K.C. Popularity: 36th

Dimension of Temperament	Level of Dimension				
	Very high	High	Med.	Low	Very low
1. Indoor activity					▬
2. Outdoor activity				▬	
3. Vigor				▬	
4. Behavioral constancy	▬				
5. Dominance to strange dogs		▬			
6. Dominance to familiar people			▬		
7. Territoriality		▬			
8. Emotional stability	▬				
9. Sociability — within family	▬				
10. Sociability — with children	▬				
11. Sociability — with strangers			▬		
12. Learning — rate				▬	
13. Learning — obedience				▬	
14. Learning — problem solving				▬	
15. Watchdog ability					▬
16. Guard-dog ability	▬				

The English Bulldog is a peculiar-looking animal familiar to most people. Its pushed-in nose, wrinkled and worried-looking forehead, and pendulous jowls give it a look of tough, aggressive disapproval. The breed stands only about 10 inches tall, but is extremely broad, with muscular shoulders, thick neck, powerful jaws and a broad stance. Some specimens may weigh as much as 60 pounds. Historically, the English used Bulldogs for the "sport" of bull baiting: hence the name. The dog's job was to sink its teeth into the nose or an appendage of the bull, driving the staked bull into a mad frenzy. This made it necessary for the dogs to be extremely ferocious, savage animals that reacted to pain by clamping on even more tightly and, if thrown, by getting up and attacking again like some living bear trap. This cruel entertainment was outlawed in England in 1835 along with dogfighting. Since then breeders have tried to "select out" this aggressive tenacity, and I suspect that they have accomplished this by selecting for extreme sluggishness and a very high stimulus threshold for biting. The result is that it takes a tremendous amount of intimidation to get a typical specimen aroused, but once aggressively aroused it can be as dangerous as its ancestors. Thus, paradoxically, the breed is a very sluggish and unsuitable watchdog, but can be a very aggressive guard dog. This is the only breed to exhibit this unusual combination of temperamental characteristics. Descriptions include "extremely sweet-natured and devoted and having a pacified and dignified demeanor" and "stubborn, but easygoing and easy to please and retentive once it learns something."

Behavior problems are few. I have encountered problems in my practice only with the exceptional specimen that is alert and has not been trained or socialized by its owners. If you have an alert Bulldog, train it early, socialize it extensively and make sure you're the boss. Otherwise you will be living with a mobile, constantly cocked bear trap. Bulldogs wheeze, snore and drool.

Chow Chow

A.K.C. Popularity: 29th

Dimension of Temperament	Level of Dimension				
	Very high	High	Med.	Low	Very low
1. Indoor activity				▨	
2. Outdoor activity		▨			
3. Vigor	▨				
4. Behavioral constancy	▨				
5. Dominance to strange dogs	▨	▨			
6. Dominance to familiar people		▨			
7. Territoriality	▨				
8. Emotional stability		▨			
9. Sociability — within family				▨	
10. Sociability — with children				▨	
11. Sociability — with strangers					▨
12. Learning — rate		▨			
13. Learning — obedience				▨	▨
14. Learning — problem solving		▨			
15. Watchdog ability	▨				
16. Guard-dog ability	▨	▨			

The Chow Chow, developed in China, is a large, densely coated breed with a lionlike mane and an unusual bluish-black tongue. Descriptions include "boldly aloof"; "Chinese hunting dog possessing scenting powers, staunchness on point, speed, stamina and cleverness in hunting tactics"; "very bossy and tends to control those about it"; "a highly independent, don't-fool-with-me animal"; aloof and not very demonstrative"; "intolerant of being crossed"; "if not socialized, trained and dominated at a very young age, will become the boss of the family"; "very stubborn, prone to willful disobedience and may become threatening to those who try to force obedience."

Behavior problems center on dominance struggles. A typical specimen may show dominance aggression toward people it considers submissive and may interpret even a friendly pat on the head as a dominance signal and react with its own dominance display. It may guard food, bones, toys and areas of the house from some or all family members. The breed is sensitive to heat and may display irritable snapping on a hot day or if annoyed. A Chow Chow may be touch-shy and refuse to be groomed. My advice to you if you want one of these dogs is to be sure you know what you are doing around it and to be sure of your own and your family's dominance before you get one. Breeders claim this is the only breed "born housebroken," but very dominant males may mark their indoor territory by squirting on chair legs.

Dalmatian

A.K.C. Popularity: 40th

Dimension of Temperament	Level of Dimension				
	Very high	High	Med.	Low	Very low
1. Indoor activity	▨				
2. Outdoor activity	▨				
3. Vigor	▨				
4. Behavioral constancy				▨	
5. Dominance to strange dogs		▨	▨		
6. Dominance to familiar people			▨		
7. Territoriality			▨		
8. Emotional stability				▨	
9. Sociability — within family			▨	▨	
10. Sociability — with children				▨	
11. Sociability — with strangers				▨	
12. Learning — rate		▨			
13. Learning — obedience		▨			
14. Learning — problem solving		▨			
15. Watchdog ability		▨			
16. Guard-dog ability		▨	▨	▨	

The Dalmatian is the breed familiar to most people as a firehouse mascot. It is the only spotted dog recognized by the A.K.C. It has been used as a watchdog, draft dog, shepherd, ratter, bird dog, trail hound, retriever, circus and stage performer and follower and guardian ("coach dog") of horse-drawn vehicles. Descriptions include "fitted for roadwork and showing speed and endurance" and "devoted, playful and responsive to training."

Behavior problems may include restlessness and, possibly, indoor destruction. Specimens of the breed may exhibit "shy-sharpness," that unfortunate combination of timidity and dominance which can lead to viciousness. Occasionally a male puppy may give every indication of being submissive and then, at puberty, begin to assert itself with more and more dominance over some family members, especially pubescent teenagers. Dalmatians are easily excitable and are prone to jump up on people.

French Bulldog

A.K.C. Popularity:
103rd

Dimension of Temperament	Level of Dimension				
	Very high	High	Med.	Low	Very low
1. Indoor activity	▦				
2. Outdoor activity			▦		
3. Vigor			▦		
4. Behavioral constancy		▦			
5. Dominance to strange dogs			▦		
6. Dominance to familiar people				▦	
7. Territoriality			▦		
8. Emotional stability		▦			
9. Sociability — within family		▦			
10. Sociability — with children				▦	
11. Sociability — with strangers					▦
12. Learning — rate		▦			
13. Learning — obedience				▦	
14. Learning — problem solving				▦	
15. Watchdog ability		▦			
16. Guard-dog ability					▦

The French Bulldog is small to medium in size. It has a Bulldog's body and pug face, but with bat ears and much less pendulous jowls. Descriptions include "remarkably intelligent, good watchdog, affectionate, sweet-tempered and dependable, alert and playful but not noisy."

Behavior problems are minimal. "Frenchies" may wheeze and snore and are sensitive to heat and cold. They may snap irritably when hot.

Keeshond

A.K.C. Popularity: 41st

Dimension of Temperament	Level of Dimension				
	Very high	High	Med.	Low	Very low
1. Indoor activity		▨			
2. Outdoor activity		▨			
3. Vigor				▨	
4. Behavioral constancy				▨	
5. Dominance to strange dogs			▨		
6. Dominance to familiar people				▨	
7. Territoriality				▨	
8. Emotional stability		▨			
9. Sociability – within family	▨				
10. Sociability – with children		▨			
11. Sociability – with strangers	▨				
12. Learning – rate		▨			
13. Learning – obedience			▨		
14. Learning – problem solving			▨		
15. Watchdog ability	▨				
16. Guard-dog ability				▨	

The Keeshond (pronounced KAZE-hond) is medium-sized and has a wolflike coat forming a lionlike mane around its foxlike face. The breed was used by the Dutch as a barge dog and became a symbol for the Dutch patriots during the eighteenth century. Descriptions include "alert, intelligent, with no desire to hunt."

Behavior problems may include trouble with housebreaking and training, some owners saying that their dogs are stubborn. Owners of the breed insist that the Keeshond's habit of baring its teeth in a menacing way is simply a submissive grin. If this is so, the Keeshond shares this behavior with the fox.

Lhasa Apso

A.K.C. Popularity: 12th

Dimension of Temperament	Level of Dimension				
	Very high	High	Med.	Low	Very low
1. Indoor activity	▨				
2. Outdoor activity		▨			
3. Vigor			▨		
4. Behavioral constancy				▨	
5. Dominance to strange dogs			▨		
6. Dominance to familiar people			▨		
7. Territoriality			▨		
8. Emotional stability				▨	
9. Sociability — within family			▨		
10. Sociability — with children				▨	
11. Sociability — with strangers					▨
12. Learning — rate		▨			
13. Learning — obedience				▨	
14. Learning — problem solving			▨		
15. Watchdog ability	▨				
16. Guard-dog ability				▨	

The Lhasa Apso is a Tibetan dog that looks like a larger version of the Shih Tzu. Descriptions include "intelligent, with quick hearing and having a finely developed instinct for distinguishing intimates from strangers, being hardy and a keen watch, gay, assertive, but chary with strangers"; "gentle with people"; "game, devoted and lively, bold and short-tempered"; "a stubborn animal showing willful disobedience"; "most obedient to anyone it trusts, easily trained and responsive to kindness." The discrepancy stems from who is doing the training. If the trainer is dominant and uses only reward, the dog will learn to obey.

Behavior problems may include irritable snapping, touch shyness and fighting when kept in pairs. Breeders claim that the breed is not prone to dog fighting, but my services have been called upon repeatedly by owners of pairs or more of these dogs to stop incessant, vicious fighting often resulting in serious damage and in locking—in which two animals bite and then clamp down their jaws on each other and neither will let

177

go. Other problems may involve dominance challenges (with larger specimens), guarding objects and places from family members, lunging in a threatening manner when approached and unpredictable aggression toward strangers and even toward family members and friends. The trainer of this dog needs to exhibit consistent dominance and use only rewards to define appropriate behavior to the dog.

Miniature and Standard Poodles*

A.K.C. Popularity: 1st

Dimension of Temperament	Level of Dimension				
	Very high	High	Med.	Low	Very low
1. Indoor activity	----	----	----		
2. Outdoor activity	----	----	----		
3. Vigor			----		
4. Behavioral constancy			----	----	
5. Dominance to strange dogs			----		
6. Dominance to familiar people			----	--	
7. Territoriality		----	----		
8. Emotional stability			----	----	
9. Sociability — within family			----		
10. Sociability — with children		----	----		
11. Sociability — with strangers			----	----	
12. Learning — rate	----	----			
13. Learning — obedience	----				
14. Learning — problem solving	----				
15. Watchdog ability	----				
16. Guard-dog ability					----

Poodles come in almost every size from the Standard, a large dog, to the Teacup Poodle, so named because of its diminutive size of 1 pound. Poodles have been used as retrievers in water, truffle finders, and circus and stage performers. They are the most popular dog in the United States, so it goes without saying that they have been subject to puppy-mill degradation, especially in the Toys and Miniatures. I have already made distinctions between well-bred and puppy-mill varieties of Toy Poodles, and the same distinctions regarding temperament apply here, so the rest of this description will focus on the well-bred varieties only. The general rule about poodles is that the larger they are, the less active they are and the more exercise they need. Also, the smaller they are (within limits) the faster they learn, although all poodles are considered very fast learners compared with other breeds.

Behavior problems, like the size of poodles, can cover the entire range. Miniatures are most likely to exhibit timidity, fear biting and the guarding of objects. Standards are less likely to exhibit problems. Puppy-mill varieties can be explosive, shy-sharp, unpredictable, vicious canine powder kegs. As you might expect, I have had numerous cases of puppy-mill poodles. Keep in mind that their potential problems can be prevented if they are raised properly and if their behavior is shaped with the appropriate procedures.

- - - - - = Miniature
▰▰▰▰▰ = Standard
*Watch out for puppy-mill dogs.

Schipperke

A.K.C. Popularity: 59th

Dimension of Temperament	Level of Dimension				
	Very high	High	Med.	Low	Very low
1. Indoor activity	▩				
2. Outdoor activity	▩				
3. Vigor		▩			
4. Behavioral constancy				▩	
5. Dominance to strange dogs			▩		
6. Dominance to familiar people			▩		
7. Territoriality		▩			
8. Emotional stability				▩	
9. Sociability — within family			▩		
10. Sociability — with children				▩	
11. Sociability — with strangers					▩
12. Learning — rate		▩			
13. Learning — obedience				▩	
14. Learning — problem solving	▩				
15. Watchdog ability	▩				
16. Guard-dog ability		▩			

The Schipperke (pronounced SKIP-er-kee) has a short, thickset body, a foxlike head with erect ears, and a thick black coat that forms a mane around its neck. It is a Belgian dog that was used for hunting and ratting. Descriptions include "agile, indefatigable, continually occupied with what is going on about it, always curious about what's going on behind closed doors and about something that has been moved, barking sharply and standing up its ruff and being mischievous"; "unaware of the limits of its size" and "quick-tempered but loyal and devoted."

Behavior problems may include house soiling, irritable snapping, stealing and guarding food and objects.

Tibetan Terrier

A.K.C. Popularity: 93rd

Dimension of Temperament	Level of Dimension				
	Very high	High	Med.	Low	Very low
1. Indoor activity	▓	▓	▓	▓	
2. Outdoor activity		▓	▓		
3. Vigor	▓				
4. Behavioral constancy		▓	▓	▓	
5. Dominance to strange dogs			▓		
6. Dominance to familiar people			▓	▓	
7. Territoriality		▓			
8. Emotional stability		▓	▓		
9. Sociability – within family			▓	▓	
10. Sociability – with children				▓	▓
11. Sociability – with strangers				▓	▓
12. Learning – rate		▓	▓		
13. Learning – obedience				▓	▓
14. Learning – problem solving			▓		
15. Watchdog ability	▓	▓			
16. Guard-dog ability		▓	▓		

The Tibetan Terrier is not actually a Terrier, nor does it have a Terrier disposition. It looks like a small Old English Sheepdog and was used to herd and to guard. There is little agreement as to the temperamental characteristics of this breed. I have therefore indicated this range of opinion by showing multiple levels on each dimension of temperament where there is disagreement.

Behavior problems may include house soiling, stealing and guarding food and objects, touch shyness and dominance challenges.

8

Selecting a Dog

Looking over all the 123 breeds of dogs described in the last six chapters, one gets a sinking feeling of consulting a very long Chinese menu written in Hungarian. Each breed can differ from the others in size, shape, strength, hair color, hair texture, length and sheddiness of coat and requirements for daily exercise, as well as the sixteen dimensions of temperament on which it is rated in the tables.

Dogs, as I have said, are the most varied species in existence. This is both good news and bad news. The bad news is that with so many choices possible, an impulsive decision can easily result in your owning a breed that doesn't begin to fit your individual personality and life-style. The good news is that there is enough diversity among dogs to match any person's uniqueness if the decision is made with a bit of rationality.

Most people, when confronted with a large number of alternatives, do things to simplify the task. There are many strategies. One is to go with your past experience. You remember the poodle that bit you when you were a child and you vow never to get near another poodle. Or you recall with fondness the summers spent with a German Shorthaired Pointer and decide that that breed is the best pet for you. These are not inappropriate ways to proceed, but they do limit your selection. It's just not possible for anyone to have experience with a large enough sample of dogs. Also, the experiences you did have were unique to that period of your life. You may be a different person now, with a completely different life-style from the one you had before.

Another way to select a dog is by its appearance. This may occur in two ways. You may have seen a specimen of a breed in a dog book or on the street that caught your fancy. Or you may use the old "How much is that doggie in the window?" technique, going to a pet shop and examining the available selection of puppies. The pet-shop selection technique has great disadvantages. I have already alluded to the problems with dogs produced in puppy mills and sold in pet shops. You're really taking a chance with these animals. You may be lucky, but there is an equal chance of getting a lemon.

Even if you get lucky with this kind of impulse shopping, you still are subjecting yourself to psychological forces that will make your decision a purely emotional one. All puppies are cute, lovable, frisky little things. Dogs are not very different in those tender first six to ten weeks. All that the pet-shop salesperson has to do is place the puppy in your arms and you will probably be hooked.

This is not to say that choosing a dog shouldn't be an emotional experience. It rightly should be, but it should be the *last* step. After you have limited your alternatives to the most suitable breed, then you can let your heart be your guide.

There are probably as many ways to limit your alternatives as there are people to give advice, but I am proposing a way that will increase the likelihood that the breed you choose will be compatible with you and how you live. I don't mean this in the superficial sense—as, for example, a woman with long, silky blond hair getting an Afghan, a dog with long, silky blond hair. These matches certainly occur, but they simply reflect the dog owner's feelings about physical appearance. The selection process I am proposing involves a matching of your basic personality characteristics and the life-style you have chosen with the kind of dog that will mesh with and contribute to your life.

In my professional experience I have found that people who succeed in matching a breed's temperamental characteristics to their life-style are less likely to experience behavior problems, turmoil and annoyances that usually arise out of a mismatch. I cannot guarantee that problems will not occur, but the matching process substantially reduces their probability of occurrence.

In the selection process I have devised, you begin with a large range of possibilities and reduce them through a series of dichotomous decisions. Each decision will put you closer to your ideal breed match.

Physical Characteristics

The four physical characteristics that are the most important to consider in choosing a dog to suit your life-style are coat quality, height, weight and strength.

Coat, Shedding and Grooming. The coats of dogs differ greatly. Some are short, some are long; some are coarse or wiry, others are silky; some dogs shed profusely all year round, some shed moderately, some shed seasonally and some very little.

Obviously, the amount of shedding will dictate the amount of hair you have lying around the house, the amount of cleaning you will have to do and the amount of brushing that both the dog and your clothes will need. It is just not possible to keep a home completely free of small amounts of dog hair that accumulate under furniture and in corners, or to keep yourself and your furniture free of hair, when you live with a heavily shedding dog like a Dalmatian or German Shepherd. There will be some loose hair on everything no matter how much you clean.

Thus, the amount of shedding should be considered in light of three personality characteristics: your desire for personal cleanliness, your desire for a clean living space and your desire to brush and comb your dog. Table 4 is a matrix that describes the amount of grooming necessary both to keep your dog healthy and to keep your house reasonably free of piles of loose hair. In each cell of the table, the breeds are arranged by height, with the tallest at the top of the cell. The assumption is that the taller the breed, the more surface area you will have to groom.

TABLE 4.

Distribution of Purebred Dogs by Number of Grooming Sessions Needed per Week and Time Needed for Each Grooming Session

NUMBER OF SESSIONS PER WEEK	5	10	15	20
7		+Ir. Wolfhnd +Ger. Shepherd +Dalmatian St. Schnauz. M. Schnauz. WH Dachshnd.	Gi. Schnauz. +The Belgians Maltese	
4	+Manchest. Terrier		+Fem. Borzoi Airedale Terrier Silky Terrier	+St. Bernard Wheaten Terrier
3		+Male Borzoi	+Nor. Elkhnd	
2	+Greyhound +Eng. Foxhnd +Am. Foxhnd +Vizsla +Whippet +Harrier +Brit. Spaniel +Field Spaniel +Beagle It. Greyhnd +Mini. Pinscher Manch. Toy Terrier +Fr. Bulldog +Sm. Dachsh. +Sm. Br. Griffon +Chihuahua	+B&T Coonhnd +Bloodhound +Weimaraner +Rh. Rdgback +Boxer +Saluki +Am. Staffordshire +Clumber Spaniel +Welsh Springer +Sussex Spaniel +Sm. Fox Terrier +Boston Terrier +Basset Hnd +Pug +Papillon +Lng. C. Dach.	+Great Dane +Mastiff +Akita +Doberman +Ber. Mt. Dog +Sm. Collie +Rottweiler +Sib. Husky +Bull Terrier +Eng. Bulldog +Schipperke +Car. W. Corgi +Pem. W. Corgi Australian Cairn Terrier Rgh. Br. Griffon	+Al. Malamute Bedlington West. High Terrier Lakeland Terrier Welsh Terrier Sealyham Terrier Affenpinsch. Dand. Dinmnt Eng. Toy Spaniel Yorkshire Terrier
1	Basenji	+Pointer +G. SH Pointer +Ches. Bay Retriever +C. Coat Retriever +Labrador Retriever +Fl. Coat Retriever +Bullmastiff +Staff. Bull	+G. WH Pointer +WH Pnt Griffon Border Terrier	

MINUTES OF GROOMING PER SESSION

30	45	60	90	120-300
	Bich. Frise			
+Gr. Pyrenees +Kuvasz +Newfoundlnd +Samoyed Irish Terrier Norwich Terrier +Pomeranian	+Chow Chow Kerry Blue +Keeshond +Eng. Cocker +Cocker Spaniel Scottish Terrier	WH Fox Terrier +Tibetan Terrier +Lhasa Apso +Shih Tzu +Pekingese +Japan. Spaniel		O.E. Sheep.
Bouv. des Fl. +Am. Water Spaniel +Shet. Sheepdog	+Sc. Deerhnd +Irish Setter +Gordon Setter +Eng. Setter +Golden Retriever +Eng. Spr. Spaniel +Skye Terrier	+Afghan Hnd Komondor +Otterhound +Rgh. Collie Ir. Water Spaniel Puli Toy Poodle	+Briard	St. Poodle Min. Poodle
30	**45**	**60**	**90**	**120-300**

+ indicates shedder

TABLE 5

Exceptional Shedders and Breeds That Require Professional Grooming

Breed	Exceptional Shedders Type of Shedding	Breeds that Need Professional Grooming
Alaskan Malamute	Heavy seasonal shedder	Airedale Terrier
Belgian Malinois,	Very heavy, once-a-year shedders	Bedlington Terrier
Sheepdog and Tervuren		Bouvier des Flandres
Collie	Sheds heavily for 3 weeks twice a year	Dandie Dinmont
Chow Chow	Heavy shedder	Giant Schnauzer
Curly-coated Retriever	Sheds once a year. Rest of the year sheds less than rest of retrievers	Irish Terrier
Dalmatian	Heavy daily shedder	Irish Water Spaniel
German Shepherd	Constant shedder	Kerry Blue Terrier
Great Pyrenees	Heavy shedder twice a year	Lakeland Terrier
Keeshond	Blows coat twice a year, requiring several hours of combing at these times	Miniature Schnauzer
Newfoundland	Heavy seasonal shedder	Miniature Poodle
Pomeranian	Heavy shedder	Standard Poodle
St. Bernard	Heavy shedder	Toy Poodle
Samoyed	Heavy seasonal shedder	Scottish Terrier
Shetland Sheepdog	Sheds heavily for 3 weeks twice a year	Standard Schnauzer
Siberian Husky	Heavy shedder	Welsh Terrier
		Wirehaired Fox Terrier

The amount of time necessary for a complete grooming session multiplied by the number of times you must groom a specimen of a breed per week will determine the total amount of dog grooming you can expect to do to keep that breed's coat healthy and beautiful. A "plus" before the breed name means that it sheds. The more they shed, the more times per week the shedders have to be groomed. The longer the hair, the longer the duration of each session. Table 5 gives a list of exceptional shedders and those breeds which need professional grooming.

As you can see from these two tables, the breeds range from the Basenji, which sheds the least of all shedding dogs and thus needs the least care, to the Dalmatians and German Shepherds, which have to be brushed every day to keep the accumulation of loose hair down to a tolerable minimum.

The type of person who should *not* consider getting the shedding breeds is someone who can't stand to have dog hairs all over his or her clothing, furniture and home and/or doesn't have the time to groom a particular breed properly. Now, with these facts of shedding and grooming in mind, respond to the following set of statements.

	T	F
1. I hate it when a dog gets hair all over me.	___	___
2. I would find it embarrassing if people came to my house clean and left with dog hair on their clothing.	___	___
3. I get very uncomfortable when my house is not scrupulously clean.	___	___
4. I enjoy being neatly dressed.	___	___
5. I feel uncomfortable in casual clothes.	___	___
6. It bugs me when I have to constantly clean up after people.	___	___
7. I couldn't rest until all the rooms in my house were clean and orderly.	___	___
8. I am concerned about what people think and say about me.	___	___
9. I don't grow house plants because I don't have time to care for them properly.	___	___
10. I usually don't have enough time in any one day to get done all that I want to.	___	___

11. I do not enjoy repetitive tasks, even if I allow my mind to wander over pleasant thoughts while I do them. ____ ____

12. There is no place in my living space where I could groom a dog easily. ____ ____

If you answered "True" to 9 out of these 12 questions, it means that you should *not* get a dog that is a shedder. The more the breed sheds, the more uncomfortable you will feel. You will find yourself getting annoyed at your dog for making it necessary to constantly clean up after it, brush it and remove the hairs from your clothing. If you answered "False" to 9 out of these 12 questions, you probably could stand to live with a shedder.

Whether a dog is a shedder or not, some dogs take a lot of grooming, like the Bichon Frise, which has to be groomed for 45 minutes a day, 7 days a week. Most of the nonshedding dogs, save the Basenji, have to be professionally groomed periodically. This can be an expensive proposition.

Obviously, if you find that you enjoy the picking, plucking, brushing and primping activities that go into grooming a dog, then the breeds needing a lot of care would be right for you. If you find that you don't enjoy these activities or that you don't have the time it takes, then you are going to have to pay for your dog's grooming needs, either in annoyance, if you do it yourself, or in money, if you pay for it to be done.

Height, Weight and Bulkiness. The other physical characteristics that can affect your life-style are your dog's potential size and strength. Figure 1 arranges all 123 breeds of dogs into levels of average height measured at the shoulder. Adult females of each breed are usually 1 to 2 inches shorter than their ideal male counterpart. This height discrepancy increases as you move into the taller breeds. Within any level, the breeds are arranged by height with the tallest breed at the beginning of the list. Thus, the tallest of the towering breeds is the Irish Wolfhound. Keep in mind that the word towering is to be taken both literally and figuratively, since the taller of these breeds

FIGURE 1.
Height Distribution of Purebred Dogs

HEIGHT IN INCHES AT THE SHOULDERS OF AVERAGE ADULT MALE			
5" - 10" SHRIMPY	Sealyham Terrier Lhasa Apso Affenpinscher Poodle, Toy Skye Terrier Scottish Terrier Norwich Terrier Cairn Terrier	Australian Terrier Shih Tzu Dandie Dinmont Dachshund English Toy Spaniel Silky Terrier Papillon Japanese Spaniel	Maltese Pekingese Brussels Griffon Yorkshire Terrier Pomeranian Chihuahua
11" - 15" LITTLE	Sussex Spaniel Fox Terrier Tibetan Terrier Lakeland Terrier Staffordshire Bull Terrier Welsh Terrier Boston Terrier Cocker Spaniel	Shetland Sheepdog Italian Greyhound Beagle Poodle, Miniature Schnauzer, Miniature Basset Hound Schipperke Border Terrier	Manchester Toy Terrier Cardigan W. Corgi Bichon Frise Pug French Bulldog Miniature Pinscher Pembroke W. Corgi West Highland White
16" - 20" SHORT	Whippet Norwegian Elkhound Chow Chow Harrier English Springer Spaniel Brittany Spaniel Schnauzer, Standard Kerry Blue Terrier	Wheaten Terrier Am. Staff. Bull Terrier Bull Terrier Puli Keeshond Irish Terrier Field Spaniel Clumber Spaniel	Basenji Welsh Springer Spaniel Manchester Terrier American Water Spaniel English Cocker Spaniel Bedlington Terrier English Bulldog
21" - 25" MIDDLE	Saluki Bouvier des Flandres Bernese Mt. Dog Otterhound Gordon Setter Rottweiler Briard German Shepherd Poodle, Standard Collie Belgian Tervuren Belgian Malinois	Belgian Sheepdog German WH Pointer English Setter Alaskan Malamute Kuvasz (small) Chesa. Bay Retriever German SH Pointer English Foxhound Boxer American Foxhound Labrador Retriever Golden Retriever	Curly-Coated Retriever Vizsla Irish Water Spaniel Airdale Terrier Flat-Coated Retriever WH Pointer Griffon Old English Sheepdog Siberian Husky Samoyed Dalmatian
26" - 30" TALL	Great Pyrenees Kuvasz Afghan Hound Borzoi Newfoundland Greyhound	Doberman Pinscher Akita Irish Setter Pointer Schnauzer, Giant Bullmastiff	Rhodesian Ridgeback Bloodhound B&T Coonhound Weimaraner

FIGURE 1 *(cont.)*

31" - 36" TOWERING	Irish Wolfhound Scottish Deerhound Great Dane Mastiff St. Bernard	

can easily stand seven feet tall when up on their hind legs and will thus tower over almost everyone. On the other hand, the smallest of the shrimpy breeds, the Chihuahua, can be so small as to go unnoticed.

Basically, the decision about height has to do with whether you or your family members would be intimidated by the taller breeds or would tend to step on the shorter ones.

In Figure 2, the breeds are arranged into levels of average weight when in trim condition. Within each level, the breeds are arranged by weight with the heaviest breed at the beginning of the list. Adult females are only slightly lighter in the tiny and miniature breeds, about 5 pounds lighter in the small to medium-sized breeds, 10 pounds lighter in the large and very large breeds and as much as 15 to 20 pounds lighter in the enormous breeds.

FIGURE 2.
Weight Distribution of Purebred Dogs

TRIM WEIGHT	POCKET 1 - 4 VI	Japanese Spaniel Pocket Poodle	Maltese Yorkshire Terrier	Pomeranian Pocket Beagle
	TINY 5 - 12	Chihuahua Pomeranian	Yorkshire Terrier Poodle, Toy	Maltese

FIGURE 2 *(cont.)*

TRIM WEIGHT IN POUNDS				
MINIATURE 13 – 25	Whippet Basenji Sealyham Terrier Boston Terrier Dandie Dinmont Scottish Terrier Welsh Terrier Bedlington Terrier Dachshund	Fox Terrier Sheltie Beagle Manchester Terrier Lakeland Terrier Westie Terrier Lhasa Apso Pug Poodle, Miniature	Schnauzer, Miniature Border Terrier Tibetan Terrier Cairn Terrier Australian Terrier Shih Tzu Bichon Frise Schipperke Pekingese
SMALL 26 – 39	American Water Spaniel Wheaten Terrier Kerry Blue Terrier Brittany Spaniel Staff. Bull Terrier	Pembroke W. Corgi Puli English Cocker Spaniel Cardigan W. Corgi Skye Terrier	French Bulldog Irish Terrier Beagle Whippet
MEDIUM 40 – 59	WH Pointing Griffon Clumber Spaniel Poodle, Standard Norwegian Elkhound Airedale Vizsla	Siberian Husky English Springer Spaniel Harrier English Bulldog Basset Hound Bull Terrier	Schnauzer, Standard Field Spaniel Welsh Springer Spaniel Keeshond
LARGE 60 – 89	Otterhound Schnauzer, Giant Alaskan Malamute Briard B&T Coonhound German Shepherd Weimaraner English Foxhound Doberman Rhodesian Ridgeback Boxer Chow Chow	Chesa. Bay Retriever Golden Retriever Belgian Malinois Belgian Sheepdog Belgian Tervuren Gordon Setter Labrador Retriever German WH Pointer Collie American Foxhound Greyhound Pointer	Samoyed English Setter Irish Setter Flat-coated Retriever Afghan Curly-coated Retriever German WH Pointer Am. Staff. Bull Terrier Dalmatian Irish Water Spaniel Poodle, Standard Saluki
VERY LARGE 90 – 100	Kuvasz Otterhound Bloodhound Bouvier des Flandres	Scottish Deerhound Borzoi Akita Bernese Mountain Dog	Komondor Old Eng. Sheepdog
ENORMOUS ≥ 110	Mastiff St. Bernard Newfoundland Great Dane	Irish Wolfhound Great Pyrenees Bullmastiff Rottweiler	Kuvasz Otterhound

You can see that the Mastiff is the heaviest of all the breeds, some individuals weighing over 180 pounds, and the Pocket Beagle is the lightest, some specimens weighing less than 2 pounds.* So you must ask yourself whether you would be comfortable living with a dog that would outweigh you. Or whether you would feel ridiculous walking a dog so tiny that it could fit comfortably into your coat pocket.

The weight dimension can also be used to calculate the amount and cost of feeding the dog. A generally accepted rule of thumb is that the daily food requirement of a mature dog will be an ounce of mixed dry and canned food for every two pounds of weight of the dog, but this rule becomes less accurate for breeds at the ends of the weight distribution. Table 6 gives the potential daily food needs for the different weight categories. To give you some representative figures, a 200-pound Mastiff will eat up to 6¼ pounds of food a day. If you buy large quantities at discount prices, you still will not be able to get away with a bill of less than $600 per year to feed one of these beasts. On the other hand, a 5-pound Chihuahua can eat less than 2½ ounces of food per day, thus a 12-ounce can of wet dog food could last five days. At 39 cents a can, it would cost, at most, $28.47 per year to maintain this little animal. This figure could be a lot less if you mixed the Chihuahua's food with less expensive dry food. If you pampered a Chihuahua with an exclusive diet of Porterhouse steak ($3/lb.), it would still cost less than $171 per year, excluding the potential veterinary-medical bills for the sickly animal that this diet would produce.†

Another informative size measure is derived from dividing the average weight of a breed by its height. This weight/height ratio gives us a different picture from that of either height or weight in isolation. The ratio describes the density, or bulkiness, or stockiness of a breed. Barring obesity, the stockier the breed, the larger the dogs are perceived and the stronger they

---

*Note: I did not include the Teacup Chihuahua or the Pocket Poodle, some specimens of these breeds weighing only 10 ounces, since I don't think they should exist. They are examples of selective breeding taken to an absurd extreme and are an expensive substitute for a hamster.

†With inflation, I am sure these cost estimates will be outdated the moment this book is published. The estimates are based on 1979 prices.

TABLE 6
Potential Daily Food Requirements for Different Weights of Dogs

Category	Average Weight (lbs.)	Daily Food (oz.)	Estimated Yearly Cost
Very Enormous	200	100	$600
Enormous	110	55	440
Very Large	95	47½	380
Large	75	37½	300
Medium	50	25	200
Small	22½	11¼	100
Miniature	19	9½	85

are. People automatically view stockier dogs as bigger, even if they are shorter in height. Stockiness also relates to the amount of musculature of a breed and the heaviness of the skeletal structure. Figure 3 arranges the breeds in ten categories of increasing stockiness. Females are on the average .2 of a bulk ratio unit less than the males of the same breed. Thus, females are in general a bit less stocky than most males. The frail animals have a bulk ratio (weight/height) of less than one, meaning that they have less weight in pounds than they have height in inches. The Italian Greyhound is the frailest of the frail. The frail breeds are easily crushed, delicate and tiny animals. They are prone to shivering and have to be protected from almost anything.

On the other hand, the St. Bernards, Mastiffs and New-foundlands are the stockiest of the breeds. The first two have a bulk ratio of 6 and the Newfs 5.83. Interestingly, the Saints and Newfs may look bigger than some Mastiffs owing to the abundance of their long hair. All three breeds are enormously powerful. Keep in mind that a dog's musculature, pound for pound, is 3 to 4 times as strong as an average man's. Thus, a well-exercised Mastiff could exert the force of three or four 180-pound men—the infielders of the New York Yankees, for example. The Mastiff's power is not to be taken lightly. Luckily, its temperament obviates excessive force to control it.

Notice that when the bulk ratio is used as a measure, the breeds become reorganized. For instance, the Irish Wolfhound,

FIGURE 3.

Distribution of Purebred Dogs by Bulk Ratio—i.e., Ratio Obtained by Dividing Weight by Height

BULK RATIO				
FRAIL	Poodle, Toy Maltese Italian Greyhound			
FRAGILE	Australian Terrier Manchester Terrier Silky Terrier Yorkshire Terrier	Chihuahua English Toy Spaniel Brussels Griffon Papillon	Pomeranian Manchester Toy Affenpinscher Japanese Spaniel	
BANTAM	Lhasa Apso Tibetan Terrier Irish Terrier Westie Terrier Pekingese Schipperke Cairn Terrier	Basenji Shih Tzu Pug Welsh Terrier Bichon Frise Sheltie Bedlington Terrier	Poodle, Miniature Whippet Schnauzer, Miniature Border Terrier Lakeland Terrier Fox Terrier Norwich Terrier	
LIGHT	Scottish Terrier Wheaten Terrier Dachshund Kerry Blue Terrier	English Cocker Spaniel Brittany Spaniel Puli Beagle	Cocker Spaniel Tibetan Terrier	
MIDDLE	Cardigan Welsh Corgi Pembroke Welsh Corgi WH Pointing Griffon Gordon Setter Irish Water Spaniel English Springer Spaniel English Setter German WH Pointer German SH Pointer Irish Setter	Sussex Spaniel Harrier Staff. Bull Terrier Pointer Greyhound Bull Terrier French Bulldog Airedale Vizsla Schnauzer, Standard	Field Spaniel Siberian Husky Saluki Afghan Welsh Springer Spaniel Sealyham Terrier Keeshond American Water Spaniel Dandie Dinmont Poodle, Standard	
SOLID	Scottish Deerhound English Foxhound Golden Retriever Weimaraner Boxer Samoyed Rhodesian Ridgeback	American Foxhound Labrador Retriever Chesa. Bay Retriever Dalmatian FC Retriever Skye Terrier Belgian Sheepdog	Belgian Tervuren Belgian Malinois CC Retriever Collie Doberman Norwegian Elkhound	

FIGURE 3 *(cont.)*

BULK RATIO				
STURDY		Bernese Mountain Dog Chow Chow Akita Alaskan Malamute Briard	Am. Staff. Bull Terrier German Shepherd Clumber Spaniel Kuvasz (s) B&T Coonhound	Schnauzer, Giant English Bulldog Borzoi
STRONG		Old English Sheepdog Basset Hound Bouvier des Flandres Bloodhound	Great Pyrenees Irish Wolfhound Komondor Otterhound	Kuvasz (1)
VERY STRONG		Bullmastiff Rottweiler Great Dane		
POWERFUL		St. Bernard Mastiff Newfoundland		

which is the tallest and one of the heaviest breeds, falls into the third category up from the bulkiest of breeds and is considered to be less stocky than the Bloodhound, Bouvier, Basset Hound and Old English Sheepdog, but stockier than the Komondor, Otterhound and Kuvasz. This is due to the fact that even though a Wolfhound is towering in height and enormous in weight, it has a different type of musculature and bone structure than Saints and Mastiffs. Its muscles and bones are long and not as bulky because the breed was designed for long-distance running.

It must be kept in mind that height, weight and bulk-ratio figures are based on the average idealized standard for specimens of a breed in good physical condition. The variation in height for any particular breed within the towering breeds can be up to 6 inches; for the large breeds it can be up to 4 inches; for the short to middle-sized breeds it can be about 2 inches; for the little it can be 1 inch and for the pockets it can be up to 4 inches. Similarly, weight may vary as much as 80 pounds for any of the enormous breeds. Thus, it is conceivably possible to get a 240-pound Mastiff or a petite one of only 150 pounds. The individual variation for the large to very large breeds can be up to 15 pounds. A 10-pound variation is typical of the medium-sized breeds, 5 to 8 pounds for the miniature to small and a few pounds for the tiny breeds. The pocket breeds can vary up to 3 pounds. Bulk rate is not as variable as height and weight unless a particular specimen is way under or, more typically, way overweight. There are only two breeds, the Otterhound and the Kuvasz, with variations large enough to stretch across categories.

Finally, I would caution you that trying to predict an adult dog's ultimate size by the size of its paws when it is a puppy is fraught with error. Aside from the fact that big dogs have big paws and vice versa, you will be more accurate in predicting adult size by breed than by paw size. Even breeders admit that they are not very accurate in judging the ultimate size of puppies, especially with puppies in the middle of the continuum. However, puppies that tower over or are dwarfed by their littermates will most probably grow up respectively larger or smaller than their siblings. Thus you can predict the potential adult size of a puppy by (a) knowledge of the typical breed size, (b) knowledge of the typical size of the breeder's line, (c) knowledge of the average size of dogs produced by a specific mated pair in the breeder's line and finally, (d) by noting extremes in any one litter.

If you go to a breeder of Mastiffs who is known to have a relatively large line and you select the largest male puppy from a litter created by a mating known to produce larger-than-average adults, you will probably end up with a dog the size of a small pony. Conversely, if you go to a breeder known to have a small line of Chihuahuas and select the smallest female puppy from the mating that usually produces the smallest dogs, you will probably end up with a "hamster"-sized dog. The moral, of course, is that reputable breeders will be able to help you select an individual puppy that is most likely to suit your needs in terms of size. You will not be able to obtain any of this information from a pet shop. There you may have only one example of a limited variety of breeds. You will have no precise way of predicting the puppy's potential size except that it may be small, medium or large.

Here is a list of questions for you to answer concerning the size of the dog you want.

	T	F
1. I want a big dog.	___	___
2. I do not care how much it will cost to feed a dog.	___	___
3. I am physically capable of walking a strong dog.	___	___
4. I live in a place with enough space for a large dog.	___	___
5. I am most interested in the "bulkier" breeds of dogs.	___	___

If you answer "false" to any of these questions, you should probably limit your selection to breeds that are average to low in height, weight and bulkiness.

Temperamental Characteristics

You now have some concept of how various breeds of dogs compare in relevant physical characteristics and you have an idea of the size, strength and coat texture of your potential pet. At this point you are ready to compare the breeds you are still considering on the sixteen temperamental characteristics previously described. These are indoor and outdoor activity levels; behavioral vigor; behavioral constancy; dominance with strange dogs and familiar people; emotional stability; sociability, including the potential reactions toward family, children and strangers; learning, including learning rate, obedience and problem-solving abilities; watchdog ability; guarddog ability.

Activity Level. Indoor and outdoor activity levels in dogs have to be considered separately, since they impact differently on an owner's life-style and type of residence. Also, indoor and outdoor activity levels are not highly correlated. A breed may be inactive indoors and potentially active outdoors or vice versa. Or a breed may be generally active or inactive both indoors and out.

INDOOR ACTIVITY. Figure 4 distributes the breeds over the five levels of indoor activity. Within each level, the breed has been ranked in terms of bulk ratio, going from the bulkiest at the beginning of the list to the least bulky at the end. Bulkiness is very relevant when indoor activity is considered because, as you can imagine, a very active but fragile Chihuahua will have

FIGURE 4.

Distribution of Purebred Dogs on Dimension of Indoor Activity with Breeds at Any One Level Rank-ordered on Bulkiness

LEVEL OF INDOOR ACTIVITY				
	VERY INACTIVE	Basset Hound Clumber Spaniel English Bulldog		
	INACTIVE	Mastiff St. Bernard (wb) Newfoundland Bullmastiff Great Dane Rottweiler Basset Hound Bloodhound Bouvier des Flandres Irish Wolfhound Great Pyrenees Otterhound Bernese Mt. Dog	Chow Chow Akita B&T Coonhound Borzoi Scottish Deerhound Chesa. Bay Retriever Rhodesian Ridgeback Curly-coated Retriever Flat-coated Retriever Skye Terrier Collie English Setter Greyhound	Saluki Vizsla Afghan Hound Poodle, Standard Sealyham Terrier Tibetan Terrier Boston Terrier Pekingese Pug Whippet English Toy Spaniel
	MODERATE	Gordon Setter		
	ACTIVE	St. Bernard (pm) Old Eng. Sheepdog (wb) Komondor German Shepherd (wb) Schnauzer, Giant Boxer Golden Retriever Labrador Retriever Belgian Malinois Belgian Sheepdog Belgian Tervuren Doberman Pinscher	Norwegian Elkhound English Springer Spaniel Irish Water Spaniel Sussex Spaniel Bull Terrier Welsh Springer Spaniel Dandie Dinmont Keeshond American Water Spaniel Kerry Blue Terrier Wheaten (soft coat) English Cocker Spaniel	Brittany Spaniel Cocker Spaniel Irish Terrier Shih Tzu Bedlington Terrier Border Terrier Shetland Sheepdog Australian Terrier Silky Terrier Papillon Japanese Spaniel Italian Greyhound

FIGURE 4 *(cont.)*

LEVEL OF INDOOR ACTIVITY	VERY ACTIVE			
		Old Eng. Sheepdog (pm)	Irish Setter	Schipperke
		Komondor	Harrier	Bichon Frise
		Kuvasz	Pointer	Welsh Terrier
		Am. Staff. Bull Terrier	Staffordshire Bull Terrier	Poodle, Miniature
		Alaskan Malamute	Airedale Terrier	Norwich Terrier
		Briard	Field Spaniel	Lakeland Terrier
		German Shepherd (pm)	French Bulldog	Fox Terrier
		Weimaraner	Samoyed	Manchester Terrier
		English Foxhound	Schnauzer, Standard	Brussels Griffon
		American Foxhound	Siberian Husky	Chihuahua
		Dalmatian	Dachshund	Yorkshire Terrier
		Samoyed	Scottish Terrier	Miniature Pinscher
		Cardigan W. Corgi	Beagle	Pomeranian
		Pembroke W. Corgi	Puli	Affenpinscher
		Doberman Pinscher	Tibetan Terrier	Manchester Toy Terrier
		WH Pointing Griffon	Lhasa Apso	Maltese
		German SH Pointer	West Highland White	Poodle, Toy (pm)
		German WH Pointer	Basenji	Poodle, Toy (wb)

less of an impact on its owner's life indoors than a very active, strong 100-pound Old English Sheepdog.

The breeds can be divided into two main categories: those which are active to very active indoors and those which are inactive. The Gordon Setter is the only breed in which a male is considered moderately active indoors; the English Bulldog, Clumber Spaniel and Basset Hound are the only ones considered very inactive indoors. Females of a breed differ from their male counterparts in the following ways. In the breeds classed as active indoors, females tend to be less active. Thus, a female of the very active breeds would be classed as active and females in the active breeds would be classed as moderate. For the breeds listed in the inactive column, females tend to be more active and should be moved one level higher in activity than their male counterparts.

There are three dimensions of human personality and lifestyle which may interact with your dog's indoor activity level. The first two relate to your own activity level. One I would describe as your need for nervous or restless activity. The second I would call your enjoyment of activity. The third dimension relates to your living accommodations.

A person who is high on the *Need for Restless Activity* dimension usually feels a need to work and move rapidly. Such people get restless whenever they have to be quiet. They can never really relax for any prolonged period of time and do things fast even when their activities do not call for speed.

The following statements will help you determine your Need for Restless Activity. Look at the next seven statements and respond to them as true or false for you.

		T	F
1.	I need to work quickly and energetically.	____	____
2.	I consider myself more restless and fidgety than most people.	____	____
3.	I speak more quickly and loudly than most people.	____	____
4.	I tend to eat rapidly even during a leisurely meal.	____	____
5.	It annoys me to drive slowly when I can go faster.	____	____
6.	I am a brisk walker and feel impatient with stragglers.	____	____
7.	I get uncomfortable with tasks that require deliberate and slow movements.	____	____

If you checked 5 or more of these statements as true of you, consider yourself high in restless activity. From 3 to 4 "true" responses is average and 2 or below indicates you are low in restless activity.

Paradoxically, a person high in Need for Restless Activity would be better off with an inactive dog. Such people should choose breeds listed in the very inactive and inactive columns of Figure 4, because such people will tend to get annoyed with an active breed that may bounce around the house and get in their way. The dog may become a nuisance because it activity may interfere with the rapid completion of its owner's tasks, a frustrating experience for restless people. In classic Gestalt psychology, this desire to complete what is started is called a need to achieve closure. People scoring low in restless activity—those who like to take a leisurely stroll, don't get impatient with stragglers, like slow, deliberate tasks, speak slowly and quietly and enjoy eating their meals at a leisurely pace—are temperamentally suited to the more active breeds. The less restless you are, the higher the canine activity level you will be able to stand. Thus very inactive people have essentially the entire list at their disposal. Their decisions would have to be based upon other criteria. People scoring in the middle range should lean toward the breeds in the inactive to active columns of Figure 4. Those people with high normal activity should choose from the inactive column; and those with low normal activity should choose from the active column.

The next human dimension may help you refine your choice. I call this dimension *Enjoyment of Activity*. People high in this dimension don't feel unhappy, anxious or restless when they are not active. They just derive a particular enjoyment from continually doing things. The next 5 statements sample your Enjoyment of Activity.

	T	F
1. I am usually full of pep and vigor.	___	___
2. I enjoy keeping busy during my leisure time.	___	___
3. I am happiest when I have a lot to do.	___	___
4. I pop out of bed in the morning ready and raring to go.	___	___
5. I enjoy working fast.	___	___

If you have checked 4 or 5 statements as true of yourself, then you rank high in Enjoyment of Activity. The higher you are, the more active the breed of dog you should contemplate. Choose from the active to very active columns of Figure 4. These breeds will suit your natural way of doing things and can join in your activities. If you have checked one or none of the statements as true of yourself, you rank low in Enjoyment of Activity. You would be better off with the inactive breeds. The more inactive you are, the more inactive the breed you should contemplate. Choose from the inactive to very inactive columns of Figure 4. Intermediately active people, those who judge 2 or 3 of the statements to be true of themselves, should choose from the inactive and active columns respectively depending upon whether you lean toward the inactive or active direction.

Obviously, when you are considering the indoor activity level of a dog, your living accommodations have to be taken into account. If your own activity scores indicate that you can tolerate or perhaps prefer the breeds rated as active or very active indoors, the next decision is based upon whether you live in a small city apartment or in a home with plenty of running room. Very active, medium to large dogs are unsuitable for small, cramped apartments. They will get restless and perhaps destructive, even if exercised a lot. Only small to tiny active breeds are suitable for apartment life. The more active the breed, the smaller it should be. Thus you should choose only the dogs rated as Fragile or Frail in stockiness or from tiny to pocket in weight if you would prefer a very active dog in an apartment. There are 11 breeds listed at the end of the very active column of Figure 4 that are suitable for apartment living. The remaining 43 breeds rated as very active indoors are suitable only for suburban or country living. The larger and stockier the breed, the more indoor space it should have.

Of the active breeds, the dogs rated up to light in stockiness or little in height or miniature in weight would be acceptable for apartment living. The remaining breeds would be more suitable for suburban or country living.

The breeds rated as inactive and very inactive can be equally at home in an apartment or suburban home regardless of their size. Interestingly, all the breeds rated as enormous in weight or powerful in stockiness are also considered inactive indoors. They could do well in an apartment, if there is enough room for them to turn around. With breeds rated inactive indoors, the consideration of whether or not they should be city dwellers depends more on their need for outdoor activity, the availability of parks and the willingness of the owners to exercise them if necessary. These factors will be discussed in the next section.

OUTDOOR ACTIVITY. Figure 5 compares the outdoor activity needs for all breeds of dogs. Since size is relevant to this dimension, the breeds in each level are listed in order of **decreasing height**.

FIGURE 5.
Distribution of Purebred Dogs on Dimension of Outdoor Activity, with Breeds at Any One Level Rank-ordered by Height

LEVEL OF OUTDOOR ACTIVITY	**INACTIVE**	Curly-coated Retriever Flat-coated Retriever English Bulldog Pug	Shih Tzu Japanese Spaniel Pekingese	
	MODERATE	Irish Wolfhound Mastiff Great Dane Great Pyrenees St. Bernard (wb) Labrador Retriever Golden Retriever Norwegian Elkhound Basenji	Tibetan Terrier Cocker Spaniel Boston Terrier Basset Hound Beagle French Bulldog Sealyham Terrier Lhasa Apso Skye Terrier	Cairn Terrier Bichon Frise English Toy Spaniel Papillon Dandie Dinmont Maltese Pomeranian
	ACTIVE	Scottish Deerhound Newfoundland St. Bernard (pm) Akita Schnauzer, Giant Bullmastiff Bloodhound B&T Coonhound Bouvier des Flandres Otterhound Rottweiler Poodle, Standard German Shepherd (wb)	German Shepherd (pm) Collie Bernese Mountain Dog Belgian Malinois Belgian Sheepdog Belgian Tervuren Boxer Vizsla WH Pointing Griffon Chow Chow Wheaten (soft coat) Kerry Blue Terrier Bull Terrier	Am. Staff. Bull Terrier Keeshond Irish Terrier Clumber Spaniel English Cocker Spaniel Bedlington Terrier Sussex Spaniel Staff. Bull Terrier Cardigan W. Corgi Border Terrier Pembroke W. Corgi Australian Terrier Silky Terrier
	VERY ACTIVE	Borzoi Afghan Hound Greyhound Irish Setter Whippet Saluki Pointer Gordon Setter Weimaraner Rhodesian Ridgeback German WH Pointer Komondor Kuvasz English Setter Doberman Pinscher Briard Alaskan Malamute English Foxhound Chesapeake Bay Ret. German SH Pointer	Irish Water Spaniel American Foxhound Airedale Terrier Samoyed Siberian Husky Old Eng. Sheepdog (wb) Old Eng. Sheepdog (pm) Dalmatian Harrier English Springer Spaniel Schnauzer, Standard Puli Field Spaniel Welsh Springer Spaniel Manchester Terrier American Water Spaniel Fox Terrier Welsh Terrier Shetland Sheepdog Lakeland Terrier	Italian Greyhound Brittany Spaniel Schnauzer, Mini. (pm) Schnauzer, Mini. (wb) Poodle, Miniature Schipperke Manchester Toy Terrier Miniature Pinscher West Highland White Scottish Terrier Poodle, Toy (pm) Poodle, Toy (wb) Norwich Affenpinscher Dachshund Brussels Griffon Yorkshire Terrier Chihuahua

As you can see, the breeds are distributed differently on the dimension of Outdoor Activity than they are on Indoor Activity, with the majority of the dogs being very active outdoors. On the dimension of outdoor activity, females of the breeds listed in the very active group should be classed as only active. Those in the active and inactive group should be classed as moderate. Females of the larger breeds in the moderate group tend to be active and females of the smaller breeds tend to be inactive.

There are a number of human personality dimensions that relate to the outdoor activity level of a breed of dog. One is the previously described dimension "enjoyment of activity." People scoring high on this scale would be better off with the breeds listed as active or very active outdoors. People scoring low on this scale would be better off with the breeds that are inactive outdoors. People scoring average would be better off with the breeds listed as needing a moderate amount of outdoor exercise.

The choice of a breed with respect to outdoor activity level may also be influenced by the availability of younger, physically active people in the family. Very active and active dogs should be owned by youthful people who participate in vigorous activities like jogging, hunting, camping, etc., and would like to take their dogs along with them. The older you feel or the more physically inactive you want to be, the less active the breed you should choose.

Active and very active dogs want, and need, and should get a lot of exercise. You should not get one of these breeds if the availability of exercise space is limited or if your working conditions would preclude you from sufficiently exercising the larger, active or very active breeds. If you live in the suburbs or country and have a large backyard, this is not as much of a concern, since the active to very active breeds can exercise themselves. The larger the active breed, the more space it needs to run.

Behavioral Vigor. This dimension relates to the force of behaviors regardless of how often they are produced; very vigorous breeds tend to do most things with excessive force, while very gentle breeds tend to perform their behaviors gently. Figure 6 compares all the breeds on this dimension.

FIGURE 6.

Distribution of Purebred Dogs on Dimension of Vigor, with Breeds at Any One Level Rank-ordered by Bulkiness

LEVEL OF BEHAVIORAL VIGOR				
VERY GENTLE	Newfoundland Papillon Japanese Spaniel Maltese Italian Greyhound			
GENTLE	Mastiff St. Bernard (wb) Great Dane Old Eng. Sheepdog (wb) Bouvier des Flandres Irish Wolfhound Otterhound Bernese Mountain Dog Am. Staff. Bull Terrier Clumber Spaniel English Bulldog Borzoi Scottish Deerhound	Golden Retriever Chesapeake Bay Ret. Belgian Malinois Belgian Sheepdog Belgian Tervuren Collie Greyhound Staff. Bull Terrier Saluki Afghan Hound American Water Spaniel Keeshond Beagle	Cocker Spaniel Boston Terrier Basenji Pub Bichon Frise Border Terrier Shetland Sheepdog Whippet Chihuahua English Toy Spaniel Affenpinscher Poodle, Toy (wb)	
MODERATE	Basset Hound Labrador Retriever Samoyed Cardigan W. Corgi Curly-coated Retriever Flat-coated Retriever Skye Terrier Doberman Pinscher Pembroke W. Corgi English Setter English Springer Spaniel French Bulldog	Siberian Husky Welsh Springer Spaniel Dandie Dinmont Scottish Terrier English Cocker Spaniel Pekingese West Highland White Cairn Terrier Shih Tzu Welsh Terrier Bedlington Terrier Lakeland Terrier	Norwich Terrier Poodle, Miniature Schnauzer, Mini. (pm) Schnauzer, Mini. (wb) Australian Terrier Manchester Terrier Silky Terrier Brussels Griffon Yorkshire Terrier Miniature Pinscher Pomeranian Manchester Toy Terrier	
VIGOROUS	St. Bernard (pm) Old Eng. Sheepdog (pm) Great Pyrenees Irish Water Spaniel Akita Briard B&T Coonhound German Shepherd (pm) German Shepherd (wb) Boxer English Foxhound American Foxhound	Chesapeake Bay Ret. Gordon Setter WH Pointer Griffon English Springer Spaniel Sussex Spaniel Harrier Pointer Airedale Terrier Field Spaniel Vizsla Poodle, Standard Sealyham Terrier	Dachshund Kerry Blue Terrier Wheaten (soft coat) Brittany Spaniel Puli Tibetan Terrier Irish Terrier Lhasa Apso Schipperke Fox Terrier (SH) Fox Terrier (WH) Poodle, Toy (pm)	

FIGURE 6 *(cont.)*

VERY VIGOROUS	Bullmastiff	Am. Staff. Bull Terrier	German SH Pointer
	Rottweiler	Schnauzer, Giant	German WH Pointer
	Bloodhound	Weimaraner	Irish Setter
	Komondor	Dalmatian	Staff. Bull Terrier
	Chow Chow	Rhodesian Ridgeback	Bull Terrier
	Alaskan Malamute	Norwegian Elkhound	Schnauzer, Standard

If you go back to Figures 1, 2 and 3 and compare them with Figure 6, you will notice that the dimensions of stockiness, strength and size of a breed are not well correlated with the level of vigor into which the breeds are categorized. Some enormous breeds, like the Mastiff and the well-bred St. Bernard, are classified as gentle, and the very gentle category includes Newfoundlands as well as some of the more fragile breeds. However, within any level, vigor is related to strength, so within each group, breeds are organized by bulk ratios with the bulkiest breeds at the beginning of the list. Thus the Bullmastiff is classified as the most vigorous of all the breeds and the Italian Greyhound as the least vigorous.

Females will tend to be less vigorous than their male counterparts. Thus, females of any breed should be shifted one level to the left of their male counterparts. Females of the very vigorous breeds would be classed as vigorous and so on.

Obviously, a consideration of this dimension is related to the physical strength of the owner. The stronger you are, the more likely you are to be able to cope with the more vigorous of the bulky breeds. This doesn't mean that stronger people necessarily would want to have a more vigorous breed, just that they could handle an emergency in which they would have to exert force to keep their dog under control. As a general guideline, you should be able to press 125 or more pounds over your head if you are considering the top five of the very vigorous breeds, and at least 100 pounds for the rest of the very vigorous breeds.

As you look down the list in Figure 6, you can locate the level of vigor for a particular breed. Within a particular level you can tell a breed's vigor relative to other breeds in that category because dogs at any one level are ranked according to bulk, with the bulkiest breeds at the beginning of the list. The Newfoundland is at the top of the very gentle dimension, and the Mastiff and St. Bernard are at the top of the gentle dimension. This means that these breeds are unlikely to exert the strength potential in their enormous bulk, but keep in mind that on rare occasions they will be forceful. At those rare times you'd better be prepared to contain them.

Now that you have determined whether you can physically handle a specimen of a particular breed, you are ready to consider what you would want to handle. Check the following six statements as true or false for you.

	T	F
1. I have enjoyed participating in wrestling, boxing, football, hockey, baseball, soccer, weight lifting, basketball, mountain climbing. (Note: Give yourself 1 point for each sport in which you have participated regularly.)	___	___
2. I have enjoyed hiking, skiing (water or snow), running, tennis, surfing, backpacking, hunting, horseback riding. (Note: Give yourself 1 point for each sport in which you have participated regularly.)	___	___
3. I am a regular and consistent jogger.	___	___
4. I enjoy work that requires physical exertion.	___	___
5. I like a race or game better when I have a bet on it.	___	___
6. I am resourceful in fixing mechanical things about the house.	___	___

If you have accumulated 7 to 10 or more points in the "true" column, you would probably be more suited to the breeds rated as very vigorous. If you have more than 10 points, you would be both suited to and probably able to handle the bulkier of the vigorous and very vigorous breeds. If you have checked one or none of the statements as true, then stick with the fragile of the very gentle breeds. Scoring from 2 to 4 makes you most suitable for the gentle breeds. The moderately vigorous breeds would be most suitable for the people who checked 5 or 6 statements as true for them.

Behavioral Constancy. Behavioral constancy relates to the "stick-to-it-iveness" of a breed. A constant breed stays with one behavior despite distraction, while variable breeds are distractable, changing one behavior for another relatively frequently. It can be an advantage or a pain in the neck to have a dog with high behavioral constancy, depending upon what behavior the animal is engaging in.

Figure 7 compares all the breeds on the dimension of behavioral constancy. In this figure, the breeds are listed in alphabetical order.

FIGURE 7.

Distribution of Purebred Dogs on Dimension of Behavioral Constancy, with Breeds at Any One Level Alphabetized

VERY VARIABLE	Dachshund	
	Doberman Pinscher	
	Golden Retriever	
	Irish Setter	
	Poodle, Toy (pm)	
	Scottish Terrier	
VARIABLE	Affenpinscher	English Foxhound	Papillon
	Alaskan Malamute	English Springer Spaniel	Pomeranian
	American Foxhound	Fox Terrier (SH)	Poodle, Miniature
	Australian Terrier	Fox Terrier (WH)	Poodle, Toy (wb)
	Basenji	German Shepherd (pm)	Puli
	Belgian Malinois	Gordon Setter	St. Bernard (pm)
	Belgian Sheepdog	Greyhound	Saluki
	Belgian Tervuren	Harrier	Samoyed
	Boxer	Keeshond	Schnauzer, Min. (pm)
	Brittany Spaniel	Komondor	Shetland Sheepdog
	Brussels Griffon	Kuvasz	Schipperke
	Chihuahua	Lhasa Apso	Tibetan Terrier
	Cocker Spaniel (pm)	Maltese	Whippet
	Cocker Spaniel (wb)	Manchester Terrier	WH Pointer Griffon
	Curly-coated Retriever	Manchester Toy Terrier	Yorkshire Terrier
	Dalmatian	Miniature Pinscher	
	English Cocker Spaniel	Old Eng. Sheepdog (pm)	

(LEVEL OF BEHAVIORAL CONSTANCY)

FIGURE 7 *(cont.)*

LEVEL OF BEHAVIORAL CONSTANCY				
MODERATE	Basset Hound Beagle Bichon Frise Boston Terrier Cairn Terrier Collie Chesapeake Bay Ret.	Dandie Dinmont Doberman Pinscher English Cocker Spaniel English Setter Flat-coated Retriever Giant Schnauzer Italian Greyhound	Japanese Spaniel Old Eng. Sheepdog (wb) Otterhound Poodle, Standard Skye Terrier	
CONSTANT	Afghan Hound Airedale Terrier Akita American Water Spaniel Bedlington Terrier Bernese Mountain Dog B&T Coonhound Border Terrier Borzoi Briard Bullmastiff Bull Terrier Cardigan W. Corgi English Toy Spaniel Field Spaniel French Bulldog	German Shepherd (wb) German SH Pointer German WH Pointer Great Pyrenees Irish Terrier Irish Water Spaniel Irish Wolfhound Kerry Blue Terrier Labrador Retriever Lakeland Terrier Norwegian Elkhound Norwich Terrier Pekingese Pembroke W. Corgi Pointer Pug	Rhodesian Ridgeback Rottweiler Schnauzer, Min. (wb) Sealyham Terrier Shih Tzu Siberian Husky Silky Terrier Scottish Deerhound Tibetan Terrier Vizsla Welsh Springer Spaniel Welsh Terrier West Highland Terrier Weimaraner Yorkshire Terrier	
VERY CONSTANT	Am. Staff. Bull Terrier Bloodhound Bouvier des Flandres Chow Chow Clumber Spaniel	English Bulldog Great Dane Mastiff Newfoundland St. Bernard (wb)	Staff. Bull Terrier Standard Schnauzer Sussex Spaniel	

212 / THE RIGHT DOG FOR YOU

Most breeds, as you can see, fall into two main groups, those which are more or less variable and those which are more or less constant.

Females of the variable breeds tend toward the constant end of the dimension, being categorized one level more constant than their male counterparts. Females in the constant breeds tend toward the variable end of the dimension, being one level more variable than the males of the same breed. The females of the breeds classed as moderate tend to be moderate. Thus the distribution for female specimens would fall into three groups—constant, moderate and variable—as compared with the two main groups for males.

The human personality dimensions of impulsiveness and responsibility can be expected to interact with the dimension of behavioral constancy in dogs. The following statements sample your impulsiveness. Check each statement as generally true or false about yourself.

	T	F
1. I usually make snap decisions.	___	___
2. I like to take a chance just for excitement.	___	___
3. I usually have a ready answer for most questions.	___	___
4. My friends consider me happy-go-lucky.	___	___
5. I like to make people laugh.	___	___
6. I prefer being at places where something is happening most of the time.	___	___
7. I usually let myself go and have a fun time at parties.	___	___
8. I like work that has a lot of excitement.	___	___
9. I enjoy competitive games more than noncompetitive ones.	___	___
10. I love to yell along with the crowd at a sports event.	___	___

If you have checked 7 or more of these statements as true, you tend to be impulsive and you would probably get more enjoyment from the variable to very variable breeds. The closer you score to 10 the more variable the breed you might like. If you have checked 3 or fewer statements as true, you would probably be happier with one of the constant or very constant breeds. The moderately constant breeds would make the people checking from 4 to 6 statements happiest.

The next set of statements relate to your responsibility. These will tell you which breeds you are more suited to, whether or not you would be happy with them. Check each statement as true or false of yourself.

	T	F
1. When I have something to do, I usually get going on it right away.	⎯⎯	⎯⎯
2. When work piles up, I get uncomfortable.	⎯⎯	⎯⎯
3. I like my surroundings to be clean and neat.	⎯⎯	⎯⎯
4. My friends can rely upon me fully.	⎯⎯	⎯⎯
5. I always try to use my time to the best advantage.	⎯⎯	⎯⎯
6. I enjoy working instead of daydreaming.	⎯⎯	⎯⎯
7. I consider myself organized.	⎯⎯	⎯⎯
8. I am usually not forgetful about important events.	⎯⎯	⎯⎯
9. I prefer to make a step-by-step contingency plan rather than deal with things as they occur.	⎯⎯	⎯⎯
10. I rarely leave things to the last moment.	⎯⎯	⎯⎯

If you have checked 7 or more of the previous statements as true, consider yourself rather responsible. You would be suited to any breed, and the more responsible you are, the more likely it is that you could handle one of the very variable breeds. However, you may get frustrated by what you feel is the irresponsibility of the variable breeds.

The fewer the statements you have checked as true of yourself, the more constant the breed you should choose. People checking from 6 to 4 statements should consider only the breeds classified as moderately or more constant. People checking 3 or fewer statements should consider only the constant breeds. The very constant breeds may be too headstrong for casual people. They would tend to let their dog have its own way and might lose control of it.

Dominance. Dominance is probably the most salient dimension with regard to how well a dog will get along with other dogs and, more importantly, in predicting a pet dog's potential position in the family social order.

DOMINANCE AND CANINE BEHAVIOR. *Canis familiaris* will signal its dominant or subordinate position in relation to another significant organism (dog or person) by both postures and facial expressions. When approached by a strange dog, a dominant canine will stand as erect and tall as possible, keeping its head high, tail up, mouth puckered; the hair on its back may be erect. Further signals in increasing order of dominance involve direct eye contact; a frontal approach; the T-position, in which a dominant animal places its head over a submissive animal; sniffing hindquarters; standing over, in which a dominant animal places its forepaws on the back of a submissive animal; standing astraddle, in which a dominant animal will stand with one leg on either side of a submissive one that is lying on its back; growling with direct eye contact and an aggressive pucker; raising the top lip, exposing the canines; placing the jaw around the submissive animal's neck; and, finally, a violent attack stimulated by behaviors interpreted as signaling dominance.

Submissive animals will produce behaviors that appear to be opposite to dominant signals. In response to an intruding dominant organism (dog or person) they may lower the body, head and tail; pull the lips back into a submissive grin; avert their eyes; approach from the side and under the dominant animal's head; lick the face and chin of the dominant animal; stand still when being sniffed or touched; roll over on their backs, exposing their necks; urinate submissively and remain on their backs as long as the dominant animal maintains its standing-over or astraddle position. If hurt, the submissive dog may snap and run away, tail tucked between its legs.

Very dominant animals may attempt to dominate familiar and unfamiliar people alike. If a very dominant dog perceives submissive behaviors in these people, it may escalate its dominance displays. It may aggressively challenge the position of those family members, including its master, whom it perceives as submissive to it. Depending upon the social position or

FIGURE 8.

Distribution of Purebred Dogs on Dimension of Dominance with Familiar People, with Breeds Within Any One Level Rank-ordered on Bulkiness

LEVEL OF DOMINANCE

VERY SUBMISSIVE

- Old Eng. Sheepdog (pm)
- Doberman Pinscher
- Maltese

SUBMISSIVE

Mastiff	Belgian Sheepdog	Keeshond
St. Bernard (wb)	Belgian Tervuren	Dachshund
Newfoundland	Cardigan W. Corgi	English Cocker Spaniel
Great Dane	Curly-coated Retriever	Beagle
Old Eng. Sheepdog (wb)	Flat-coated Retriever	Cocker Spaniel (wb)
Basset Hound	Collie	Boston Terrier
Bloodhound	Pembroke W. Corgi	Pug
Bouvier des Flandres	WH Pointing Griffon	Bichon Frise
Otterhound	English Setter	Border Terrier
Bernese Mountain Dog	English Springer Spaniel	Poodle, Miniature
B&T Coonhound	German SH Pointer	Shetland Sheepdog
Welsh Springer Spaniel	Irish Setter	Whippet
Borzoi	Greyhound	Australian Terrier
Scottish Deerhound	Harrier	Silky Terrier
Boxer	French Bulldog	Chihuahua
English Foxhound	Saluki	English Toy Spaniel
Golden Retriever	Siberian Husky	Papillon
American Foxhound	Vizsla	Japanese Spaniel
Samoyed	Afghan Hound	Poodle, Toy (wb)
Belgian Malinois	Field Spaniel	Italian Greyhound

INTERMEDIATE

Mastiff	Skye Terrier	Pekingese
St. Bernard (wb)	Gordon Setter	Tibetan Terrier
Newfoundland	German SH Pointer	West Highland White
Bull Mastiff	German WH Pointer	Basenji
Great Pyrenees	Irish Water Spaniel	Cairn Terrier
Irish Wolfhound	Pointer	Schipperke
Akita	Staff. Bull Terrier	Welsh Terrier
Alaskan Malamute	Airedale Terrier	Bedlington Terrier
Am. Staff. Bull Terrier	Bull Terrier	Lakeland Terrier
Briard	Dandie Dinmont	Norwich
Clumber Spaniel	Poodle, Standard	Schnauzer, Mini. (wb)
German Shepherd (wb)	Sealyham Terrier	Manchester Terrier
English Bulldog	American Water Spaniel	Yorkshire Terrier
Chesapeake Bay Ret.	Scottish Terrier	Pomeranian
Dalmatian	Wheaten (soft coat)	Affenpinscher
Labrador Retriever	Brittany Spaniel	Manchester Toy Terrier
Samoyed	Lhasa Apso	

FIGURE 8 *(cont.)*

DOMINANT	St. Bernard (pm) Rottweiler Chow Chow German Shepherd (pm) Kuvasz Schnauzer, Giant Weimaraner Rhodesian Ridgeback	Norwegian Elkhound Sussex Spaniel Schnauzer, Standard Kerry Blue Terrier Cocker Spaniel (pm) Puli Irish Terrier Shih Tzu	SH Fox Terrier WH Fox Terrier Schnauzer, Mini. (wb) Schnauzer, Mini. (pm) Brussels Griffon Miniature Pinscher Poodle, Toy (pm)
VERY DOMINANT	Old Eng. Sheepdog (pm) Am. Staff. Bull Terrier Doberman Pinscher Staff. Bull Terrier		

dominance of the family members, such animals may dominate one, several or the entire family. They may attack a person who inadvertently or consciously signals dominance, especially if the person's position is uncertain.

Dominant breeds attempt to dominate many intruding dogs, and some familiar and most unfamiliar people. Breeds characterized as intermediate modulate their behavior according to their perception of the dominance or submissiveness of the organisms they encounter. They will dominate submissive ones and be submissive to dominant ones.

FIGURE 9.

Distribution of Purebred Dogs on Dimension of Dominance with Strange Dogs, with Breeds Within Any One Level Rank-ordered on Bulkiness

LEVEL OF DOMINANCE	**VERY SUB-MISSIVE**	Old Eng. Sheepdog (pm) German Shepherd (pm) Irish Water Spaniel		
	SUBMISSIVE	Golden Retriever English Foxhound American Foxhound Flat-coated Retriever Collie English Springer Spaniel Irish Setter Greyhound	Harrier Afghan Hound Keeshond Beagle Brittany Spaniel Cocker Spaniel (wb) English Cocker Spaniel Bichon Frise	Shetland Sheepdog Whippet Silky Terrier English Toy Spaniel Papillon Japanese Spaniel Poodle, Toy (wb) Italian Greyhound

FIGURE 9 *(cont.)*

LEVEL OF DOMINANCE	**INTERMEDIATE**	St. Bernard (wb) Newfoundland Great Dane Basset Hound Old Eng. Sheepdog (wb) Bouvier des Flandres Great Pyrenees Irish Wolfhound Otterhound Bernese Mountain Dog Clumber Spaniel Scottish Deerhound Borzoi Chesa. Bay Retriever Dalmatian Labrador Retriever Samoyed Curly-coated Retriever Skye Terrier	Cardigan W. Corgi Pembroke W. Corgi WH Pointer Griffon English Setter German SH Pointer Pointer Field Spaniel French Bulldog Saluki Siberian Husky Vizsla Welsh Springer Spaniel Manchester Terrier Poodle, Standard Skye Terrier Dachshund Wheaten (soft coat) Boston Terrier Lhasa Apso	Pekingese Tibetan Terrier West Highland White Cairn Terrier Pug Schipperke Border Terrier Norwich Terrier Poodle, Miniature Schnauzer, Mini. (pm) Schnauzer, Mini. (wb) Australian Terrier Manchester Terrier Brussels Griffon Chihuahua Affenpinscher Maltese
	DOMINANT	Mastiff Bullmastiff Rottweiler Bloodhound Irish Wolfhound Komondor Chow Chow Akita Alaskan Malamute Briard B&T Coonhound German Shepherd (wb) Kuvasz English Bulldog Boxer Weimaraner	Belgian Malinois Belgian Sheepdog Belgian Tervuren Doberman Pinscher Gordon Setter Norwegian Elkhound German WH Pointer Sussex Spaniel Pointer Airedale Terrier Bull Terrier Afghan Hound American Water Spaniel Kerry Blue Terrier Scottish Terrier Cocker Spaniel (pm)	Puli Irish Terrier Basenji Shih Tzu Bedlington Terrier Fox Terrier (SH) Fox Terrier (WH) Lakeland Terrier Yorkshire Terrier Pomeranian Poodle, Toy (wb) Manchester Toy Terrier Poodle, Toy (pm) Poodle, Toy (wb)
	VERY DOMINANT	St. Bernard (pm) Old Eng. Sheepdog (pm) Am. Staff. Bull Terrier	German Shepherd (pm) Schnauzer, Giant Rhodesian Ridgeback	Staff. Bull Terrier Schnauzer, Standard Basenji

Submissive breeds approach most familiar and unfamiliar people and dogs with submissive displays. Very submissive dogs approach all organisms submissively.

Figures 8 and 9 distribute the purebred dogs on the dimensions of potential for dominance toward (1) familiar people and (2) strange dogs, respectively. The size and strength of a breed are not highly correlated with its potential for dominance across levels, but strength or stockiness may be related to dominance potential within a level. Thus within a level, the breeds are organized in terms of decreasing bulk ratio, with the breed having the highest ratio at the top of each column. Females are generally more submissive than males in all levels of dominance toward familiar and strange dogs and people. They are more likely to be submissive to males than to females.

The following statements will sample your tendency for dominance, a human personality dimension that is clearly relevant to dominance in canines. Respond to the following 12 statements to estimate your own level of dominance.

	T	F
1. I am ready to argue a point when I think I'm right.	___	___
2. In a pinch I can bluff my way through.	___	___
3. I enjoy being the boss and supervising the work of others.	___	___
4. I do or would get a kick out of public speaking.	___	___
5. I can and usually do take the lead in group projects and decision making.	___	___
6. I usually stand erect and look the person I am talking to right in the eye.	___	___
7. I would prefer to lead rather than to follow.	___	___
8. I usually feel comfortable talking to "superiors" or "important people."	___	___
9. I don't mind asking an obviously innocuous stranger questions concerning directions or the time of day or for a match.	___	___

10. I prefer a job that involves initiative, one
    where I make the decisions.   ____ ____
11. I don't mind being conspicuous, and it
    doesn't bother me to attract attention.   ____ ____
12. I would prefer to take the initiative rather
    than wait and let others take it.   ____ ____

If you have checked 8 or more of the previous statements as true, you should consider yourself dominant and assertive. You would probably be successful in controlling the breeds classified up to the level of intermediately dominant toward familiar people regardless of the breed's size and strength. Those of you who take pride in your own dominance may be embarrassed with dogs that are submissive or even intermediately dominant toward strange dogs. Feeling the dog is an extension of your own ego, a frequent outgrowth of owning a dog, you will probably want one that is assertive over strange dogs. If you are like this, be prepared for dogfights. If you have checked 10 or more statements as true, you would probably be able to dominate the dominant and very dominant breeds if you know what you are doing and are very familiar with the dog. People scoring 10 to 12 are also more likely to be attacked by the larger of the dominant and very dominant dogs, especially when they first meet them, since these people will be signaling dominance with their body cues.

If you checked 4 or fewer statements as true, you would be better off with the breeds classed as submissive toward familiar people. You are likely to be dominated by dogs rated intermediate to very dominant; the higher the rating of the dog, the higher the likelihood that you will be dominated. The more submissive you are, the smaller the submissive breed you should get. Choose breeds from the end of the submissive group on Figure 8. It would also not be advisable for you to have dogs that are dominant to very dominant over strange dogs. These dogs may be more likely to get into dogfights, and since you are submissive, you wouldn't be able to control your dog or break up the fight in these situations.

You would also have to deal, perhaps, with the angry owner of the dog yours attacked. Some timid, submissive people, knowing their own fears or fearing harm from other people, obtain a dominant breed for "protection." Some of these people get what they are looking for, but they may not be able to control their dog's protectiveness. Others may wind up needing protection from their canine protectors.

If you checked 5 to 7 statements as true, you are average in dominance. You should choose breeds that are rated as intermeditate or submissive to familiar people. You would also be better off with dogs that are submissive to intermediate toward strange dogs, since you may not be able to handle the dogfight potential in the dominant and very dominant breeds. People average in dominance may want a dominant to very dominant breed for protection, but they may wind up in the same submissive position as submissive people, being unable to control their dog and sometimes dominated by it. The difference is that people of average dominance may perceive their lack of control as a failure and feel frustrated. They may confront their dog's dominance. If the animal is large and dominant enough, they may loose the struggle, thereby suffering injury and a further reduction in dominance, whereas very submissive people would tend to accept their position in relation to a dominant dog and not challenge it, thereby avoiding an aggressive attack.

Territoriality. A dimension that relates to a breed's ability to function as a watchdog or guard dog is territoriality. This dimension relates to the likelihood that a dog will stake out a territory and to the size of the territory once established. A dog high in territoriality will rapidly stake out a territory by marking bushes, trees, buildings and posts in the outdoor area with urine. Its territory may extend far beyond the boundaries of its own home. A dog very high in territoriality acts as if it owned the world. Its territory is wherever it is at any particular time. Dogs moderate in territoriality usually stake out an area in and around their owner's home, whereas dogs low in this dimension may consider only the inside of their owner's house or apartment as their own. Dogs very low in territoriality may have only a small space around their bodies that they will guard.

Figure 10 compares all breeds on the dimension of their potential level of territoriality. Within each level the breeds are arranged in decreasing bulk ratio. The assumption is that within any one level, the more powerful the dog, the more able it will be to defend its territory. The Chow Chow is the most powerful of the very territorial breeds. Essentially, this means that if a male Chow Chow wanders into your backyard and starts urinating on your azalea bushes, you'd think twice before shooing it away. It will treat your yard as its own and you as an intruder.

FIGURE 10.
Distribution of Purebred Dogs on Dimension of Territoriality, with Breeds at Any One Level Rank-ordered on Bulkiness

LEVEL OF TERRITORIALITY				
VERY LOW	Old Eng. Sheepdog (wb)	Golden Retriever	Harrier	
	English Foxhound	American Foxhound	Beagle	
LOW	St. Bernard (wb)	Irish Setter	West Highland White	
	Newfoundland	Greyhound	Shih Tzu	
	Basset Hound	Pointer	Bichon Frise	
	Otterhound	Field Spaniel	Border Terrier	
	Clumber Spaniel	Siberian Husky	Shetland Sheepdog	
	Borzoi	Vizsla	Whippet	
	Scottish Deerhound	Saluki	English Toy Spaniel	
	Flat-coated Retriever	Keeshond	Silky Terrier	
	Collie	Wheaten (soft coat)	Papillon	
	English Setter	English Cocker Spaniel	Japanese Spaniel	
	English Springer Spaniel	Cocker Spaniel (wb)	Poodle, Toy (wb)	
	German SH Pointer	Boston Terrier	Italian Greyhound	
MODERATE	Mastiff	Curly-coated Retriever	Brittany Spaniel	
	St. Bernard (pm)	Skye Terrier	Lhasa Apso	
	Great Dane	Gordon Setter	Pekingese	
	Bloodhound	Pembroke W. Corgi	Tibetan Terrier	
	Bouvier des Flandres	WH Pointing Griffon	Cairn Terrier	
	Great Pyrenees	German WH Pointer	Pug	
	Irish Wolfhound	Irish Water Spaniel	Welsh Terrier	
	Bernese Mountain Dog	Airedale Terrier	Bedlington Terrier	
	B&T Coonhound	French Bulldog	Norwich Terrier	
	Samoyed	Afghan Hound	Poodle, Miniature	
	Boxer	Welsh Springer Spaniel	Schnauzer, Miniature	
	Dalmatian	American Water Spaniel	Australian Terrier	
	Labrador Retriever	Dandie Dinmont	Manchester Terrier	
	Belgian Malinois	Poodle, Standard	Brussels Griffon	
	Belgian Sheepdog	Sealyham Terrier	Affenpinscher	
	Belgian Tervuren	Dachshund	Maltese	

FIGURE 10 *(cont.)*

HIGH	Bullmastiff	Rhodesian Ridgeback	Tibetan Terrier
	Rottweiler	Cardigan W. Corgi	Basenji
	Old Eng. Sheepdog (pm)	Doberman Pinscher	Schipperke
	Komondor	Norwegian Elkhound	SH Fox Terrier
	Akita	German WH Pointer	WH Fox Terrier
	Alaskan Malamute	Sussex Spaniel	Lakeland Terrier
	Briard	Bull Terrier	Chihuahua
	German Shepherd (pm)	Scottish Terrier	Yorkshire Terrier
	German Shepherd (wb)	Kerry Blue Terrier	Pomeranian
	English Bulldog	Cocker Spaniel (pm)	Miniature Pinscher
	Weimaraner	Puli	Manchester Toy Terrier
	Chesapeake Bay Ret.	Irish Terrier	Poodle, Toy (pm)
VERY HIGH	Chow Chow	Kuvasz	Staff. Bull Terrier
	Am. Staff. Bull Terrier	Schnauzer, Giant	Schnauzer, Standard

Keep in mind that the territory of a dog is also a function of the territory within which it lives. A dog will have a different territorial configuration depending upon whether it lives in a high-rise apartment or a suburban home. City dogs will have their territories compressed by virtue of living in that type of environment. The rule of thumb is that the more you compress a dog's territory, the more alert and aggressive it will be. Very territorial dogs living in the city may become savage when they sense an intrusion. Dogs of low territoriality that would ignore intruders in the country may threaten them in the city. Thus, compression of space where territoriality occurs magnifies that territoriality.

Emotional Stability. Emotional stability is defined by how frequently an animal changes from one emotional state to another. A breed classed as greatly vacillating will tend to be high-strung and nervous; some of the bolder ones would be called "shy-sharp." They may be subject to extreme timidity, irritable snapping, fear biting and other manifestations of nervousness. Emotionally vacillating breeds are typically described as high-spirited. Very stable animals react calmly to most potentially exciting situations. Emotionally stable ani-

FIGURE 11.

Distribution of Purebred Dogs on Dimension of Emotional Stability with Breeds at Any One Level Arranged Alphabetically

LEVEL OF EMOTIONAL STABILITY			
GREATLY VACILLATING	Cocker Spaniel (pm) Doberman Pinscher	Italian Greyhound Old Eng. Sheepdog (pm)	Poodle, Toy (pm) St. Bernard (pm)
VACILLATING	Affenpinscher Afghan Hound Bedlington Terrier Belgian Malinois Belgian Sheepdog Belgian Tervuren Borzoi Boston Terrier Brittany Spaniel Brussels Griffon Chihuahua Collie Dachshund	Dalmatian German Shepherd (pm) Greyhound Irish Terrier Irish Setter Irish Water Spaniel Lhasa Apso Manchester Terrier Manchester Toy Terrier Miniature Pinscher Mini. Schnauzer (pm) Papillon Poodle, Miniature	Poodle, Toy (wb) Puli Saluki Shetland Sheepdog Schipperke Skye Terrier Sussex Spaniel Tibetan Terrier Vizsla West Highland White Whippet WH Pointing Griffon Yorkshire Terrier
NORMAL	Briard Cocker Spaniel (wb) Doberman Pinscher English Toy Spaniel	German Shepherd (wb) Gordon Setter Kerry Blue Terrier Maltese	Old Eng. Sheepdog (wb) Pekingese Samoyed Welsh Springer Spaniel
STABLE	Afghan Hound Airedale Terrier Akita Alaskan Malamute American Foxhound Am. Staff. Bull Terrier American Water Spaniel Australian Terrier Basenji Beagle Bernese Mountain Dog Bichon Frise B&T Coonhound Bouvier des Flandres Boxer Bullmastiff Bull Terrier Cairn Terrier Cardigan W. Corgi Chesapeake Bay Ret. Chow Chow Collie	Curly-coated Retriever Dandie Dinmont English Cocker Spaniel English Foxhound English Springer Spaniel Field Spaniel Fox Terrier French Bulldog German Shepherd (wb) German SH Pointer German WH Pointer Golden Retriever Harrier Irish Wolfhound Japanese Spaniel Keeshond Komondor Kuvasz Labrador Retriever Lakeland Terrier Norwegian Elkhound Norwich Terrier	Otterhound Pembroke W. Corgi Pointer Pomeranian Poodle, Standard Pug Rhodesian Ridgeback Rottweiler Schnauzer, Giant Schnauzer, Mini. (wb) Schnauzer, Standard Scottish Terrier Shih Tzu Siberian Husky Silky Terrier Staff. Bull Terrier Tibetan Terrier Weimaraner Welsh Terrier Wheaten (soft coat)

FIGURE 11 *(cont.)*

	Basset Hound	English Setter	Newfoundland
VERY STABLE	Bloodhound	Flat-coated Retriever	St. Bernard (wb)
	Border Terrier	Great Dane	Scottish Deerhound
	Clumber Spaniel	Great Pyrenees	Sealyham Terrier
	English Bulldog	Mastiff	

mals will stay calm in at least 75% of the potentially exciting situations they encounter.

Figure 11 compares all breeds on the dimension of emotional stability. You can see that most breeds fall into two groups: those which are classed as normal to very stable, with the highest preponderance of breeds in the group being listed as stable; and those which are ranked as vacillating or very vacillating. Within each level, the breeds are listed alphabetically. Females of the vacillating to normal breeds are generally more vacillating than the males. Females of the stable breeds are generally more stable than the males.

In my opinion, most people would be better off with the stable to very stable breeds. Irritable or emotional people would do best with only the very stable breeds. Some very placid, unemotional people could handle the vacillating breeds, but they still would be better off with the normal to stable animals.

If you don't already know, the following statements will help you decide whether you are more or less placid.

	T	F
1. I am not bothered easily and generally don't get ruffled.	___	___
2. I consider myself an easygoing, even-tempered person.	___	___
3. I try to avoid arguments and rarely get into a dispute.	___	___
4. I seldom hold a grudge.	___	___
5. I don't mind having noisy children or active dogs around me.	___	___
6. I stay calm when things go wrong.	___	___

7. I'm not bothered when I am in a hurry and
   I just miss the bus.   ____ ____
8. I don't mind waiting in a line or being
   stuck in traffic.   ____ ____
9. When someone does something stupid, I
   refrain from "chewing him out."   ____ ____
10. I find it easy to forget a slight.   ____ ____
11. I find there is hardly anyone I just can't
    stand.   ____ ____
12. It is easy for me to control my temper.   ____ ____

If you checked 4 or fewer of the previous statements as true, consider yourself an irritable person. Only a very stable dog would be suited to you. Furthermore, you are more likely to get irritated and lose your temper with the behaviorally active and very active breeds. Also, it would be best for you to have a behaviorally constant and moderately vigorous animal.

If you checked none of the statements as true, you probably should forget about having any dog. You are too irritable to put up with the inevitable problems of living with another species.

If you checked 8 or more statements as true, consider yourself very placid. You may be able to handle even the very vacillating animals. You also wouldn't be bothered by the active or very active breeds or the behaviorally variable and vigorous breeds.

If you have checked from 5 to 7 statements as true, consider yourself normally placid. You could probably take one of the emotionally vacillating breeds, but you would be happier with one of the normal or stable ones. You could probably stand one of the breeds classed as active indoors, behaviorally variable and vigorous.

Sociability. The meaning of sociability in canines can vary. It can mean the speed and number of people with whom a dog is able to permanently bond. It can mean playfulness even if no bond is formed. A dog can be considered sociable if it is friendly to strangers, but a dog can be friendly in a dominant or submissive way. A dog may be sociable only with a certain class of organisms or with almost all living things. Thus a breed could be friendly to adults but downright dangerous to children, or vice versa. A dog may be playful with most other dogs or, like the Chihuahua, act "clannish" and interact well only with its own kind. A breed may be friendly to humans and not to other dogs, or vice versa.

What I am saying is that the sociability dimension may interact with other dimensions to form a unique type of sociability. In this section we will examine sociability in general and then look at various kinds of sociability.

SOCIABILITY IN GENERAL. By "sociability in general" I mean the number of people a breed can tolerate in one location. A very sociable dog can tolerate, even enjoy crowds. A very solitary dog would get irritable, fearful or aggressive in a crowd. Moderately sociable dogs can be trusted in small gatherings, especially if the owner is around to control them.

Figure 12 compares all the breeds on the dimension of sociability. The breeds are listed alphabetically within each level of the dimension. As you can see, the breeds fall into four groups. Those which are generally sociable vary from moderate to very sociable; those breeds which are classed as solitary vary from very solitary to moderate.

TABLE 7
Sociability of Female Dogs Given the Sociability and Dominance of Their Male Counterparts and the Person with Whom the Dog Interacts

Dominance of Typical Male of Breed	Sociability of Typical Male of Breed			
	Solitary		Sociable	
	Person with Whom Female Dog Is Interacting		Person with Whom Female Dog Is Interacting	
	Man	Woman	Man	Woman
Dominant	Female dog is more *sociable* than male counterpart	Female dog is more *solitary* than male counterpart	Female dog is more *sociable* than male counterpart	Female dog is more *solitary* than male counterpart
Submissive	Female dog is more *solitary* than male counterpart	Female dog is more *sociable* than male counterpart	Female dog is more *solitary* than male counterpart	Female dog is more *solitary* than male counterpart

FIGURE 12.

Distribution of Purebred Dogs on Dimension of Sociability, with Breeds at Any One Level Arranged Alphabetically

LEVEL OF SOCIABILITY	**VERY SOLITARY**	Afghan Hound American Water Spaniel Belgian Malinois Belgian Sheepdog Belgian Tervuren Chihuahua Chow Chow	Cocker Spaniel (pm) Doberman Pinscher Irish Water Spaniel Kuvasz Miniature Pinscher Old Eng. Sheepdog (pm) Pekingese	Pomeranian Poodle, Toy (pm) Puli Saluki Schipperke Tibetan Terrier
	SOLITARY	Afghan Hound Akita Am. Staff. Bull Terrier Australian Terrier Basenji Bernese Mountain Dog Bouvier des Flandres Briard Bullmastiff Bull Terrier Cardigan W. Corgi Dachshund Dalmatian Dandie Dinmont Doberman Pinscher English Toy Spaniel	French Bulldog German Shepherd (pm) Giant Schnauzer Great Pyrenees Irish Terrier Italian Greyhound Komondor Lhasa Apso Maltese Manchester Terrier Manchester Toy Terrier Min. Schnauzer (pm) Min. Schnauzer (wb) Norwegian Elkhound Pembroke W. Corgi Poodle, Miniature	Poodle, Toy (pm) Pug Rhodesian Ridgeback Rottweiler St. Bernard (pm) Samoyed Scottish Terrier Sealyham Terrier Shetland Sheepdog Skye Terrier Staff. Bull Terrier Standard Schnauzer Tibetan Terrier Whippet WH Pointing Griffon
	MODERATE	B&T Coonhound Borzoi Chesapeake Bay Ret. Curly-coated Retriever English Bulldog German Shepherd (wb)	German SH Pointer German WH Pointer Gordon Setter Greyhound Pointer Poodle, Standard	Sussex Spaniel Welsh Springer Spaniel Weimaraner WH Pointing Griffon
	SOCIABLE	Affenpinscher Airedale Terrier Alaskan Malamute Basset Hound Bedlington Terrier Bloodhound Boston Terrier Boxer Brittany Spaniel Brussels Griffon Cairn Terrier Collie English Setter English Springer Spaniel	Field Spaniel Flat-coated Retriever Fox Terrier (SH) Fox Terrier (WH) Great Dane Harrier Irish Wolfhound Keeshond Kerry Blue Terrier Labrador Retriever Lakeland Terrier Mastiff Min. Schnauzer (pm) Min. Schnauzer (wb)	Norwegian Elkhound Norwich Terrier Papillon St. Bernard (wb) Scottish Deerhound Shih Tzu Silky Terrier Vizsla Welsh Terrier West Highland White Wheaton (soft coat) Yorkshire Terrier

FIGURE 12 *(cont.)*

		American Fox Terrier	Cocker Spaniel (wb)	Japanese Spaniel
VERY SOCIABLE		Beagle	English Cocker Spaniel	Newfoundland
		Bichon Frise	English Fox Terrier	Old Eng. Sheepdog (wb)
		Border Terrier	Golden Retriever	Otterhound
		Clumber Spaniel	Irish Setter	Siberian Husky

Now let's consider sociability as a dimension of human personality. The following statements are grouped into two sets, each having to do with a different aspect of human sociability. The first set of statements has to do with the presence or absence of sociable behaviors. The second set taps the desire for friendships.

HUMAN SOCIAL SKILLS. Respond to the following twelve statements to get an estimate of the level of your social skills.

	T	F
1. I can make friends easily.	——	——
2. I can be the life of the party.	——	——
3. I find it easy to express myself in conversation.	——	——
4. I tend to put strangers at ease.	——	——
5. People readily tell me about their personal troubles.	——	——
6. I often praise and encourage my friends.	——	——
7. When people talk to me I can listen instead of thinking of the next comment.	——	——
8. I can hear the feelings behind people's words as well as what they literally are saying.	——	——
9. I can be sensitive and sympathetic to people's moods.	——	——
10. I am aware of and generally sensitive to other people's tone of voice and body posture when they interact with me.	——	——

11. I can change my behavior/mood to match
or help the people I am interacting with. ___ ___
12. I can smile readily when people interact
with me. ___ ___

If you have checked 8 or more of the above statements as true of you, then consider yourself to have an abundant repertoire of social skills. If you have checked 3 or less, consider your social skills to be deficient. From 4 to 7 is about average.

HUMAN SOCIAL DESIRE. The next set of statements will allow you to estimate your desire to be socially active. It relates to the number of people you are willing to and/or want to interact with.

	T	F
1. Usually I would rather go to a party than watch TV or a movie or go to the theater.	___	___
2. I dislike eating alone.	___	___
3. I would like to and/or do join many organizations and/or clubs.	___	___
4. I would like to and/or do get acquainted with my neighbors.	___	___
5. I like work that puts me in contact with many people.	___	___
6. I would like to and/or do spend many evenings with friends.	___	___
7. I would like to have or do have many friends.	___	___
8. I would mind living by myself.	___	___
9. Usually I prefer to work with people rather than with things and ideas.	___	___
10. Having people around me most of the time would not get on my nerves.	___	___
11. I depend very much on others for company.	___	___
12. I would rather talk to someone than read a book or watch TV.	___	___
13. I consider myself a social lion.	___	___
14. I prefer a large number of acquaintances to a small number of close friends.	___	___

If you have checked 10 or more of the previous statements as true, then consider yourself to be a social butterfly or someone who wants to be one. You have or desire many friends and acquaintances. If you have checked 4 or fewer statements as true, then consider yourself to be more of a lone wolf. You are most comfortable by yourself or with a few close friends. From 5 to 9 statements checked is average.

Now we are ready to put the human personality dimensions of Social Skills and Social Desire together. To do this I have formed a 3 × 3 matrix in Table 8 combining the two human social dimensions. The recommendation for the type of breed most suitable to you, based on your Social Skill and Social Desire scores, is given in the cells of the matrix.

TABLE 8
Recommended Sociability Level of Dog Based on Human Social-skill and Social-desire Scores

Human Social-desire Score	Human Social-skill Score		
	Low	Average	High
Low	Very sociable dog	Very solitary dog	Very solitary dog
Average	Sociable dog	Moderate to solitary dog	Moderate to solitary dog
High	Very sociable dog	Sociable dog	Very sociable dog

This matrix represents my recommendations and may not reflect the desires of the people so categorized. For instance, people low in both social skill and social desire might think they would be best with some of the solitary and very solitary breeds because they feel empathy for their dog's aloofness and secure in the safety engendered by their dog's protective aggressiveness toward strangers. A solitary to very solitary breed will indeed help such people maintain their own reserve and not embarrass or annoy them by being overly friendly to strangers. However, I think that these people would be better with breeds from the other end of the spectrum, since they may lack the social skills to interact appropriately even with a dog. The combination of antisocial dog and socially unskilled person may result in a further isolated individual or one who can't get along even with his or her dog. If this type of person gets a very sociable dog, he or she will probably wind up making the dog less sociable anyway. If a solitary person gets a very solitary dog, that person could wind up making it a menace to society.

On the other hand, people high in both social skill and social desire would want, and I would recommend, a very sociable breed. These people probably have a lot of friends coming and going, go to and throw many parties, etc. They would feel their social life confined by any breed other than the very sociable type. This type of person could probably do all right with anything down to the moderately solitary breeds, since such a person would tend to transform his or her pet's temperament in the direction of his or her own personality.

People low in social skills but high in social desire may think they want one of the solitary breeds, since it might give them an excuse for their lack of friends. However, they would do best with a very sociable breed. First, these people don't need any more handicaps in making friends, and second, a very sociable dog may be helpful in making friends.

People high in social skills but low in social desire are those who have freely chosen to live a solitary to semisolitary life. They can have friends but prefer to have none or only a few. These people probably have the social skills to handle the very solitary dog. With their desire for solitude, such people would be most compatible with one of the solitary to very solitary breeds, depending respectively on whether they want to entertain a few close friends or none at all.

People average in both social skill and social desire are probably accurately assessing their capabilities to make and sustain acquaintances and friends. They would probably desire a moderately sociable breed, but would be better off with the sociable breeds.

Those high in social skill but average in social desire have also chosen to limit their interactions. They would probably desire and be best off with a moderate to solitary breed, depending upon the amount of solitude they desire.

Finally, those people having an average desire for social contact but low social skills would probably desire a solitary to moderate breed, depending upon the desire for friendship, but they would be better off with a moderate to sociable breed. The very sociable breeds would embarrass them and the solitary and very solitary breeds would confine them, and be a handicap.

SOCIABILITY IN DOGS AND THE SAFETY OF VISITORS: After you have decided upon the degree of sociability of the dog you are considering, it may be wise to consider the potential reaction of your dog to visiting strangers. This reaction is a function of your dog's breed characteristics and the amount of training and socialization your dog has. Figure 13 distributes the breeds according to their reactions to strangers.

FIGURE 13.

Distribution of Purebred Dogs Regarding Potential Reaction to Visiting Strangers, with Overlap of Levels of the Sociability Dimension Indicated

SOCIABLE / **VERY SOCIABLE**	**THE SOCIABILITY DIMENSION**	**VERY FRIENDLY**	Affenpinscher American Foxhound Beagle Bichon-Frise Clumber Spaniel English Cocker Spaniel	English Foxhound Golden Retriever Irish Setter Newfoundland Old Eng. Sheepdog (wb) Otterhound	Siberian Husky SH Fox Terrier WH Fox Terrier Sussex Spaniel
		FRIENDLY	Airedale Terrier Alaskan Malamute American Water Spaniel Basset Hound Bedlington Bloodhound Border Borzoi Boston Terrier Boxer Brittany Spaniel Brussels Griffon Cocker Spaniel (wb)	Collie English Setter English Springer Spaniel Field Spaniel Flat-coated Retriever German SH Pointer Great Dane Japanese Spaniel Keeshond Labrador Retriever Lakeland Terrier Mastiff Min. Schnauzer (wb)	Norwegian Elkhound Papillon Pembroke W. Corgi St. Bernard (wb) Scottish Deerhound Shih Tzu Silky Terrier Standard Poodle Vizsla Welsh Terrier Yorkshire Terrier

FIGURE 13 *(cont.)*

NEUTRAL	Am. Staff. Bull Terrier Basset Hound	Borzoi English Bulldog	Irish Wolfhound
RESERVED	Afghan Hound Airedale Terrier Australian Terrier Basenji Belgian Malinois Belgian Sheepdog Belgian Tervuren Bernese Mountain Dog B&T Coonhound Bouvier des Flandres Briard Bullmastiff Bull Terrier Cairn Terrier Cardigan W. Corgi Chesa. Bay Retriever Dachshund Dalmatian Dandie Dinmont Doberman Pinscher English Bulldog	English Toy Spaniel French Bulldog German Shepherd (wb) German SH Pointer German WH Pointer Giant Schnauzer Gordon Setter Great Pyrenees Greyhound Harrier Irish Terrier Irish Water Spaniel Irish Wolfhound Kerry Blue Komondor Lhasa Apso Maltese Manchester Terrier Miniature Poodle M. Schnauzer (wb) Norwegian Elkhound	Pekingese Pointer Pomeranian Pug Puli Rhodesian Ridgeback Rottweiler Saluki Samoyed Shetland Sheepdog Schipperke St. Bernard (pm) Standard Poodle Standard Schnauzer Tibetan Terrier Toy Manchester Toy Poodle (wb) Weimaraner Welsh Springer Spaniel Whippet
FEARFUL	Belgian Malinois Belgian Sheepdog Belgian Tervuren	Cocker Spaniel (pm) German Shepherd (pm) Puli	Shetland Sheepdog Toy Poodle (pm) WH Pointing Griffon
SUSPICIOUS	Akita Chihuahua Chow Chow	German Shepherd (pm) Kuvasz Miniature Pinscher	Old Eng. Sheepdog (pm) Schipperke Tibetan Terrier
AGGRESSIVE	Am. Staff. Bull Terrier Cardigan W. Corgi Chesa. Bay Retriever Doberman Pinscher	Irish Water Spaniel German Shepherd (pm) Komondor Pomeranian	Rhodesian Ridgeback Rottweiler Toy Poodle (pm)

Left margin vertical labels: SOLITARY · VERY SOLITARY · MODERATE · SOCIABLE · THE SOCIABILITY DIMENSION

As you can see, there is some overlap between the sociability of a breed and its potential reaction to strangers. Very sociable dogs may range from friendly to very friendly toward strangers. Sociable dogs may vary from friendly to reserved with strangers. Moderately sociable range from neutral to fearful of strangers. Solitary dogs vary from fearful to suspicious of visitors. Finally, very solitary dogs may be either suspicious or aggressive toward strangers. This is not contradictory, since the sociability of a breed is a function of many characteristics, only one of which is its reaction to visiting strangers.

In order for you to decide which type of reaction toward strangers you would want, it would be best if I defined these terms more fully. The following are definitions of a breed's potential reaction to strangers:

1. *Very friendly:* These breeds are described with the following terms: "likes everybody," "very friendly" and "likes people." These breeds may be very playful and jump on people who enter and continuously nuzzle, smell and rub up against visitors. They are basically indiscriminate in their friendliness. They can be a pleasure to people who love dogs but an annoyance to people who do not. So choosing this breed may reduce visitations from your dog-hating friends.

2. *Friendly:* These breeds are variously called "friendly," "sociable," "liking almost everyone," "accepting" or "mildly friendly." They are slightly more discriminating toward people with whom they interact. They may jump up on people, but they will rapidly get the message from certain people that this is unacceptable behavior.

3. *Neutral:* These breeds are described as "tolerant," "ignoring" or "oblivious of visiting strangers." They don't seem to care who comes or goes. Note: four out of five of these breeds appear in more than one category. The American Staffordshire is aggressive with strangers, especially if left alone with them. The Irish Wolfhound is also classed as reserved. The Borzoi and Basset (usually the females) are classed as friendly. This may mean that a specimen of a breed alternates between these behaviors, and/or that the breed varies from one specimen to another.

4. *Reserved:* These breeds are also described as "aloof." Basically they hang back and don't immediately approach strangers, but will warm up to visitors who encourage them after one or two visits. With some socialization these breeds can be friendly to visitors.

5. *Suspicious:* These breeds take a rather long time to trust visiting strangers. They may growl if petted, approached or stared at by strangers. They are usually not aggressive unless provoked. Unfortunately, the provocation may be friendly overtures made by pushy or naive visitors. With extensive socialization and training these dogs may be made less suspicious of visitors.

6. *Fearful:* These breeds are also called "submissive, timid or shy." Most of these breeds also appear in two categories, being classified as either reserved or aggressive. These animals tend to hide when visitors enter. If left alone they will slowly come out of their hiding place. They may become friendly to friendly visitors over a long period of time, but usually they become more assertive, snapping at visitors if they walk or move. If rebuked, shouted at, stared at or punished by the visitors, they will almost permanently fear them. They are generally a source of irritation—and so are their owners if they tolerate or excuse this behavior. These dogs need extensive training and socialization to reduce their fearfulness.

7. *Aggressive:* These breeds have been called "mildly aggressive," "forbidding," "aggressive," "very aggressive," "dangerous," "vicious" and "ill-tempered" toward visiting strangers. The potential danger to visitors varies with the breed's size and strength and the amount of socialization and training a dog receives. If you get any of the breeds in the Aggressive category, socialize early and extensively, and train exhaustively, if you want to protect the physical integrity of visitors and/or if you want people to visit at all. If you plan to be a hermit, living in a cave on a deserted island, you may not have to be as diligent.

CHILDREN AND BREED SOCIABILITY. Figure 14 categorizes all the breeds on their potential behavior toward children.

FIGURE 14.

Distribution of Purebred Dogs Regarding Potential Interaction with Children, with Breeds within a Given Level Rank-ordered on Bulkiness

LEVEL OF SOCIABILITY WITH CHILDREN	**DANGEROUS**	St. Bernard (pm) Old Eng. Sheepdog (pm)	Alaskan Malamute Am. Staff. Bull Terrier	Staff. Bull Terrier Poodle, Toy (pm)
	BAD	Rottweiler Old Eng. Sheepdog (pm) Komondor Chow Chow German Shepherd (pm) Kuvasz Borzoi Rhodesian Ridgeback Doberman Norwegian Elkhound German WH Pointer	Irish Water Spaniel Greyhound French Bulldog Saluki American Water Spaniel Dandie Dinmont Dachshund Cocker Spaniel (pm) Puli Lhasa Apso Tibetan Terrier	Pekingese Shipperke Schnauzer, Min. (pm) Whippet Manchester Terrier Chihuahua Pomeranian Affenpinscher Manchester Toy Terrier Poodle, Toy (wb) Italian Greyhound
	UNSUITED	Schnauzer, Giant Dalmatian Doberman + German SH Pointer Italian Greyhound		
	TOLERANT	✓?◄Alaskan Malamute ✓◄Borzoi *✓ Komondor ◄Rottweiler + Weimaraner Norwegian Elkhound ✓◄Rhodesian Ridgeback ✓ Cardigan W. Corgi Belgian Malinois Belgian Sheepdog Belgian Tervuren ✓ Skye Terrier *◄Doberman ✓ Pembroke W. Corgi * WH Pointing Griffon SH Pointing Griffon ✓◄Greyhound * Pointer Airedale	+✓ Bull Terrier Field Spaniel ✓◄Saluki ✓ Schnauzer, Standard ✓ Afghan ✓ Welsh Springer Spaniel ✓ Sealyham Terrier ✓ Scottish Terrier ✓◄Dachshund ✓ Kerry Blue Terrier +✓Irish Terrier ◄Tibetan Terrier ✓ Westie ✓ Basenji ✓ Cairn Terrier ✓ Shih Tzu ✓ Welsh Terrier ✓ Bedlington ✓ Fox Terrier SH	✓ Fox Terrier WH ✓ Lakeland Terrier ✓ Norwich Terrier ◄Poodle, Miniature ✓ Schnauzer, M. (wb) ✓ Sheltie ✓◄Whippet ✓ Australian ✓ Manchester Terrier ✓ English Toy Spaniel ✓ Silky Terrier ✓ Yorkshire Terrier ✓ Brussels Griffon * Miniature Pinscher ✓ Papillon ✓ Japanese Spaniel ✓ Maltese

FIGURE 14 *(cont.)*

LEVEL OF SOCIABILITY WITH CHILDREN				

	EXCEPTIONALLY GOOD WITH PROVISO	←St. Bernard (wb)
		* Bullmastiff
		+ Great Dane
		←Old Eng. Sheepdog (wb)
		✔Basset Hound
		* Great Pyrenees
		+ Irish Wolfhound
		+ Otterhound
			* Akita
			** Am. Staff. Bull
			* Briard
			? German Shepherd (wb)
			* Golden Retriever
			←Belgian Malinois
			←Belgian Sheepdog
			←Belgian Tervuren
				* Curly-coated
				   Retriever
				* Flat-coated
				   Retriever
				* Collie
				+ Irish Setter
				? Wheaten
				←Cocker Spaniel (wb)

	EXCEPTIONALLY GOOD	Mastiff Boxer Newfoundland Bloodhound Bouvier des Flandres Bernese Mountain Dog B&T Coonhound Clumber Spaniel English Bulldog Scottish Deerhound English Foxhound	Samoyed American Foxhound Chesa. Bay Retriever Labrador Retriever Gordon Setter Sussex Spaniel English Setter English Springer Spaniel Harrier Field Spaniel Siberian Husky	Vizsla Keeshond Poodle, Standard English Cocker Spaniel Brittany Spaniel Beagle Boston Terrier Pug Bichon Frise Border Terrier

LEGEND:

  ? Questionable
  + Too clumsy, impetuous or vigorous
    for small ones
  ✔ Considerate, respectful, careful children
  ✔ Considerate, respectful, careful older
    children
  * Must be raised with children
  ← Multiple listing

In each category the breeds are arranged in terms of bulk, with the stockiest breed at the start. This is done for two reasons. In the exceptionally good column it is assumed that the stockier the breed, the more it will be able to withstand the punishment that some children can dish out. In the bad to dangerous category, the opposite is true: the stockier the breed, the more potential the dog has to inflict physical harm.

In the exceptionally good group are breeds that usually can withstand the physical taunts of children; be calm in response to rapid movements; react unemotionally to loud and sometimes peculiar noises and modulate their physical strength in relation to the size of the child, either being more gentle with smaller children or generally gentle and, if necessary, being protective of the children.

I was very careful in selecting breeds that appear in the exceptionally good group. If there was any proviso attached to a breed, it was not listed in this group. As an owner of a Mastiff, I am still ambivalent about listing Mastiffs in this category. Despite their enormous size, they are not clumsy. The Mastiff is usually a gentle, placid beast that is prone to sleep through a child's racket and lie quietly as a toddler uses its body as a footstool or its cavernous chest as a drum. My ambivalence comes from the fact that it could knock a child down with its tail.

Any other breed that would normally be rated as exceptionally good, but had a proviso, was listed in the next group. The provisos include being too clumsy for small children, being exceptionally good with considerate and/or older children, needing to be raised with the child to be exceptionally good or any suspicion I have that some of the specimens of a breed may not be good with children. Some of these suspicions may be based on only a minimum of evidence, but I feel it is best to use maximally conservative criteria where children are concerned. For instance, well-bred Old English Sheepdogs, St. Bernards and Cocker Spaniels are generally considered to be very good with children. But the fact that some naive pet owners might obtain the unpredictable puppy-mill varieties was enough to rate these breeds with a proviso. German Shepherds and Wheaten Terriers are also considered to be exceptionally good with children. However, I have had a number of cases in my professional experience in which a specimen from one of these breeds has attacked a child. Usually the aggression was directed toward a boy or girl entering puberty and had a lot to do with a dominance struggle between the child and dog. The specimens that gave their owners this kind of trouble were ill trained and poorly socialized. These dogs showed signs of dominance problems from early puppyhood which the owners either chose to ignore or were too naive to recognize. Thus these breeds are listed in the exceptionally good category with a question mark after the breed name.

In the exceptionally good with proviso column, there are some breed names marked with an asterisk, meaning that they must be raised with children if the breed is to be expected to be good with children. This has implications for couples who intend to have children and are contemplating getting a dog. If they are going to get a dog before they have children, they would be better off choosing from the breeds without this proviso. If you are set on getting a breed that must be raised with children, then you'd better make sure that this pet has a significant amount of advance socialization and playful experiences with other children.

One final comment about the breeds rated exceptionally good with or without proviso. I have made the assumption that they are owned by intelligent owners who supervise their children's interactions with the dog and their dog's interactions with the children. The children should be taught the appropriate way of playing with the dog, and the dog should be well trained and well socialized with many children. As soon as possible, the children should be involved in training the dog so that they too can control it.

The breeds rated as only tolerant of children also come with many provisos and may be classed as bad or even dangerous with children. Some specimens in the tolerant category may turn out to be good with children owing to natural variation in temperament from dog to dog within a particular breed. Females in this category are more likely to be good with children. Some specimens in this category may be taught to be good with children. The breeds were listed in this column to remind potential parents to be careful.

Any of the breeds listed as unsuitable or worse should be

avoided by people who have children, expect to have children or are visited by children frequently. These breeds are not necessarily bloodthirsty child abusers. They are just too aggressive, dominant, high-strung, snappy or fragile to be around youngsters.

SOCIABILITY WITH THE OWNER AND FAMILY. Breeds may vary from a no-person dog, which may be aloof, independent and undemonstrative to its owners even when raised with them from puppyhood, to an any-person dog which quickly forms weak bonds with any person with whom it playfully interacts. Any-person dogs are frequently described as fickle by their amused or jealous owners.

Between these extremes we have the one-person breeds that appear to be able to form strong bonds with one individual. This exclusivity may make a one-person dog strongly attached to its master, sometimes protective of him/her even against other family members, timid or aggressive toward strangers and prone to separation anxiety if the master must leave it for any period of time. Separation anxiety may manifest itself in fearfulness, barking and/or howling, elimination and destruction if left alone. The type of reaction depends upon the amount of early socialization and training, the dominance or submissiveness and the emotional stability of the breed. One-person dogs are described as loyal, faithful and dependent by their owners.

A one-family dog is like a one-person dog except that it is able to form lasting and strong bonds to a number of people it lives with and sees regularly. In this category there are small-family dogs, which bond with no more than two individuals, and large-family dogs. The rest are limited to about four to five strong bonds. One-family dogs can form bonds with other people, but usually these are weaker and take some time to form.

Depending upon their emotional stability, dominance and lack of socialization, these breeds may also show separation anxiety when left alone and protectiveness of family members. They usually attach themselves most strongly to the family member with whom they spend most time or the one who is dominant in the family.

Open-family dogs can discriminate between family members and non–family members. However, they readily accept new members into the family after one or two playful experiences with them. Whether or not these new members are in reality a part of the family is of no importance to open-family dogs. Once they have accepted them, they will greet these adopted family members with exuberance even if they haven't seen them for long periods of time.

Figure 15 compares all the breeds on the dimension of sociability with owners and family. The breeds are listed alphabetically within each level of the dimension. Over half of the breeds are classified as more or less one-family dogs, and the rest of the breeds are symmetrically distributed in categories above and below the one-family breeds.

Your choice along this dimension of canine temperament is related to your willingness to be accepting or critical of other people. Accepting people would lean toward the open-family or any-person dogs. Critical people would probably be more comfortable with the less trusting breeds. The following statements will sample your tendency to be accepting or critical.

	T	F
1. I sincerely believe that most people mean well.	___	___
2. I expect an honor system to work well in most situations.	___	___
3. For me, logic is less important than faith in human interactions.	___	___
4. I have found that I can trust people.	___	___
5. If I lost my wallet or purse, I believe the finder would try to return it to me.	___	___
6. In my experience, automobile drivers are usually courteous and considerate.	___	___
7. I believe that one has to be sensitive to others to get on in this world.	___	___
8. I am confident that most people look out for other people.	___	___

T   F

9. I believe that most people will not cheat,
   even if they can get away with it.   ____ ____

10. I feel the only road to success is through
    the willing help of others.   ____ ____

11. In my opinion, most people will do more
    work than is expected of them.   ____ ____

12. I feel that if I let my guard down, people will
    feel closer to me.   ____ ____

If you have checked 10 or more statements as true, consider yourself as very accepting to other people. You would probably feel comfortable only with an accepting dog. Choose from the any-person group of Figure 15. With 8 to 10 statements checked as true, you are generally accepting. You would probably want a breed that is mildly discriminating but accepts people readily especially if you do. Choose a breed from the open-family group of the table.

A score of 5 to 7 is average. You are accepting in some situations and critical in others. Depending upon how threatened you feel by intruding strangers, you should choose from the breeds that are more or less one-family dogs.

FIGURE 15.

Distribution of Purebred Dogs on Dimension of Sociability with Family, with Breeds in Any One Level Alphabetized

SOCIABILITY WITH FAMILY	NO-PERSON ALOOF WITH OWNER			
		Borzoi	German Shepherd (pm)	Poodle, Toy (pm)
		Chow Chow	Kuvasz	Saluki
		Cocker Spaniel (pm)	Miniature Pinscher	
	ONE-PERSON	American Water Spaniel	Irish Water Spaniel	Pug
		Belgian Malinois	Komondor	Rottweiler
		Belgian Sheepdog	Manchester Toy Terrier	St. Bernard (pm)
		Belgian Tervuren	Norwegian Elkhound	Schnauzer, Giant
		Bernese Mountain Dog	Norwich Terrier	Schnauzer, Standard
		Chihuahua	Old Eng. Sheepdog (pm)	Scottish Terrier
		Chow Chow	Pekingese	Skye Terrier
		Doberman Pinscher	Pomeranian	

FIGURE 15 *(cont.)*

LEVEL OF SOCIABILITY WITH FAMILY				
ONE-FAMILY	Afghan Hound	French Bulldog	Poodle, Standard	
	Airedale	German Shepherd (wb)	Poodle, Toy (pm)	
	Akita	German SH Pointer	Poodle, Toy (wb)	
	s Am. Staff. Bull Terrier	German WH Pointer	Pug	
	Australian Terrier	Giant Schnauzer	Puli	
	Basenji	Gordon Setter	Rhodesian Ridgeback	
	Basset Hound	Great Pyrenees	Rottweiler	
	Bedlington Terrier	Greyhound	St. Bernard (pm)	
	s Belgian Malinois	Harrier	St. Bernard (wb)	
	s Belgian Sheepdog	Irish Setter	Samoyed	
	s Belgian Tervuren	Irish Terrier	Schipperke	
	s Bernese Mountain Dog	Irish Wolfhound	Scottish Deerhound	
	B&T Coonhound	Italian Greyhound	Scottish Terrier	
	Border Terrier	Kerry Blue	Sealyham Terrier	
	Boston Terrier	Komondor	Shetland Sheepdog	
	l Bouvier des Flandres	Labrador Retriever	Silky Terrier	
	Briard	Lakeland Terrier	Skye Terrier	
	Bullmastiff	Lhasa Apso	s Staff. Bull Terrier	
	Bull Terrier	Maltese	Schnauzer, Min. (pm)	
	Cairn Terrier	s Manchester Terrier	Schnauzer, Min. (wb)	
	Cardigan W. Corgi	Manchester Toy Terrier	Schnauzer, Standard	
	Chesa. Bay Retriever	Mastiff	Tibetan Terrier	
	Collie	Miniature Pinscher	Weimaraner	
	Cury-coated Retriever	Norwegian Elkhound	Welsh Springer Spaniel	
	Dachshund	s Pekingese	Welsh Terrier	
	Dalmatian	Pembroke W. Corgi	Whippet	
	Dandie Dinmont	Pointer	WH Pointing Griffon	
	Doberman Pinscher	s Pomeranian	Yorkshire Terrier	
	English Toy Spaniel	Poodle, Miniature		
OPEN-FAMILY	Affenpinscher	Field Spaniel	Schnauzer, Min. (pm)	
	Bichon Frise	Flat-coated Retriever	Shih Tzu	
	Brittany Spaniel	Golden Retriever	Siberian Husky	
	Brussels Griffon	Great Dane	Sussex Spaniel	
	Clumber Spaniel	Japanese Spaniel	Vizsla	
	Cocker Spaniel (wb)	Keeshond	West Highland White	
	English Bulldog	Newfoundland	SH Fox Terrier	
	English Cocker Spaniel	Old Eng. Sheepdog (wb)	WH Fox Terrier	
	English Setter	Papillon	Wheaten Terrier	
	English Springer Spaniel	Schnauzer, Min. (wb)		
ANY-PERSON	Alaskan Malamute	Beagle	English Foxhound	
	American Foxhound	Bloodhound	Otterhound	

Key: **s = small-family**
l = large-family

A score of 2 to 4 would put you more toward the untrusting and critical side of this personality dimension. The small-family or one-person dogs are more likely to suit your tastes. You may become annoyed by the tendency of the open and trusting breeds to befriend strangers. Also, you will probably feel more protected by a dog that is attached only to you.

If you have checked fewer than two statements as true, consider yourself to be very critical. You would probably be better off with a one-person dog. Its discrimination would comfort you.

People wanting the no-person dogs are so insular that they prefer a dog that would not need to be petted or cared for. Or they could be people who work during the day and want a dog that could stand to be left alone for periods of time. Some people find themselves attracted to aloofness and independence. Many cat lovers would like these breeds. In fact, owners of the no-person dogs say their dogs are catlike in their temperament.

Obviously, your ability to be accepting of others is not the only consideration relevant to Figure 15. Another consideration is the size or potential size of your family, the number of friends and/or relatives who visit you and their feelings about dogs, etc. The larger the family, the better it is to have larger- or open-family dogs. If you don't want your dog bothering relatives or friends, you should choose in the direction of the small-family or one-person dogs. The aloof breeds will not annoy any visitor with solicitations for play or affection. However, these breeds may become annoyed at visitors and even the owner if they become overly demonstrative.

Learning Abilities. The next dimensions on which the breeds are to be compared are the various learning abilities that determine the breed's potential as a house dog and pet. These abilities include the breed's receptivity to training, its ability to solve problems and its willingness to be obedient.

LEARNING RATE. The ease with which a breed is able to form associations between two or more events determines its trainability. These events may be a response and a subsequent reinforcement (reward). You may think that fast learners will be the best choice, but this is not necessarily so. It all depends upon *what* your dog is likely to learn when living with you and your family.

Knowing *what* an animal is learning can be a tricky business. For example, some breeds may rapidly associate their barking behavior with the consequent dog biscuit their owners give them to quiet them down. Other breeds may form this association very slowly. In either case, however, what the dog is being reinforced for is barking, the very thing the owner is trying to stop.

The learning events may consist of a response and a subsequent punishment. Thus, some breeds may rapidly learn an avoidance response from sniffing a candle and the consequent burning sensation on their noses, while other breeds may learn the association more slowly, roasting their noses regularly until the association is finally made.

These events may consist of stimuli that reliably follow each other. The grinding sound of the electric can opener may consistently precede the smell of dog food. The sight of a person putting on his or her coat with leash in hand, or the words "Do you want to go for a walk?" may reliably signal a walk. Owners of fast learners may find themselves bugged by an excited dog when they operate the can opener or even when they spell the word "walk." Slow-learning dogs may have to be dragged to the door and forced outside before they are aware that it is walk time.

Other situations may involve the animal's learning the effects of its behavior on the environment. For example, If I push on a door with my nose, it usually opens; or, If I chew on the doorknob, then the door will open. Or, If I dig in the sofa, the stuffing comes out. Or, If my owner leaves me alone, I am free to run around the house. Some dogs may learn these associations rapidly and others slowly or not at all.

There are constraints on the types of associations that certain breeds will form. These constraints frequently can be related to the function the animals were bred to perform. Thus sight hounds, which are coursing dogs, may rapidly form associations between visual stimuli and a running response, but only slowly form associations between odors and these responses. Conversely, Bloodhounds may be particularly

FIGURE 16.

Distribution of Purebred Dogs on Dimension of Learning Rate, with Breeds in Any One Level Alphabetized

VERY SLOW	Boston Terrier English Bulldog			
SLOW	Afghan Hound Alaskan Malamute American Fox Terrier Basset Hound B&T Coonhound Bloodhound Briard Bull Terrier Chesapeake Bay Ret.	Clumber Spaniel Cocker Spaniel (pm) Doberman Pinscher English Fox Terrier English Setter Great Dane Great Pyrenees Komondor Mastiff	Old Eng. Sheepdog (wb) Otterhound Pointer Rottweiler Saluki Scottish Deerhound Sussex Spaniel Tibetan Terrier	

LEARNING RATE

FAST

Affenpinscher	Field Spaniel	Norwich Terrier
Airedale Terrier	Flat-coated Retriever	Old Eng. Sheepdog (pm)
Akita	SH Fox Terrier	Papillon
Am. Staff. Bull Terrier	French Bulldog	Pekingese
American Water Spaniel	German SH Pointer	Pomeranian
Australian Terrier	German WH Pointer	Pug
Basenji	Giant Schnauzer	Rhodesian Ridgeback
Beagle	Gordon Setter	Samoyed
Bedlington Terrier	Greyhound	Scottish Terrier
Bichon Frise	Harrier	Sealyham Terrier
Border Terrier	Irish Setter	Schipperke
Borzoi	Irish Terrier	Shih Tzu
Boston Terrier	Irish Water Spaniel	Siberian Husky
Boxer	Irish Wolfhound	Silky Terrier
Brittany Spaniel	Italian Greyhound	Staff. Bull Terrier
Brussels Griffon	Japanese Spaniel	St. Bernard (pm)
Bullmastiff	Keeshond	St. Bernard (wb)
Cairn Terrier	Kerry Blue Terrier	Standard Schnauzer
Chihuahua	Kuvasz	Tibetan Terrier
Chow Chow	Lakeland Terrier	Vizsla
Cocker Spaniel (wb)	Lhasa Apso	Weimaraner
Collie	Maltese	Welsh Springer Spaniel
Curly-coated Retriever	Manchester Terrier	Welsh Terrier
Dachshund	Manchester Toy Terrier	West Highland White
Dalmatian	Miniature Pinscher	Wheaton Terrier
English Cocker Spaniel	Min. Schnauzer (pm)	Whippet
English Springer Spaniel	Min. Schnauzer (wb)	
English Toy Spaniel	Newfoundland	

FIGURE 16 *(cont.)*

LEARNING RATE	VERY FAST			
		Belgian Malinois	Dandie Dinmont	Pembroke W. Corgi
		Belgian Sheepdog	Doberman Pinscher	Poodle, Mini. (very)
		Belgian Tervuren	German Shepherd (pm)	Poodle, Standard
		Bernese Mountain Dog	German Shepherd (wb)	Poodle, Toy (pm)
		Bichon Frise	Golden Retriever	Poodle, Toy (wb)
		Bouvier des Flandres	Labrador Retriever	Puli
		Cardigan W. Corgi	Norwegian Elkhound	Shetland Sheepdog

suited to forming associations between odors and their tracking behavior. Pointers may form their most rapid associations between the odor and/or the sight of something and standing still. Guard dogs may rapidly associate their threats and aggression with the behavior of people around them. They may learn that they can dominate these people by growls, and this may reinforce their tendency to control people.

Figure 16 compares all breeds on their potential to form the associations involved in training. The breeds are organized alphabetically within a level. As you can see, most breeds are classified as fast learners. Interestingly, the breeds fall into a dichotomous distribution—those which are fast to very fast learners and those which are slow to very slow learners.

OBEDIENCE. Figure 17 compares all breeds on the obedience dimension. As you can see, this dimension is distributed differently from the learning-rate dimension, with the majority of breeds being classed as fair or poor in obedience. This dimension relates to your dog's willingness to obey your commands. It is a social learning dimension and is not well correlated with learning rate or problem solving. For example, a breed may be an excellent problem solver but poor in obedience, figuring out clever ways to avoid obeying your commands. Or a dog may be a fast learner, rapidly associating a command with a particular response, but may refuse to comply with the owner's commands. Owners sometimes say of this kind of dog, "He knows what to do, but won't do it for me." Also, some disobedient breeds may differentiate between people, complying with the commands of those they consider dominant and ignoring the

FIGURE 17.

Distribution of Purebred Dogs on Dimension of Obedience, with Breeds at Any One Level Rank-ordered on Bulkiness

LEVEL OF OBEDIENCE			
VERY POOR	Chow Chow Briard Kuvasz	Doberman Pinscher Greyhound Boston Terrier	Pekingese Miniature Pinscher Pomeranian
POOR	St. Bernard (pm) Bullmastiff Rottweiler Old Eng. Sheepdog (wb) B&T Coonhound Great Pyrenees Komondor Alaskan Malamute Akita Am. Staff. Bull Terrier German Shepherd (pm) English Bulldog Schnauzer, Giant Boxer Weimaraner Rhodesian Ridgeback Samoyed Norwegian Elkhound	German SH Pointer Irish Water Spaniel Sussex Spaniel Harrier Staff. Bull Terrier Airedale Terrier Bull Terrier French Bulldog Schnauzer, Standard Siberian Husky Afghan Hound Dandie Dinmont Sealyham Terrier Dachshund Kerry Blue Scottish Terrier Beagle Cocker Spaniel	Puli Norwich Terrier Irish Terrier Lhasa Apso Tibetan Terrier Schipperke Welsh Terrier SH Fox Terrier WH Fox Terrier Lakeland Terrier Schnauzer, Miniature Manchester Terrier Brussels Griffon Chihuahua Yorkshire Terrier Manchester Toy Terrier Poodle, Toy (pm)
FAIR	St. Bernard (pm) St. Bernard (wb) Mastiff Great Dane Basset Hound Bloodhound Great Pyrenees Otterhound Clumber Spaniel Schnauzer, Giant Scottish Deerhound Borzoi English Foxhound Chesapeake Bay Ret.	American Foxhound Skye Terrier English Setter English Springer Spaniel German SH Pointer German WH Pointer Pointer Airedale Terrier Saluki Schnauzer, Standard Welsh Springer Spaniel American Water Spaniel Dandie Dinmont Keeshond	Wheaton Terrier Boston Terrier Basenji Cairn Terrier Pug Shih Tzu Bedlington Terrier Schnauzer, Miniature Whippet English Toy Spaniel Silky Terrier Yorkshire Terrier Affenpinscher

FIGURE 17 *(cont.)*

LEVEL OF OBEDIENCE	**GOOD**	Newfoundland Bouvier des Flandres Irish Wolfhound Bernese Mountain Dog German Shepherd (wb) Golden Retriever Dalmatian Labrador Retriever	Curly-coated Retriever Flat-coated Retriever Pembroke W. Corgi WH Pointing Griffon Irish Setter Field Spaniel Vizsla English Cocker Spaniel	Brittany Spaniel Cocker Spaniel West Highland White Border Terrier Australian Terrier Maltese Italian Greyhound
	VERY GOOD	German Shepherd (wb) Belgian Malinois Belgian Sheepdog Belgian Tervuren Cardigan W. Corgi	Collie Doberman Pinscher Poodle, Standard Bichon Frise Poodle, Miniature	Shetland Sheepdog Chihuahua Papillon Japanese Spaniel Poodle, Toy (wb)

commands of those they consider submissive. Thus learning rate, problem solving, obedience and the potential for dominance or submission interact.

PROBLEM-SOLVING ABILITY. Problem solving is not completely correlated with trainability. For example, some dogs may rapidly associate the sight of a flame with being burned. Good problem solvers that have formed this association can produce novel responses to deal with the fear engendered by a burning match. I once knew a Standard Poodle that had learned to sneeze on a lighted match, thereby putting it out. When this dog was confronted with a campfire, it initially sneezed at it, and when this didn't work it turned and started digging, throwing earth on the fire, which ultimately extinguished it. The dog then walked up to the smoldering embers, lifted its leg and urinated on them. Poor problem solvers would react to this event by hiding in terror, even if this behavior produced no effective improvement in their situation.

The difference between good and poor problem solvers is not necessarily whether they form associations rapidly, but what they do about these associations once they are formed. The payoff of associations indicates to good problem solvers what is important in their environment and what can be ignored. The good problem solver can abandon ineffective behaviors and readily try new behaviors. Poor problem solvers persevere; once they have found a solution, they stay with it whether it works or not.

Figure 18 compares all breeds on their potential problem-solving ability. As you can see, these abilities are distributed differently from learning rate. There is some overlap, especially at the extremes of each dimension. Seven of the 27 breeds ranked as very good problem solvers are also classed as very fast learners. Paradoxically, the puppy-mill Old English Sheepdog is considered to be a very good problem solver but a very poor learner. This means that specimens of this breed will form associations slowly, but once they are formed the dogs will be able to vary their behavior to solve problems on the basis of these associations, even if the payoff involved in the associations is no longer in effect. In other words, such dogs could be solving problems that aren't really there.

FIGURE 18.

Distribution of Purebred Dogs on Dimension of Problem-solving Ability, with Breeds at Any One Level Arranged Alphabetically

PROBLEM-SOLVING ABILITY				
	VERY POOR	Boston Terrier English Bulldog Old Eng. Sheepdog (pm)		
	POOR	Am. Staff. Bull Terrier Basset Hound B&T Coonhound Borzoi Boxer Bull Terrier Clumber Spaniel Cocker Spaniel (pm) English Toy Spaniel	French Bulldog Great Dane Greyhound Italian Greyhound Mastiff Pekingese Pointer Pug St. Bernard (pm)	Saluki Scottish Deerhound Sealyham Terrier Shih Tzu Skye Terrier Staff. Bull Terrier Sussex Spaniel

FIGURE 18 *(cont.)*

LEVEL OF PROBLEM-SOLVING ABILITY				
FAIR	Akita	English Springer Spaniel	Mastiff	
	American Foxhound	Flat-coated Retriever	Min. Schnauzer (pm)	
	Bedlington Terrier	German Shepherd (pm)	Min. Schnauzer (wb)	
	Bloodhound	German WH Pointer	Otterhound	
	Briard	Golden Retriever	Rottweiler	
	Bullmastiff	Gordon Setter	Scottish Terrier	
	Chesapeake Bay Ret.	Irish Setter	Tibetan Terrier	
	Clumber Spaniel	Irish Water Spaniel	Vizsla	
	Cocker Spaniel (wb)	Irish Wolfhound	Welsh Springer Spaniel	
	Curly-coated Retriever	Keeshond	Whippet	
	English Cocker Spaniel	Labrador Retriever	WH Pointing Griffon	
	English Foxhound	Lhasa Apso		
	English Setter	Manchester Terrier		
GOOD	Affenpinscher	Collie	Newfoundland	
	Afghan Hound	Dachshund	Norwich Terrier	
	Airedale Terrier	Dalmatian	Old Eng. Sheepdog (wb)	
	American Water Spaniel	English Setter	Papillon	
	Beagle	Field Spaniel	Pembroke W. Corgi	
	Belgian Malinois	German SH Pointer	Pomeranian	
	Belgian Sheepdog	Great Pyrenees	Rhodesian Ridgeback	
	Belgian Tervuren	Harrier	St. Bernard (wb)	
	Bernese Mountain Dog	Irish Setter	Silky Terrier	
	Border Terrier	Irish Terrier	Standard Schnauzer	
	Boston Terrier	Komondor	Welsh Terrier	
	Bouvier des Flandres	Kuvasz	Weimaraner	
	Brittany Spaniel	Lakeland Terrier	Wheaten (soft coat)	
	Cardigan W. Corgi	Maltese	Yorkshire Terrier	
	Chow Chow	Manchester Toy Terrier		
	Cocker Spaniel (wb)	Miniature Pinscher		
VERY GOOD	Alaskan Malamute	Fox Terrier (SH)	Poodle, Standard	
	Australian Terrier	Fox Terrier (WH)	Poodle, Toy (pm)	
	Basenji	German Shepherd (wb)	Poodle, Toy (wb)	
	Bichon Frise	Giant Schnauzer	Puli	
	Brussels Griffon	Japanese Spaniel	Samoyed	
	Cairn Terrier	Kerry Blue Terrier	Shetland Sheepdog	
	Chihuahua	Norwegian Elkhound	Schipperke	
	Dandie Dinmont	Old Eng. Sheepdog (pm)	Siberian Husky	
	Doberman	Poodle, Miniature	West Highland Terrier	

THE LEARNING DIMENSIONS SUMMARIZED. I am assuming that you have already narrowed down your choices to a few representative breeds. You can now determine what you may be facing in terms of training.

Obviously the more obedient the breed, the less time you will have to spend in training it. Thus, if your personality or life-style suits one of the less obedient breeds, make sure you have the time available to train it.

In relation to dominance, you already know that the more submissive you are, the more submissive the breed you should choose. Submissiveness also relates to obedience to family members. The more submissive the breed, the more likely it will obey all the family members. Breeds intermediate in dominance will obey only those members it perceives as dominant. Thus if you have a family with children, it's best to choose one of the submissive breeds. This will guarantee that almost everyone will be able to control the family pet.

One would think that it would always be best to obtain a good problem solver and a fast learner. However, this may not be the case. It depends upon what problems the dog will be faced with and what it has available to learn. Large dogs that are left alone and are either emotionally attached to their owners or active indoors are faced with the problem of how to get out when locked up indoors. Poor problem solvers will try a few things, fail and give up. Very good problem solvers may succeed in escaping or fail but persist. This can wreak havoc on someone's walls or floor as the dog attempts to dig through the floorboards, chew through the wall, chew off doorknobs and so on. It would be better to have a poor problem solver if you need to leave the dog home alone for long periods of time.

Among problems a good problem solver can readily solve are How do I open the refrigerator? How do I get at the dog biscuits on the top shelf of the kitchen cabinet? What is the best way to chew up the couch so that I will have the most fun? How do I get my owners to stay with me? What is the best way to attract attention? and so on. If your dog will be faced with these problems, stick with the fair to poor problem solvers and avoid a potential financial catastrophe.

Fast learners may be faced with such associations as Every time I'm taken for a car ride I wind up at the vet's office. They thus balk at entering the car. Or, Every time my owners argue I get hit, so I'll hide under the bed, lunging when anyone passes by. Or, Every time the phone rings everyone gets excited, so I will bark continuously and protectively while my owners are trying to carry on a conversation. Then these fast learners may learn that if they bark when someone's on the phone, they will be calmed down, distracted, and attended to, which is what they wanted in the first place. If you have the type of chaotic family life in which these associations are common, then it would be best to choose from the slow-learning breeds.

In summary, the degree of learning rate, problem solving and obedience will interact with your skill and assertiveness as a trainer, your motivation to train, the associations that are common in your family and the types of problems with which your animal will be faced. Choose wisely or else you will wind up needing to see me or one of my colleagues.

WATCHDOG AND GUARD-DOG CAPABILITY. Figure 19 compares all breeds on their watchdog capabilities. Within each level, the breeds are listed alphabetically. As you can see, the majority of the breeds are considered to be very alert watchdogs. The next-largest group are ranked as alert watchdogs. There are only 7 breeds considered less than alert. Thus almost any breed should do to alert the owner to the possibility of intruders. The very alert, small and emotionally vacillating breeds that are submissive or timid may make too much of a racket for some people. These breeds are marked with an asterisk in Table C-4 of the Appendix (pp. 370-71).

Figure 20 compares all breeds on their suitability for guard work. The breeds are listed in order of sturdiness. A natural guard may threaten intruders without any training. Such a breed would have to be trained to perform this function reliably, but the training would be in the direction of the dog's natural tendency and would proceed rapidly. An aggressive guard may attack intruders without training. In fact, training and socialization may be necessary to gain control of the dog's potentially aggressive tendencies. A dog with strong guarding instinct may have to be trained not to be aggressive to visitors.

Moderate guards may or may not be naturally protective. They would have to be trained to perform this function with any degree of reliability. The training would not be so easy as with the natural guard dogs.

Breeds rated as unsuited for guard work are categorized this way because their diminutive size or mild temperament precludes their effectiveness. Some of the larger, more territorial of these breeds could be trained for guard work, but only with great difficulty and probably only if the animal is brutalized into not trusting humans.

FIGURE 19.

Distribution of Purebred Dogs on Dimension of Watchdog Ability, with Breeds at Any One Level Arranged Alphabetically

VERY SLUGGISH	English Bulldog	
SLUGGISH	Clumber Spaniel Irish Wolfhound Scottish Deerhound	
ATTENTIVE	Alaskan Malamute Borzoi Siberian Husky	
ALERT	Afghan Hound American Foxhound American Water Spaniel Basset Hound Beagle B&T Coonhound Bloodhound Bichon Frise Border Terrier Boxer Brittany Spaniel Cocker Spaniel (pm) Cocker Spaniel (wb) Curly-coated Retriever Dalmatian	Dandie Dinmont English Cocker Spaniel English Foxhound English Setter English Springer Spaniel English Toy Spaniel Flat-coated Retriever French Bulldog Golden Retriever Gordon Setter Greyhound Irish Setter Italian Greyhound Labrador Retriever Newfoundland	Old Eng. Sheepdog (wb) Otterhound Papillon Pointer Pug Saluki Sealyham Terrier Wheaten Terrier Sussex Spaniel Tibetan Terrier Vizsla Welsh Springer Spaniel West Highland White Whippet

LEVEL OF WATCHFULNESS

FIGURE 19 (cont.)

LEVEL OF WATCHFULNESS	VERY ALERT	Affenpinscher	WH Fox Terrier	Old Eng. Sheepdog (pm)
		Akita	German SH Pointer	Pekingese
		Airedale Terrier	German WH Pointer	Pembroke W. Corgi
		Am. Staff. Bull Terrier	German Shepherd (pm)	Pomeranian
		Australian Terrier	German Shepherd (wb)	Poodle, Miniature
		Basenji	Giant Schnauzer	Poodle, Standard
		Bedlington Terrier	Great Dane	Poodle, Toy (pm)
		Belgian Malinois	Great Pyrenees	Poodle, Toy (wb)
		Belgian Sheepdog	Harrier	Puli
		Belgian Tervuren	Irish Terrier	Rhodesian Ridgeback
		Bernese Mountain Dog	Irish Water Spaniel	Rottweiler
		Boston Terrier	Japanese Spaniel	Samoyed
		Bouvier des Flangres	Keeshond	Schipperke
		Briard	Kerry Blue	Scottish Terrier
		Brussels Griffon	Komondor	Shetland Sheepdog
		Bullmastiff	Kuvasz	Shih Tzu
		Bull Terrier	Lakeland Terrier	Silky Terrier
		Cairn Terrier	Lhasa Apso	Skye Terrier
		Cardigan W. Corgi	Maltese	Staff. Bull Terrier
		Chesapeake Bay Ret.	Manchester Terrier	Standard Schnauzer
		Chihuahua	Manchester Toy Terrier	St. Bernard (pm)
		Chow Chow	Mastiff	St. Bernard (wb)
		Collie	Miniature Pinscher	Tibetan Terrier
		Dachshund	Mini. Schnauzer (pm)	Weimaraner
		Doberman Pinscher	Mini. Schnauzer (wb)	Welsh Terrier
		Field Spaniel	Norwegian Elkhound	WH Pointing Griffon
		SH Fox Terrier	Norwich Terrier	Yorkshire Terrier

FIGURE 20.

Distribution of Purebred Dogs on Dimension of Guard-dog Ability, with Breeds at Any One Level Rank-ordered on Bulkiness

LEVEL OF GUARDING ABILITY				
VERY UNSUITABLE	Clumber Spaniel Irish Setter Shetland Sheepdog			
UNSUITED	St. Bernard (pm) St. Bernard (wb) Newfoundland Great Dane Old Eng. Sheepdog (pm) Old Eng. Sheepdog (wb) Basset Hound B&T Coonhound Bloodhound Irish Water Spaniel Otterhound Borzoi Scottish Deerhound English Foxhound Golden Retriever American Foxhound Dalmatian Labrador Retriever Samoyed Skye Terrier Curly-coated Retriever Flat-coated Retriever Collie Gordon Setter English Setter English Springer Spaniel Greyhound Harrier Pointer	Field Spaniel French Bulldog Saluki Siberian Husky Vizsla Afghan Hound American Water Spaniel Dandie Dinmont Keeshond Sealyham Terrier Dachshund Scottish Terrier Wheaten Terrier English Cocker Spaniel Beagle Brittany Spaniel Cocker Spaniel (pm) Cocker Spaniel (wb) Boston Terrier Norwich Terrier Lhasa Apso Pekingese Tibetan Terrier West Highland White Basenji Cairn Terrier Pug Shih Tzu Bichon Frise	Welsh Terrier Bedlington Terrier Border Terrier SH Fox Terrier WH Fox Terrier Lakeland Terrier Poodle, Miniature Schnauzer, Mini. (pm) Schnauzer, Mini. (wb) Whippet Australian Terrier Manchester Terrier Brussels Griffon Chihuahua English Toy Spaniel Silky Terrier Yorkshire Terrier Manchester Toy Terrier Miniature Pinscher Papillon Pomeranian Affenpinscher Japanese Spaniel Maltese Poodle, Toy (pm) Poodle, Toy (wb) Italian Greyhound	

FIGURE 20 *(cont.)*

LEVEL OF GUARDING ABILITY	**MODERATE**	Irish Wolfhound WH Pointing Griffon	German SH Pointer Sussex Spaniel	Welsh Springer Spaniel
	NATURAL	Mastiff Bouvier des Flandres Irish Wolfhound Great Pyrenees Bernese Mountain Dog Akita German Shepherd (wb) Boxer Weimaraner	Chesa. Bay Retriever Dalmatian Labrador Retriever Cardigan W. Corgi Gordon Setter Norwegian Elkhound Pembroke W. Corgi German WH Pointer Irish Water Spaniel	Pointer Airedale Terrier Bull Terrier Am. Staff. Bull Terrier Poodle, Standard Kerry Blue Terrier Irish Terrier Tibetan Terrier Schipperke
	AGGRESSIVE	St. Bernard (pm) Bullmastiff Rottweiler Komondor Chow Chow Am. Staff. Bull Terrier Briard	German Shepherd (pm) Kuvasz English Bulldog Schnauzer, Giant Rhodesian Ridgeback Belgian Malinois Belgian Sheepdog	Belgian Tervuren Doberman Pinscher Staff. Bull Terrier Schnauzer, Standard Puli

9

Each Dog Is an Individual

The descriptions and comparisons of breeds in the previous chapters were based on the average temperament of a physically and sexually mature "ideal" male specimen of the breed. Pay close attention to seven key words in the last sentence: *sexually* and *physically mature, ideal specimen, male* and *breed*. It is important to keep these terms in mind as you use this book to select a dog that will fit into the environment created by your personality and life-style.

Most male dogs become *sexually* mature at about 12 months of age. At this time, testosterone (the male hormone) is secreted into the bloodstream from the testes at a level that produces sufficient sperm for procreation. Behavioral changes accompanying this sexual maturity include leg lifting when urinating and an increase in territoriality, dominance and other male behaviors. *Physical* maturity, the point at which your dog reaches its full size and strength, may come later. The rule of thumb is, the larger the breed, the longer it takes to reach physical maturity. Minuscule Chihuahuas may become physically mature in less than a year. Monstrous Mastiffs and gigantic Irish Wolfhounds take more than three years to reach their full physical proportions and adult temperament. Thus if you have an ideal, male specimen of any breed, its temperament will change as it grows, and its mature, breed-typical behavior may not show for quite a while.

The next consideration is the sex of your dog. Male and female purebred dogs differ, sometimes dramatically, in temperament. You may ask why, if this is true, I chose to generate a set of standards of temperament using males as the anchor points. The answer to this question is simple. Dogs have been bred selectively for centuries. The standards developed have always been on males of the breed, probably because the cultural systems of the people involved were, in general, male-dominated. In other words, the choice to use the male dog as the standard of the breed was an arbitrary one based on values that were probably tainted by male chauvinism. It seems to me that it would be entirely possible to develop, through selective breeding, a type of dog in which the females were reliably larger, more dominant and more aggressive than the males. This remains to be done. Perhaps someone will do it. Perhaps someone else will develop a set of standards based on females of the breeds. Neither of those activities was, however, the purpose of this book, and I am thus left to sift through a historical collection of information that has led both the A.K.C. and most experts to focus their attention on the males, using them as the standard for the breed. There is simply more information on males than on females. However, ideal female specimens differ predictably from males both physically and temperamentally. These differences were described in the last chapter. You will have to keep them in mind when choosing the gender of the breed you are interested in.

Finally, consider the words "ideal specimen" of a breed. The "ideal" for a breed is established in the United States by the writing of a breed standard. This standard, when accepted by the American Kennel Club, is supposed to guide judges in evaluating a specimen of the breed in the show ring. Since reputable breeders usually want to produce prizewinning animals, they will try to make their breeding selections more or less in accordance with the standard. They will try to "improve" their line of dogs by mating them with the winners, attempting to create "ideal" dogs. Once they believe they have succeeded, they will not want to tamper with success and will inbreed to maintain the "quality" they believe they have created.

There is a lot of room for error in this system, since it is based on the subjective judgment of many people. For example, the A.K.C.'s standards are confusing when they describe temperament. Judges vary in their application of the standard when making their show-ring evaluations. A dog may be considered optimal by one judge and less so by another. Individual judges may vary in their judgment over time, depending on factors that may include the time of day, phases of the moon and whether a judge had a good breakfast that morning. Also, there is a halo effect that surrounds breeders and individual dogs with a reputation of winning. An "ideal" dog may lose simply because it doesn't have a "rep." In addition, the evaluation by the judges is a function of the skill of the handler showing the dog and the handler's relationship with the dog.

Further, breeders will vary in their perception of the standard, their judgment of their own dog's standard characteristics and their skill at selective mating. This variation from breeder to breeder means that different breeders actually create different types or lines of the same breed. Variation will also occur within a breeder's line because the results of any one mating are only partially predictable by the nature of the mated pair. Just as each child in a family is genetically different from its siblings, it is likely for a specific mated pair of dogs to produce a somewhat different litter of puppies with each mating. This variation will occur both between and within litters. Each individual puppy from a litter has a somewhat different genetic makeup, since each is the product of a unique combination of the genes carried by different eggs and spermatozoa. In dogs, most commonly several ova are fertilized at once to produce the litter.

Finally, each individual dog will have some experiences that are different from its littermates'—and all other dogs', for that matter. These different experiences start in utero, even before the puppies are born, and become progressively magnified as the dog is born, develops, is weaned and matures. These experiences will interact with its genetic heritage, with the result that each dog is a unique individual, the joint product of its heredity and its environment.

A dog's temperamental uniqueness will be a function of the interaction of the behavioral characteristics of its family (Canidae), genus *(Canis)*, species *(familiaris)*, breed, line, litter, sex, stage of development, initial social position within the litter, ultimate social position in the family and lifetime of unique experiences.

Obviously this book cannot detail this uniqueness, since that task would take a book in itself, but I can give some general rules concerning age, litter, social position within the litter and types of unique experiences that will allow you to predict the potential temperamental characteristics of an individual dog given the anchor point of its membership in a particular breed. I have already discussed the interaction of sex and temperament in the previous chapter and will not recapitulate that information here.

Stage of Development

There are a large number of researchers who have examined the development of dogs from birth to maturity. Scott and Fuller (1965) performed the most extensive breed comparison on development. Michael Fox (1971) performed an analysis of the development of behavior and the growth of the brain. Table 9 summarizes the stages of development in puppies. Much of the puppy's behaviors serve only to get attention and solicit

TABLE 9
Natural Periods of Development in Dogs

Stage	Initial Point	Major Process	Change in Social Relationships
Neonatal	Birth	Neonatal nutrition	Begin
Transition	(2 weeks) eyes open	Transition to adult sensory, motor and psychological capacities	Increasing complexity based on new behavior patterns
Socialization	(3 weeks) Rapid, stable conditioning, startle to sound, tail wagging	Formation of primary social relationships	Partial independence of mother, increasing response to littermates
Juvenile	(12 weeks)	Rapid growth, development of motor skills	Increasing independence of mother

care. Usually these behaviors consist of whining and yelping, rudimentary investigation, elimination and sucking. Puppies react to things that make them uncomfortable with the few behaviors they have at their disposal, yelping and moving randomly. They also exhibit a number of involuntary reflexes.

During this stage their eyes are closed and all their behavior serves two functions, obtaining nutrition and obtaining warmth by snuggling.

The puppy is not self-sufficient. It needs its mother for food, to maintain its temperature and even to urinate and defecate. Its mother must lick its hindquarters to stimulate that reflex. A puppy in this stage of development can be considered a bundle of reflexes and tropisms all directed toward maintaining its bodily needs through its mother. A summary of these reflexes is presented in Table 10.

What you are able to observe during the neonatal stage is the relative inactivity among puppies. Perhaps you will also be able to identify neurological damage if the puppy doesn't exhibit the appropriate reflexes at the right time. However, this would not be the best time to choose a puppy.

As the puppy gets older, some of its reflexes disappear and others develop. At about 14 days of age, puppies open their eyes and enter the transitional stage. This lasts for about seven days, or until the puppy is 20 to 21 days old. During this stage the puppy is profoundly reorganizing its behavior and beginning to sense more of the environment. It can also move around on its own.

The most important stage for you as a potential owner to observe and participate in begins at three weeks of age and ends at twelve weeks. During this time the puppy forms permanent social relationships. This is called the imprinting period. Most students of dog behavior fix 7 weeks of age as the optimal imprinting time. It is the time in your dog's life when it is most susceptible to behavioral shaping by its caretakers. If during this time the dog is isolated in a cage, it will not readily be able thereafter to form social relationships with you or other dogs. If your puppy is kept exclusively with dogs, then it will not be able to form a bond easily with its human owners. Thus it is best for a pet during this period to have plenty of human contact but also to have contact with other dogs.

TABLE 10
Summary of Puppy Reflexes

Age in Days	Stimulus	Response
1–15	1. *Crossed extensor:* Pinch one hind foot between your fingers.	The pinched foot withdraws while the other foot extends.
1–17	2. *Magnus:* Turn the head to one side.	The legs on the side to which the head is turned extend while the others withdraw.
1–13	3. *Rooting:* Form a cup with your hand and touch both sides of the puppy's muzzle with the cupped hand.	The puppy will crawl forward, maintaining contact with the cupped hand.
1–22	4. *Urination:* Tickling or stroking external genitalia.	Urination.
1–4	5. *Breathing:* Rubbing the puppy's belly.	Causes the puppy to take a breath.
1–18	6. *Head Turning:* Stroking one side of the face or behind the ear.	Head is turned toward the side of stimulation.
Puppylike: 1–19 Adultlike: 24–	7. *Touch Muscle:* Stroking skin on back.	Rapid contraction of skin.
Puppylike: 1–15 Adultlike: 25–	8. *Pain Withdrawal:* Pinching foot between toes.	Withdrawal of limb, distress cries and avoidance.
1–	9. *Touch Blink Reflex:* Touching of closed eye.	The muscles around the eye contract in a blink.
4–	10. *Light Blink Reflex:* Light shining in eyes.	Blink.
1–4	11. *Flexor Dominance:* When animal is picked up by back of neck.	All legs withdrawn to body.
4–18	12. *Extensor Dominance:* When puppy is picked up by back of neck.	All four legs extended outward.
Placing: 5 days ± 1.25 Supporting: 10 days ± 1	13. *Forelimb Placing and Supporting:* Lowering a blindfolded puppy to table surface.	Forelegs extended to hold weight of puppy when they touch surface.
Placing: 8 days ± 1.25 Supporting: 15 days ± 1	14. *Hind-limb Placing and Supporting:* Lowering blindfolded puppy to table surface.	Hind legs extended to hold weight of puppy when they touch surface.
15 days 2	15. *Sitting Upright.*	Puppy is able to balance while sitting.
21 days 1	16. *Standing Upright.*	Puppy is able to stand on all fours.
24 days 2	17. *Auditory Startle:* Loud sudden noise like clapping of hands.	The legs and head are pulled in toward the body, and eyes blink.
24 days 1.5	18. *Auditory Orientation:* A sound stimulus to side of puppy.	Head is turned toward the source of the sound.
24 days 1	19. *Visual Orientation:* A light or moving object to side of puppy.	The head is turned toward source of visual stimulation.
27 days 1	20. *Visual Cliff:* The puppy is placed on the edge of table or bed.	Puppy hesitates or pulls back from edge; will not step off edge.

The last two stages are the juvenile period, from 12 weeks to 6 months, and adulthood, when any tendencies seen in the socialization period become more fixed. It is during the juvenile period that your puppy is most susceptible to change, so problem behavior should be discouraged and good behavior encouraged. If this is not done at this point, it becomes much harder, although not impossible, to change. An example is aggressive food guarding. Many puppies during the juvenile period will aggressively snap and bite if you approach while they are eating or chewing a bone. This is natural, especially for the more aggressive and/or territorial breeds. You have the best opportunity to change this behavior when your puppy is still relatively small. His teeth, although sharp, are not formidable. You could stand a few bites by this fuzzy little monster while you teach him to allow you and every member of the family to take food or a bone away from him. Then you can eliminate these problems before they get worse. Remember, if problems are not corrected, they will grow as your dog grows. Biting is a problem that is directly proportional to the length of your dog's teeth and the strength of his jaws. Running away is a problem that is directly proportional to the length and strength of your dog's legs.

Temperament and Learning

Whatever behavior patterns your dog has because of genetic endowment usually can be modified through learning. Just as a sculptor shapes his clay, so do the processes of learning shape behavior. And what is the clay? What is modified by the environment? The answer is genetically organized species-typical and breed-typical behavior.

Conversely, each breed's genetic endowment will shape the direction in which the environment affects the breed. This happens in a number of ways. One way relates to the direction of change. Active breeds are more readily changed in the direction of being more active than are inactive breeds, and vice versa. Also, it is more difficult to make dominant breeds submissive, gentle breeds vigorous, variable breeds constant, emotionally vacillating breeds stable, solitary breeds sociable than it would be to push them further along on these dimensions. This means that it takes a concerted effort to change a breed in a direction opposite to its natural tendencies, but no effort at all to change a breed in a direction that increases its temperamental propensities.

I have tried to build this concept into my recommendations to you. A good match between breed temperament and owner personality should naturally accentuate canine qualities the owner regards as positive and decrease those considered negative. However, a bad match may do the opposite. Read pages 75 to 99 of my previous book, *Help! This Animal Is Driving Me Crazy** for a discussion of the effects of reward and punishment on changing behavior.

Obviously, all this interacts with the learning-ability dimensions of trainability, problem-solving ability and obedience. The better a dog's trainability and obedience, the easier it is to change its basic temperamental characteristics. Conversely, if a dog is a slow learner, poor in obedience but a good problem solver, it may react to your attempts to change its temperament as a problem to solve. It may solve this problem in ways that you may not expect. For example, a dominant breed that is typically aggressive toward strange dogs may inhibit its aggression in your presence, but lash out and savagely attack the dog to which it has been made to submit when you are not around. The variations on this theme are practically unlimited.

Line and Litter

As I have already mentioned, some breeders may have developed special temperamental characteristics in their specific line. Reputable breeders may inform you of this, but take what they say with a grain of salt. Most people have a tendency to highlight the positive and underplay the negative, especially if they have a vested interest in the product they are selling. Good breeders have both an economic interest and an emotional investment in their product. They may be genuinely proud of

*Tortora, D. F. *Help! This Animal Is Driving Me Crazy.* 1977. Hardcover: New York, Playboy Press ($10.95). Paperback: New York, Wideview Press ($4.95).

what they have worked to perfect and may be insulted or defensive at the slightest suggestion of a problem with their line.

Thus it may take a modicum of people savvy to tease out the truth. For example, if a male breeder of the more aggressive breeds comes on to you as Mr. Macho and he is the one making the breeding decision, it's probably a good bet that he is consciously or, at the very least, unconsciously breeding for dominance, aggression, vigor, etc. The converse may also be true. So pay close attention not only to what breeders say about their specific line, but also what they don't say. What they communicate nonverbally may be as important as what they tell you.

This brings me to variation within and between litters. Most likely you will not have direct access to information about between-litter variation. If the breeders are observant, and the good ones usually are, they will be able to tell you that _____ bitch usually throws _____ puppies. The blanks refer to the name of the delivering bitch and the characteristics of the puppies. They may also be able to tell you that "this litter of puppies seems quieter (or more active, or what-have-you) than usual." This would be valuable information.

If you have the opportunity, you should observe the entire litter as early as three weeks of age. I don't mean you should play with them. Just sit quietly and watch for a couple of hours. If you can do this, you may be able to form some idea about the behavior of individual puppies in comparison with the rest of the litter. Keep in mind your point of reference. If you observe that a particular puppy is inactive, you are really saying that the puppy is inactive for that specific litter. If the breed is one of the very active types and the litter is generally active, your inactive puppy may turn out to be a very active dog in comparison with other dogs.

Also keep in mind that one observation is not enough to enable you to form an opinion. You would need to go back repeatedly and observe the litter at various times of day and at various ages of development to form a reliable judgment. The judgments you will be forming should include consideration of the temperamental dimensions described in the previous chapters.

Here are some examples of the questions you will be endeavoring to answer: How active are the puppies? Does one or more of the puppies stand out by doing more things per unit of time than the rest? Does a puppy seem to sleep more than the rest? Are these differences consistent over time or do they change as the puppies mature? You will notice that all the puppies get more active as they mature, but remember that you are evaluating relative activity. If you are suited to an inactive dog, then choose one of the most consistently inactive puppies. This will be difficult; there is a natural tendency to choose the most active puppies, since they appear to be the most playful. Keep in mind that a playful puppy is going to mature, and if you or your family are not prepared for continuous activity, this playfulness may drive you crazy in the adult dog.

Most puppies are gentle and variable in behavior, but some are more so than others. Observe the relative vigor and variability of their behavior. Some puppies may jump and pound into their littermates and others may behave quite demurely. Some puppies are more readily distractable than others. When they are playing, make a noise and see which puppies stop what they are doing and which do not. Again, you are looking for consistency over time.

Dominance within the litter may be related to the relative size of the puppies. The largest puppy has probably won the battle for the most productive teat and thus, being better nursed, has been able to grow faster than its littermates. Dominance is also related to who eats first at the food bowl, who gets the bone or chew toy and is able to keep it, and who literally winds up on top—that is, standing over most of the other puppies. Dominance toward people can be predicted by observing which puppy assertively approaches a stranger and which timidly hangs back. The key, of course, is consistency over time.

Territoriality is related to guarding food or objects from littermates and people: the more territoriality, the more guarding. Can you walk up and take a bone from a puppy with impunity, or does it growl and snap at you? These tendencies become more pronounced as the puppy matures.

Emotional stability may be related to irritable snapping in

puppies. If the puppy gets hurt, does it snap? Can it be picked up and held without snapping? Can it be played with roughly without snapping and/or shying away?

Sociability refers to the speed of formation of affectional bonds. During their seventh week most puppies are starting to form bonds. The more people a puppy comes in contact with, the more bonds it will form. Sociable behavior may be predicted also from the tendency in a puppy to follow the person with whom it has just played. If you have just played with all the puppies in the litter, having made sure to give each equal treatment, and you get up and walk away, which puppies will follow you? And which puppies will follow you consistently over time?

Now here's the rub. After you have made all these painstaking observations, you still cannot be sure of the puppy's potential adult behavior. This is true for two reasons.

First, adult behavior in a dog is a product of accumulated experience interacting with the breed's and the individual puppy's temperament. Thus one can turn a comparatively quiet puppy into a hellion by consistently rewarding active playful behaviors. Or you could change a very solitary puppy into a more sociable animal by making sure it has plenty of pleasant experiences with a lot of people. Or conversely, you could turn a very sociable puppy into a fearful hermit by arranging that it rarely interacts with others besides you and when it does it gets hurt. However, I must repeat that the probability and degree of change are a function of the basic temperament of the breed and the puppy. It is far easier to make a moderate to solitary breed very solitary than to make a very sociable breed equally solitary.

Second, changes in puppy behavior, barring extremes in experience, are a function of the breed's characteristic pattern of development. Scott and Fuller (1965) measured the changes in behavior of five breeds as they developed. Let's consider their results concerning the changes in one measurement, the occurrence of fights and one-sided attacks on other puppies in two different breeds: the Basenji, a breed that is aggressive toward strange dogs; and the Sheltie, which is quite the opposite.

Basenjis at five weeks of age fight more but attack less than Shelties. Basenjis attack more often as they grow older and Shelties attack less as they grow older. At fifty-two weeks the Basenjis are acting characteristically aggressive and the Shelties characteristically unaggressive. This means that if you put together a mixed litter of Basenjis and Shelties and you used attack rate as your measure of aggression, you would probably judge the Basenji puppy as unaggressive and the Sheltie puppy as a very aggressive pup. If you wanted a dog that was unaggressive with strange dogs, and you mistakenly chose the Basenji, you would be sadly disappointed when the dog matured.

The problem, as I have said before, is that we really don't have data on the development of all 123 breeds of dogs. In fact, we have extensive data on only 5 breeds. So we really don't know for sure how to predict adult behavior from puppy behavior. Therefore, right now the best predictor of adult behavior is the typical behavior of the breed.

However, I can give you a rule of thumb based on my accumulated experiences as a psychologist and on the principle of *behavioral* divergence. Behavioral divergence means that barring extreme experiences and training, a puppy will tend to develop in the direction of the breed's characteristic temperament. This rule can be summarized as follows: The more a puppy exhibits the typical characteristics of the breed, the more it will when it matures. Conversely, if a puppy shows characteristics opposite to those of the breed, it will change toward the breed's characteristics as it matures. I have indicated this relationship in Table 11 for a number of dimensions of temperament.

Now that you have selected a puppy, the fun really begins. Since you already have some idea of how your puppy is going to turn out, you can start intelligently arranging its environment so that it will have appropriate experiences. These experiences, the training, the socialization and so on can complement a puppy's basic breed-specific temperament, thereby accentuating desired characteristics. Extensively socializing a sociable puppy will make it more sociable than is typical for the breed. Or you can arrange to give your puppy experiences

TABLE 11

Prediction of Adult Behavior Based upon the Breed's Typical Temperament and the Puppy's Individual Behavior

Puppy Behavior	Breed Type	The Adult Will Become:
Active	Active	Most active
Inactive	Active	More active
Active	Inactive	Less active
Inactive	Inactive	Least active
Vigorous	Vigorous	Most vigorous
Gentle	Vigorous	More vigorous
Vigorous	Gentle	More gentle
Gentle	Gentle	Most gentle
Variable	Variable	Most variable
Constant	Variable	More variable
Variable	Constant	More constant
Constant	Constant	Most constant
Dominant	Dominant	Most dominant
Submissive	Dominant	More dominant
Dominant	Submissive	More submissive
Submissive	Submissive	Most submissive
Emotionally stable	Stable	Most stable
Emotionally vacillant	Stable	More stable
Emotionally stable	Vacillant	More vacillant
Emotionally vacillant	Vacillant	Most vacillant
Sociable	Sociable	Most sociable
Solitary	Sociable	More sociable
Sociable	Solitary	More solitary
Solitary	Solitary	Most solitary

opposite to its breed characteristics, thereby reducing them somewhat.

If you arrange its experiences intelligently, you will be able, within limits, to change your puppy's personality. Not only can you select a puppy to suit your personality and life-style: you can shape a puppy to form a perfect match to your uniqueness. Unfortunately, you can also change your puppy's temperament to be unsuitable to your life-style. It's all up to you.

Appendix A

Summary Table of the Physical Characteristics and Behavioral Descriptions of All Purebred Dogs, Arranged According to the Six Breed Types: Sporting Dogs, Hounds, Working Dogs, Terriers, Toy Dogs, Non-Sporting Dogs.

Breed Type	Breed	Height/Weight	Coat
Sporting	**Pointer** BR: Male 2.45 Female 2.24	Male: 25–28" 55–75 lbs. Fem: 23–26" 45–65 lbs.	Short
Sporting	**German Shorthaired Pointer** BR: Male 2.65 Female 2.39	Male: 23–25" 55–70 lbs. Fem: 21–23" 45–60 lbs.	Short
Sporting	**German Wirehaired Pointer** BR: Male 2.60 Female 2.39	Male: 24–26" 60–75 lbs. Fem: 22–24" 50–60 lbs.	Short, wiry
Sporting	**Chesapeake Bay Retriever** BR: Male 2.86 Female 2.67	Male: 23–26" 65–75 lbs. Fem: 21–24" 55–65 lbs.	Thick, short; tends to wave over body
Sporting	**Curly-coated Retriever** BR: Male 2.77 Female 2.57	23½" 65 lbs.	Tight curl
Sporting	**Flat-coated Retriever** BR: Male 2.83 Female 2.61	23" 60–70 lbs.	Dense and flat
Sporting	**Golden Retriever** BR: Male 2.98 Female 2.89	Male: 23–24" 65–75 lbs. Fem: 21½–22½" 60–70 lbs.	Dense and straight or wavy
Sporting	**Labrador Retriever** BR: Male 2.87 Female 2.79	Male: 22½–24½" 60–75 lbs. Fem: 21½–23½" 55–70 lbs.	Short and dense
Sporting	**English Setter** BR: Male 2.60 Female 2.29	Male: 25" 60–70 lbs. Fem: 24" 50–60 lbs.	Flat and long
Sporting	**Gordon Setter** BR: Male 2.65 Female 2.35	Male: 24–27" 55–80 lbs. Fem: 23–26" 40–70 lbs.	Med. long, wavy, silky

BR = Bulk Ratio

Color	Grooming	Function	Behavioral Description According to AKC
Liver; black; lemon; orange or combo. with white	2 × 10 min. Trim: None Shed: Ordinary	Points	Even-tempered, congenial.
Solid liver; liver and white spotted	2 × 10 min. Trim: None Shed: Ordinary	Points bird dog and retriever	Sound temperament.
Solid liver; liver and white; liver roan	2 × 15 min. Trim: Some Shed: Ordinary	Points	Energetic and aloof, but not unfriendly; one-family dog.
Dark brown to faded tan to dead-grass to dull straw	2 × 10 min. Trim: None Shed: Ordinary	Retrieves	Prowess in icy water, courageous and willing to work.
Black or liver	2 × 10 min. Trim: Some Shed: Ordinary	Retrieves	Strong, smart, upstanding, active, faithful companion, enduring and intelligent; affectionate; loves water.
Black or liver	2 × 10 min. Trim: Some Shed: Ordinary	Retrieves	Bright, active and loves water.
Shades of gold	1 × 45 min. Trim: Some Shed: Ordinary	Retrieves Guides the blind	Excellent swimmer, eager, alert, self-confident, powerful, active.
Black; yellow; chocolate	2 × 10 min. Trim: None Shed: Ordinary	Retrieves Guides the blind	Active and strong.
Black, white and tan; black, lemon, orange or liver with white; blue, lemon, orange, or liver belton; solid white	1 × 45 min. Trim: Some Shed: Ordinary	Pointing and flushing	Mild, sweet disposition, intelligent, aristocratic, ideal companion, needs exercise, better in suburbs than city.
Black with tan markings; chestnut; mahogany	1 × 45 min. Trim: Some Shed: Ordinary	Pointing and flushing	Good pet, faithful gun dog, mannerly, eager to please, gentle with children, most pettable pet, loyal family guard.

Breed Type	Breed	Height/Weight	Coat
Sporting	**Irish Setter** BR: Male 2.57 Female 2.40	Male: 27" 70 lbs. Fem: 25" 60 lbs.	Long, silky and feathery
Sporting	**American Water** **Spaniel** BR: Male 2.21 Female 1.97	Male: 15–18" 28–45 lbs. Fem: 15–18" 25–40 lbs.	Close curl
Sporting	**Brittany Spaniel** BR: Male 1.84 Female 1.61	17½–20½" 30–40 lbs.	Short, dense, flat or wavy
Sporting	**Clumber Spaniel** BR: Male 3.29 Female 2.57	17–18" Male: 55–60 lbs. Fem: 35–55 lbs.	Short, silky, wavy
Sporting	**Cocker Spaniel** BR: Male 1.77 Female 1.79	Male: 15" 25–28 lbs. Fem: 14" 25 lbs.	Soft, long, slightly wavy
Sporting	**English Cocker** **Spaniel** BR: Male 1.88 Female 1.87	Male: 16–17" 28–34 lbs. Fem: 15–16" 26–32 lbs.	Flat or wavy, med. in length
Sporting	**English Springer** **Spaniel** BR: Male 2.60 Female 2.47	Male: 20" 49–55 lbs. Fem. 19" 44–50 lbs.	Long, smooth coat
Sporting	**Field Spaniel** BR: Male 2.36 Female 2.18	18" 35–50 lbs.	Short to med., slightly wavy or flat
Sporting	**Irish Water** **Spaniel** BR: Male 2.61 Female 2.46	Male: 22–24" 55–65 lbs. Fem: 21–23" 45–58 lbs.	Tight curls

BR = Bulk Ratio

Color	Grooming	Function	Behavioral Description According to A.K.C.
Mahogany; chestnut red	1 × 45 min. Trim: Some Shed: Ordinary	Pointing and flushing	Good hunting companion, gay, courageous, devil-may-care, bold & gentle sweet-natured, rollicking personality.
Solid liver; dark chocolate	1 × 30 min. Trim: Some Shed: Ordinary	Flushing and retrieving	Good swimmer, great hunter, desire to please, learns quickly, efficient watchdog, fits family circle.
Orange or liver with white	2 × 5 min. Trim: Some Shed: Ordinary	Pointing and retrieving	Strong, virorous, energetic and quick.
Lemon or orange with white	2 × 10 min. Trim: Some Shed: Ordinary	Flushing and retrieving	Slow worker, sure finder, splendid retriever.
Black, tan or any solid color	2 × 45 min. Trim: Some Shed: Ordinary	Flushing and retrieving	Great lover of family and home, ordinarily trustworthy and adaptable
Solid colors; parti-colored	2 × 45 Trim: Some Shed: Ordinary	Flushing and retrieving	Loving and faithful to master and household, alert, courageous, intelligent, merry disposition, not quarrelsome, responsive and willing worker
Liver or black with white; tricolors	1 × 45 min. Trim: Some Shed: Ordinary	Flushing and retrieving	Friendly, eager to please, quick to learn, willing to obey.
Black; liver; golden liver; mahogany red; roan	2 × 5 min. Trim: Some Shed: Ordinary	Flushing and retrieving	Well-balanced, noble, upstanding, built for activity & endurance, beauty, utility, unusual docility & instinct.
Solid liver	1 × 60 min. Trim: Profess. Shed: Little	Flushing and retrieving	Loyal to master, forbidding to strangers, grand water dog, smart, upstanding, strong, intelligent, rugged endurance, bolt eagerness of temperament.

Breed Type	Breed	Height/Weight	Coat
Sporting	**Sussex Spaniel** BR: Male 2.50 Female 2.28	15–16" 35–45 lbs.	Med.-long, wavy
Sporting	**Welsh Springer Spaniel** BR: Male 2.29 Female 2.09	17" 40 lbs.	Med.-long, flat, silky
Sporting	**Vizsla (Hungarian Pointer)** BR: Male 2.39 Female 2.16	Male: 22–24" 50–60 lbs. Fem: 21–23"	Short, silky
Sporting	**Weimaraner** BR: Male 2.98 Female 2.60	Male: 25–27" 70–85 lbs. Fem: 23–25" 55–70 lbs.	Short, sleek
Sporting	**Wirehaired Pointing Griffon** BR: Male 2.67 Female 2.44	Male: 21½–23½" 60 lbs. Fem: 19½–21½" 50 lbs.	Short, wiry
Hound	**Afghan Hound** BR: Male 2.32 Female 2.00	Male: 27–29" 60–70 lbs. Fem: 25" 50 lbs.	Long, soft and flowing
Hound	**Basenji** BR: Male 1.40 Female 1.36	Male: 17–28" 24 lbs.–25 lbs. Fem: 16–17" 22 lbs.–23 lbs.	Short
Hound	**Basset Hound** BR: Male 4.00 Female 3.86	11–14" 40–60 lbs.	Short
Hound	**Beagle** (2 classes) BR: Male 1.79 Female 1.65	13" and under 15–20 lbs. Over 13–15" 20–30 lbs.	Short

BR = Bulk Ratio

Color	Grooming	Function	Behavioral Description According to A.K.C.
Golden liver	2 × 10 min. Trim: Some Shed: Ordinary	Flushing and retrieving	Normal dog, not too difficult to train; when properly taught, becomes excellent hunter, mostly abroad; cheerful and tractable disposition.
Dark, rich red and white	2 × 10 min. Trim: Some Shed: Ordinary	Flushing and retrieving	Excellent water dog, hardworking, faithful, willing worker, excellent nose, but if not trained becomes lone hunter and difficult to handle.
Solid rusty gold; dark sandy yellow	2 × 5 min. Trim: None Shed: Ordinary	Pointing and retrieving	Power and drive in the field, tractable and affectionate companion in the home, above average learning, lively, gentle and demonstratively affectionate, fearless and protective.
Mouse gray; silver gray	2 × 10 min. Trim: None Shed: Ordinary	Pointing and retrieving	Friendly, fearless, alert and obedient. This dog is not happy when kenneled; is accustomed to being member of family.
Gray and chestnut; chestnut	1 × 15 min. Trim: Some Shed: Ordinary	Pointing and retrieving	Strong, vigorous.
All colors	1 × 60 min. Trim: None Shed: Ordinary	Hunting by sight and scent	Withstands any temperatures, splendid all-around dog. Aloof and dignified, yet gay.
Red, black or tan with white	1 × 5 min. Trim: None Shed: Little	Pointing, tracking, and retrieving	Loves children and tireless at play. Quits easily when master stops. Should not bark, but is not mute.
Any hound color; black, tan and white	2 × 10 min. Trim: None Shed: Ordinary	Hunting by scent	Temperament is mild, never sharp or timid. Capable of great endurance in the field and is extreme in its devotion.
Any hound color; black, tan and white	2 × 5 min. Trim: None Shed: Ordinary	Hunting by scent	Solid and big for his inches, with the wear-and-tear look of the hound.

Breed Type	Breed	Height/Weight	Coat
Hound	**Black and Tan Coonhound** BR: Male 3.27 Female 2.92	Male: 25–27″ 80–90 lbs. Fem: 23–25″ 65–75 lbs.	Short
Hound	**Bloodhound** BR: Male 3.85 Female 3.75	Male: 25–27″ 90–110 lbs. Fem: 23–25″ 80–100 lbs.	Short
Hound	**Borzoi** **(Russian Wolf-** **hound)** BR: Male 3.13 Female 2.73	Male: 27½–30″ 75–105 lbs. Fem: 25½–29½″ 60–90 lbs.	Long, silky flat or wavy
Hound	**Dachshund** **(Standard)** **(Miniature)** BR: Male 2.0 Female 1.8	9½″ 6–22 lbs. 5″ less than 10 lbs.	1. Long 2. Short 3. Wiry
Hound	**American** **Foxhound** BR: Male 2.87 Female 2.78	Male: 22–25″ 65–70 lbs. Fem: 21–24″ 60–65 lbs.	Short
Hound	**English** **Foxhound** BR: Male 3.02 Female 2.82	Male: 24″ 70–75 lbs. Fem: 23″	Short
Hound	**Greyhound** BR: Male 2.45 Female 2.27	Male: 27–28″ 65–70 lbs. Fem: 27–28″ 60–65 lbs.	Short
Hound	**Harrier** BR: Male 2.5 Female 2.3	19–21″ 40–60 lbs.	Short
Hound	**Irish Wolf-** **hound** BR: Male 3.75 Female 3.50	Male: 32″+ 120 lbs.+ Fem: 30″+ 105 lbs.+	Short, med. rough
Hound	**Norwegian** **Elkhound** BR: Male 2.68 Female 2.46	Male: 20½″ 55 lbs. Fem: 19½″ 48 lbs.	Long, dense

BR = Bulk Ratio

Color	Grooming	Function	Behavioral Description According to A.K.C.
Black with tan markings	2 × 10 min. Trim: None Shed: Ordinary	Hunting by scent	Good for hunting deer, mt. lions, bears, and other large game. Powerful, agile, alert, friendly, eager and aggressive.
Black or red with tan; tawny	2 × 10 min. Trim: None Shed: Ordinary	Hunting by scent	Extremely affectionate, not quarrelsome with companions or other dogs. somewhat shy and equally sensitive to kindness or correction; one of the most docile breeds. Does not attack what it is trailing.
Any color or combination	3 × 10 min. Trim: Some Shed: Male ordinary Female heavy	Hunting by scent	Courageous, agile and elegant.
Red; black and tan	2 × 10 min. 2 × 5 min. 7 × 10 min. Only wiry needs trim Shed: Ordinary	House pet	Odorless, clever, alert. Outdoors: hardy, vigorous, tireless. Indoors: affectionate, responsive and companionable in restful mood, hilarious in play.
Any color	2 × 5 min. Trim: None Shed: Ordinary	Hunting by scent	Field-trial hounds. Speed and jealous nature. Gun hounds: slow trailing and good voice. Race hounds: very fast. Packhounds: safe in packs.
Any hound color: black, tan and white	2 × 5 min. Trim: None Shed: Ordinary	Hunting by scent	(None)
Any color	2 × 5 min. Trim: None Shed: Ordinary	Hunting by sight and racing	Has always had cultural and aristocratic background. Lovable and tractable.
Black, tan and white	2 × 5 min. Trim: None Shed: Ordinary	Hunting by scent	Active, full of strength and quality.
Gray; brindle; red; black; white; fawn	7 × 10 min. Trim: Some Shed: Ordinary	Pet	Gentle-hearted, quiet-mannered, dignified.
Silver gray tipped with black	2 × 15 min. Trim: None Shed: Ordinary to heavy	Hunting by scent; guarding	Bold, energetic, effective guardian, yet normally friendly; great dignity; independent in character. Quick to learn, reliable, fearless

Breed Type	Breed	Height/Weight	Coat
Hound	**Otterhound** BR: Male 3.73 Female 3.44	Male: 24–27″ 75–115 lbs. Fem: 22–26″ 65–100 lbs.	Long, rough and woolly
Hound	**Rhodesian** **Ridgeback** BR: Male 2.88 Female 2.60	Male: 25–27″ 75 lbs. Fem. 24–26″ 65 lbs.	Short, dense, sleek, glossy

Hound	**Saluki**
	BR: Male 2.35
	      Female 2.15
		Male: 23–28″
		60 lbs.
		Fem: Somewhat
		   smaller
			Short on body,
			long on ears
			and tail, silky

Hound	**Scottish Deer-** **hound** BR: Male 3.145 Female 3.04	Male: 30–32″ 85–110 lbs. Fem. 28″+ 75–95 lbs.	Wiry, harsh, medium
Hound	**Whippet** BR: Male 1.22 Female 1.12	Male: 19–22″ 25 lbs. Fem: 18–21″ around 25 lbs.	Short
Working	**Akita** BR: Male 3.43 Female 3.20	Male 26–28″ 85–100 lbs. Fem: 24–26″ 75–85 lbs.	Short, thick, and harsh
Working	**Alaskan Mala-** **mute** BR: Male 3.40 Female 3.26	Male: 25″ 85 lbs. Fem: 23″ 75 lbs.	Dense, med.- long

BR = Bulk Ratio

Color	Grooming	Function	Behavioral Description According to A.K.C.
Any color or combination	1 × 60 min. Trim: None Shed: Ordinary	Hunting by scent	Not very popular in U.S. Good working qualities and unfailing devotion to master; amiable and boisterous; inquisitive; good in water.
Light wheaten to red wheaten	2 × 10 min. Trim: None Shed: Ordinary	Hunting by scent and guarding	Active, great endurance, clean, easy to keep, never noisy or quarrelsome; desire to please, trains easily; good nature and likes children.
Any color but black	2 × 10 min. Trim: None Shed: Ordinary	Hunting by sight	Tremendous speed, great attachment to master, affectionate without being demonstrative, good watchdog but not aggressive.
Dark blue; gray; brindle; yellow; red; sandy; red fawn	1 × 45 min. Trim: Some Shed: Ordinary	Hunting by sight	Keen scent; strong, quiet, dignified, alert and although not agressive has great persistence and courage when necessary.
Any color	2 × 5 min. Trim: None Shed: Ordinary	Hunting by sight, racing	Charming, affectionate, and intelligent. Keen when racing. In the home is quiet, dignified, unobtrusive, highly decorative, never snappy or barky though excellent watchdog, not delicate or difficult to care for–ideal dual-purpose small dog.
White; brindle; pinto	2 × 15 min. Trim: None Shed: Ordinary	Guarding	Dignity, good nature, alert, courageous, docile, very affectionate with family and friends and thrives on companionship. Aggressive toward other dogs
Black; gray; cinnamon, all with white	2 × 20 min. Trim: None Shed: Ordinary	Pulling sleds	Very fond of people and especially children, who enjoy driving them to sleds.

Breed Type	Breed	Height/Weight	Coat
Working	**Belgian Malinois** BR: Male 2.80 Female 2.61	Male: 24–26″ 65–75 lbs. Fem: 22–24″ 55–65 lbs.	Dense, short and straight
Working	**Belgian Sheep- dog** BR: Male 2.80 Female 2.61	Male: 24–26″ 65–75 lbs. Fem: 22–24″ 55–65 lbs.	Dense, long
Working	**Belgian Tervuren** BR: Male 2.80 Female 2.61	Male: 24–26″ 65–75 lbs. Fem: 22–24″ 55–65 lbs.	Dense, long
Working	**Bernese Moun- tain Dog** BR: Male 3.63 Female 3.51	Male: 23–27½″ 80–105 lbs. Fem: 21–26″ 75–90 lbs.	Med.-long, silky, wavy
Working	**Bouvier des Flandres** BR: Male 3.92 Female 3.52	Male: 23½–27½″ 90–110 lbs. Fem: 22¾″ + 90–95 lbs.	Med, rough, wiry and thick
Working	**Boxer** BR: Male 2.95 Female 2.65	Male: 22½–25″ around 70 lbs. Fem: 21–23½″	Short
Working	**Briard** BR: Male 3.40 Female 3.16	Male: 23–27″ 80–90 lbs. Fem. 22–25½″ 70–80 lbs.	Long, slightly wavy

BR = Bulk Ratio

Color	Grooming	Function	Behavioral Description According to A.K.C.
Similar to German Shepherd	7 × 20 min. Trim: None Shed: Ordinary; Seasonally heavy	Herding and guarding	Strong, agile, well muscled, alert and full of life.
Black	7 × 20 min. Trim: None Shed: Ordinary	Herding and guarding	Intelligent, devoted to master, alert, protective of person and property. Watchful, attentive and always in motion. Affectionate with those it knows. Friendly, zealous and possessive.
Rich fawn to mahogany with black overlay	7 × 20 min. Trim: None Shed: Ordinary	Herding and guarding	Same as above.
Black with russet brown or deep tan markings	2 × 15 min. Trim: Some Shed: Ordinary	Hauling, herding and guarding	Hardy, not too much grooming, exceptionally faithful and once having centered its affection on an individual does not fawn upon or make friends with strangers.
Fawn to black; pepper and salt; gray and brindle	1 × 30 min. Trim: Profess. Shed: Little	Herding, guarding and guiding the blind	Compact body, powerful and alert.
Fawn; brindle	2 × 10 min. Trim: None Shed: Ordinary	Guarding	Large degree of courage, ability to defend, as well as aggressiveness when needed. Is devoted to master. With family and friends is playful, yet patient and stoical with children. Wary of strangers. Fearless if threatened. Responds to friendly overtures. Intelligent, affectionate and tractable to discipline.
Any color but white	1 × 90 min. Trim: Some Shed: Ordinary	Herding and guarding	Learns slowly, but has retentive memory. Not difficult to raise, seldom barks unless necessary as warning. Does not wander. Is well mannered, vigorous, alert.

Breed Type	Breed	Height/Weight	Coat
Working	**Bullmastiff** BR: Male 4.62 Female 4.40	Male: 25–27″ 110–130 lbs. Fem: 24–26″ 100–120 lbs.	Short
Working	**Collie (Modern Rough- coated)**	Male: 24–26″ 60–75 lbs. Fem: 22–24″ 50–65 lbs.	Long, dense, straight
Working	**Collie (Smooth-coated)** BR: Male 2.70 Female 2.50	Male: 24–26″ 60–75 lbs. Fem: 22–24″ 50–65 lbs.	Short and straight
Working	**Doberman Pinscher** BR: Male 2.69 Female 2.50	Male: 26–28″ 70–75 lbs. Fem: 24–26″ 60–65 lbs.	Short
Working	**German Shep- herd** BR: Male 3.30 Female 2.93	Male: 24–26″ 80–85 lbs. Fem: 22–24″ 65–70 lbs.	Med.-dense
Working	**Giant Schnauzer** BR: Male 3.21 Female 3.00	Male: 25½–27½″ 75–95 lbs. Fem: 23½–25½″	In part, kept short, dense and wiry
Working	**Great Dane** BR: Male 4.50 Female 4.29	Male: 30″+ 135–150 lbs. Fem: 28″+ 120–135 lbs.	Short

BR = Bulk Ratio

Color	Grooming	Function	Behavioral Description According to A.K.C.
Red; fawn; brindle	2 × 10 min. Trim: None Shed: Ordinary	Guarding	Great strength. Dog is fearless yet docile, has endurance and alertness; 60% Mastiff, 40% Bulldog.
Sable and white; tricolor; blue merle and white	1 × 60 min. Trim: Some Shed: Ordinary	Herding	Lithe, strong, responsible, active.
Same as above	2 × 15 min. Trim: None Shed: Ordinary	Herding	Not as popular as Rough-coated.
Black; blue; red; fawn, all with rust markings	2 × 15 min. Trim: None Shed: Ordinary	Guarding	Alert, agile and muscular. Looks upon strangers boldly and judges with unerring instincts. Ready to give prompt alarm and defend master and property, yet affectionate, obedient and loyal.
Black and tan; black; gray	7 × 10 min. Trim: None Shed: Ordinary	Guarding and guiding the blind	Distinguished for loyalty, courage, intelligence. Not a brawler, but bold and punishing if need be. Does not give affection lightly; has dignity, some suspicion of strangers, but his friendship, once given, is given for life.
Solid black; salt and pepper	7 × 15 min. Trim: Profess. Shed: Little	Guarding	Spirited, alert, intelligent and reliable. Composed, watchful, courageous, easily trained, loyal to family, playful, amiable in repose and commanding when aroused.
Brindle; fawn; blue; black; harlequin	2 × 15 min. Trim: None Shed: Ordinary	Companion	Friendly, dependable, a great home lover; responds to proper training, devoted follower.

Breed Type	Breed	Height/Weight	Coat
Working	**Great Pyrenees** BR: Male 3.81 Female 3.80	Male: 27–32″ 100–125 lbs. Fem: 25–29″ 90–115 lbs.	Long, heavy
Working	**Komondor** BR: Male 3.73 Female 3.40	Male: 25½″+ 95 lbs. Fem: 23½″+ 80 lbs.	Long, corded

Working	**Kuvasz (2)**
	BR: Male 3.27
	      Female 3.19
	
	BR: Male 3.71
	      Female 2.96
		Small:
		Male: 23–26″
		80–100 lbs.
		Fem: 22–25″
		75–90 lbs.
		
		Large:
		Male: 28–30″
		100–115 lbs.
		Fem: 26–28″
		70–90 lbs.
			Med.-long,
			wavy

Working	**Mastiff:** BR: Male 6.00 Female 6.18	Male: 30″+ 180 lbs. Fem: 27½″+ 170 lbs.	Short
Working	**Newfoundland** BR: Male 5.36 Female 4.62	Male: 28″ 150 lbs. Fem: 26″ 120 lbs.	Med.-long, dense, flat

Working	**Old English
	Sheepdog**
	BR: Male 4.09
	      Female 3.75
		Male: 22″+
		90 lbs.
		Fem: slightly
		    less
		75 lbs.
			Long, profuse,
			shaggy

BR = Bulk Ratio

Color	Grooming	Function	Behavioral Description According to A.K.C.
White	2 × 30 min. Trim: Some Shed: Ordinary	Guarding and herding	Immense size, great majesty, keen intelligence. Exemplification of gentleness and docility with those he knows; faithful, devoted to master to point of self-sacrifice, protective of the ones he loves.
White	1 × 60 min. Trim: None Shed: Little	Guarding	Tassel-like cords natural; no care except for washing. Excellent house guard, wary of strangers. Earnest, courageous and very faithful. Devoted to master and defends against attack. Readily mingles with friends of master.
White	2 × 30 min. Trim: None Shed: Ordinary	Guarding	Spirited, keen intelligence, courageous, curious. One-family dog, devoted, gentle and patient. Protects loved ones, extremely strong instinct to protect children, suspicious of strangers.
Apricot; silver fawn; dark fawn; brindle	2 × 15 min. Trim: None Shed: Ordinary	Guarding	Large, massive, good-natured, courageous and docile.
Black (most common); gray; bronze; white and black	2 × 30 min. Trim: None Shed: Ordinary	Dragging, guarding, rescuing	At home on land and water. Companion, sweet-natured, intelligent and friendly. Children's protector and playmate, not easily hurt, takes on nursemaiding without training.
White with blue-gray, blue merle, steel-blue-gray or black	2 × 2 hours Trim: Some Shed: Ordinary	Herding	Home-loving, not roamer or fighter. Easy to care for, intelligent, affectionate, not boisterous. Ideal house dog, tender mouth, may be trained as retriever. Equally at home in house, apt. or anywhere.

Breed Type	Breed	Height/Weight	Coat
Working	**Puli** BR: Male 1.81 Female 1.76	Male: 17–19″ 30–35 lbs. Fem: 16–18″ 30 lbs.	Long, corded
Working	**Rottweiler** BR: Male 4.53 Female 4.21	Male: 23¾–27″ 115 lbs. Fem: 21¾– 25¾″ 100 lbs.	Short
Working	**St. Bernard** BR: Male 6.00 Female 5.69	Male: 27½″+ 165 lbs. Fem: 25½″+ 145 lbs.	Short or long
Working	**Samoyed** BR: Male 2.92 Female 2.38	Male: 21–23½″ 55–75 lbs. Fem: 19–21″ 40–55 lbs.	Med.-long, straight
Working	**Shetland Sheepdog** BR: Male 1.24	Standard 13–16″ 18 lbs.	Long, straight, dense
Working	**Siberian Husky** BR: Male 2.36 Female 2.02	Male: 21–23½″ 45–60 lbs. Fem: 20–22″ 35–50 lbs.	Med., dense
Working	**Standard Schnauzer** BR: Male 2.37 Female 1.94	Male: 18½–19½″ 40–50 lbs. Fem: 17½–18½″ 30–40 lbs.	In part, short, wiry

BR = Bulk Ratio

Color	Grooming	Function	Behavioral Description According to A.K.C.
Dull black; rusty black; shades of gray; white	1 × 1 hour Trim: None Shed: Little	Herding and guarding	Medium size, vigorous, alert, extremely active, affectionate, devoted, home-loving. Companion. Suspicious of strangers.
Black with tan markings	2 × 15 min. Trim: None Shed: Ordinary	Herding, tracking, guarding	Good-sized, strong, active dog. Affectionate, intelligent, easily trained to work, obedient. Extremely faithful, not quarrelsome, possesses courage and makes splendid guard.
White and red with black markings	30 min. every other day Trim: Some on long coat Shed: Ordinary, heavy	Rescue	Powerful, strong, muscular and intelligent.
White; biscuit	2 × 30 min. Trim: None Shed: Ordinary	Sled dog and guarding	Intelligent, gentle, loyal, adaptable, alert, full of action, eager to serve, friendly but conservative, not distrustful or shy, not overly aggressive.
Collie colors	1 × 30 min. Trim: Some Shed: Ordinary	Herding	Obeys, willing and natural learner, guards property, devoted, docile nature, keen and all but human intelligence and understanding, small and alert.
All colors	2 × 15 min. Trim: None Shed: Ordinary, heavy	Sled dog	Friendly and gentle, but also alert, outgoing. Does not display the possessive qualities of a guard dog; not overly suspicious of strangers or aggressive with other dogs. Intelligent, agreeable companion and willing worker.
Salt and pepper; black	7 × 10 min. Trim: Profess. Shed: Little	Guarding	High-spirited temperament with unusual intelligence and reliability.

Breed Type	Breed	Height/Weight	Coat
Working	**Welsh Corgi, Cardigan** BR: 2.75	Average: 12″ 33 lbs.	Short, harsh
Working	**Welsh Corgi, Pembroke** BR: Male 2.73 Female 2.55	Male: 10–12″ 30 lbs. or less Fem: 10–12″ 28 lbs. or less	Short
Terrier	**Airedale Terrier** BR: Male 2.39	Male: 23″ 50–60 lbs. Fem: Slightly less 45–55 lbs.	Short, wiry
Terrier	**American Staffordshire Terrier** BR: Male 3.38 Female 2.71	Male: 18–19″ 55–70 lbs. Fem: 17–18″ 40–55 lbs.	Short
Terrier	**Australian Terrier** BR: 1.10	10″ 12–14 lbs.	Harsh, straight
Terrier	**Bedlington Terrier** BR: Male 1.23 Female 1.29	Male: 16½″ 17–23 lbs. Fem: 15½″ 17–23 lbs.	Curly, kept short
Terrier	**Border Terrier** BR: Male 1.19 Female 1.28	Male: 12″ 13–15½ lbs. Fem: 10″ 11½–14 lbs.	Short, harsh

BR = Bulk Ratio

Color	Grooming	Function	Behavioral Description According to A.K.C.
Any color except all white	2 × 15 min. Trim: None Shed: Ordinary	Herding	A handsome, powerful small dog; intelligent.
Red and white; red, black, white; sable and white	2 × 15 min. Trim: None Shed: Ordinary	Herding	Affectionate house dog, but does not force its attention. Intelligent, alert, ever-viligant guard. Outlook bold but kindly, not shy or vicious.
Black or grizzled with tan extremities	15 minutes every other day Trim: Profess. Shed: Little	Guarding	Dignified aloofness with both strangers and its own kind. Disposition can be molded by patience of master, but when trained for defense and attack is unbeatable for its weight.
Any color, solid, parti- or patched	2 × 10 min. Trim: None Shed: Ordinary	Pit fighting and guarding	Docile and with little training is tractable around other dogs. Intelligent, excellent guard, protects master and property. Easily discriminates between strangers who mean well and those who do not. When sold or changes hands, accepts new master in short time.
Blue and black; silver/black with tan markings; sandy on clear red	2 × 15 min. Trim: Some Shed: Little	Herding, pet	Small, affectionate and rather quiet; accepts responsibility for home and household. Harsh coat is good for any weather. Slight shedding is only one point in its favor as indoor companion.
Liver-white; blue-white	2 × 20 min. Trim: Profess. Shed: Little	Once for hunting and fighting. Now, pet.	Noted for great heart and lovable nature. Hardy and not difficult to raise.
Red; grizzle and tan; blue and tan; wheaten	1 × 15 min. Trim: Some Shed: Little	Protecting	Active terrier, alert, good-tempered, affectionate, obedient, easily trained.

Breed Type	Breed	Height / Weight	Coat
Terrier	**Bull Terrier** BR: 2.43	18½″ 35–55 lbs.	Short
Terrier	**Cairn Terrier** BR: Male 1.40 　　　Female 1.37	Male: 10″ 14 lbs. Fem: 9½″ 13 lbs.	Harsh, pro- fuse, short
Terrier	**Dandie Dinmont** BR: 2.21	Standard 8–11″ Standard 18– 24 lbs.	Rough, med. length
Terrier	**Fox Terrier,** Smooth BR: 1.16	Male: 15½″ 18 lbs. Fem: Slightly 　　less 16 lbs.	Short, smooth
	Fox Terrier, Wirehaired	Same as above	Short, wiry
Terrier	**Irish Terrier** BR: Male 1.50 　　　Female 1.39	Standard: 18″ Male: 27 lbs. Fem: 25 lbs.	Wiry, short
Terrier	**Kerry Blue Terrier** BR: Male 1.95	Male: 18–19½″ 33–40 lbs. Fem: 17½–19″ Slightly less	Short, silky, wavy

BR = Bulk Ratio

Color	Grooming	Function	Behavioral Description According to A.K.C.
1. White 2. Colored: brindle, fawn, etc. all with white chest, feet and blaze.	2 × 15 min. Trim: None Shed: Ordinary	Pit fighting and guarding	Exceedingly friendly, thrives on affection yet is always ready for a fight or frolic. Full of fire but of sweet disposition.
Any color but white	2 × 15 min. Trim: Some Shed: Little	Hunting otters, pet	Active, game, hardy small working dog.
Pepper; mustard	2 × 20 min. Trim: Profess. Shed: Ordinary	Hunting otters, pet	Fits anywhere, from rough outdoor life to the confines of city apartment. Small to fit apartment, yet a dog big in character.
White with markings	2 × 10 min. Trim: None Shed: Ordinary	Hunting	Gay, lively and active.
White with markings	2 × 1 hour Trim: Profess. Shed: Little	Hunting	Same as above.
Bright red; golden red; red wheaten; wheaten	1 × 30 min. Trim: Profess. Shed: Little	Guarding	Alert, trim, an incomparable friend, loyal and unyielding, protector of those it loves. At home in city apartment, camp or country home. Playmate and protector of children, eager to join their fun, born guard, tender. Is ever on guard between home and all that threatens.
Any shade of blue	2× 45 min. Trim; Profess. Shed: Little	Guarding	Gentle, lovable, intelligent; instinctive trailer and retrieves well. Adaptable to farmwork, an indomitable foe and cannot be surpassed as watchdog and companion. With proper treatment, food and exercise is very long-lived, and will retain activeness until end.

Breed Type	Breed	Height/Weight	Coat
Terrier	**Lakeland Terrier** BR: Male 1.17 Female 1.19	Male: 13½–15½" 17 lbs. Fem: 13–14" 10 lbs.	Short, wiry
Terrier	**Manchester** BR: 1.03	Standard: 17" Standard: 13–22 lbs.	Short
Terrier	**Miniature Schnauzer** BR: 1.19	Standard: 12–14" Standard: 14– 17 lbs.	Short, hard, wiry
Terrier	**Norwich Terrier** BR: 1.15	Standard: 10" Standard: 11– 12 lbs.	Short, rough
Terrier	**Scottish Terrier** BR: Male 2.05 Female 1.95	Standard: 10" Male: 19–22 lbs. Fem: 18–21 lbs.	Long on sides; wiry
Terrier	**Sealyham Terrier** BR: 2.24	Standard: 10½" Male: 23–24 lbs. Fem: slightly less	Med. length, wiry
Terrier	**Skye Terrier** BR: 2.80	Male: 10" 28 lbs. Fem: 9½" 28 lbs.	Long, straight
Terrier	**Staffordshire Bull Terrier** BR: 2.54	Standard: 14–16" Male: 28–38 lbs. Fem: 24–34 lbs.	Short

BR = Bulk Ratio

Color	Grooming	Function	Behavioral Description According to A.K.C.
Blue; black; liver; black or blue with tan; red; red grizzle, grizzle and tan; wheaten	2 × 30 min. Trim: Profess. Shed: Little	Hunting	Quiet disposition, bold, gay, friendly, a self-confident, cock-of-the-walk attitude.
Black and tan	5 min. every other day Trim: None Shed: Ordinary	Rat killing, rabbit coursing	Intelligent house pet and companion; clean habits and sleek, short coat admit it to homes that might shut out its rough-haired brothers.
Salt and pepper; black and silver; solid black	7 × 10 min. Trim: Profess. Shed: Little	Ratter, now pet	Robust, active, alert good guard dog. Intelligent, fond of children, good for town life and small quarters. Not a fighter but can hold its own.
Red; wheaten; black and tan; grizzle	2 × 30 min. Trim: Some Shed: Little	Rabbit dog	Ideal house dog because hard, close coat does not collect dirt and needs no trimming. One-man dog; once loyalty is given, never swerves.
Black; all shades of brindle; wheaten	2 × 45 min. Trim: Profess. Shed: Little		A compact, will-muscled and powerful dog, giving the impression of immense power in small size.
All white with head markings	2 × 30 min. Trim: Profess. Shed: Little	Quarrying badgers, otters, and foxes	Powerful, determined, keen and alert.
Black; blue; dark or light gray; silver; platinum; fawn; cream	1 × 45 min. Trim: None Shed: Ordinary	Once challenged vicious animals. Now, pet.	Displays stamina, courage, strength and agility. Fearless, good-tempered loyal and canny. Friendly and gay with those it knows; reserved and cautious with strangers.
Any color except black and tan or liver	2 × 10 min. Trim: None Shed: Ordinary	Pit fighting and guarding	Indomitable courage, high intelligence and tenacity. Affection for friends and children quietness and trustworthy stability, makes all-purpose dog.

Breed Type	Breed	Height/Weight	Coat
Terrier	**Welsh Terrier** BR: Male 1.33 Female 1.43	Male: 15″ 20 lbs. Fem: 14″ 20 lbs.	Short, wiry
Terrier	**West Highland** **White Terrier** BR: Male 1.50 Female 1.65	Male: 11″ 15–18 lbs. Fem: 10″ 15–18 lbs.	Med., hard
Terrier	**Wheaten** (Soft- coated) BR: 2.03	Male: 18–19″ 35–40 lbs.	Med. length, soft, wavy
Toy	**Affenpinscher** BR: .73	Standard: No more than 10¼″ No more than 7–8 lbs.	Shaggy, wiry
Toy	**Brussels Griffon** (Smooth coat) BR: .89	Average: 8″ 8–10 lbs.	Smooth
	(Rough coat) BR: .89	Average: 8″ 8–10 lbs.	Rough
Toy	**Chihuahua** (Short- or long-coated) BR: .92	Average 5–6″ Not over 6 lbs.	Short Long

BR = Bulk Ratio

Color	Grooming	Function	Behavioral Description According to A.K.C.
Black and tan; grizzle and tan	2 × 30 min. Trim: Profess. Shed: Little	Hunting otters and foxes	Not quarrelsome, well-mannered and easy to handle
White	2 × 20 min. Trim: Some Shed: Little	Hunting	Spunk, determination and devotion. Small, sporty, intelligent, good hunter, speedy and cunning. Faithful, understanding and devoted, yet gay and lighthearted. Needs no pampering, loves to romp and play in snow and will follow skaters or walkers across frozen lakes.
Wheaten	20 min. every other day Trim: Some Shed: Little	Pet	Companion and protector to its owners. Attractive medium-sized dog, quick-witted and responsive. Good-tempered, spirited, game, alert and intelligent.
Black; black and tan; red; gray, wheaten	2 × 20 min. Trim: Some Shed: Little	Ratting, now pet	A game, alert, intelligent and sturdy little "terrier type." Carries itself with comical seriousness. Generally quiet, devoted pal. Can get vehemently excited when attacked and is fearless toward any aggressor.
Reddish brown; black and reddish brown; solid black	2 × 5 min. Trim: None Shed: Ordinary	Ratting, now pet	A small, compact dog with harsh coat, short upturned face, gay carriage, intelligent, sensitive. Although obedient and easily managed, difficult to break to leash, which should be done at early age. Comrade.
Same as above	2 × 20 min. Trim: Some Shed: Little	Same	
Any color	2 × 5 min. Trim: None Shed: Ordinary	Religious, now pet	Clannish, liking its own kind; does not like dogs of other breeds.

Breed Type	Breed	Height/Weight	Coat
Toy	**English Toy Spaniel (King Charles)** BR: .90	Average: 9½" 9–12 lbs.	Long, soft and wavy
	(Ruby) BR: .90	Same	Same
	(Blenheim) BR: .90	Same	Same
	(Prince Charles) BR: .90	Same	Same
Toy	**Italian Greyhound** BR: .50	Standard: 13–15" 6–8 lbs.	Short
Toy	**Japanese Spaniel** BR: .72	Average: 9" 4–9 lbs.	Long, profuse
Toy	**Maltese** BR: .59	Standard: 7–10" 4–6 lbs.	Long, flat, silky
Toy	**Manchester (Toy)** BR: .74	Standard: 12" Not over 12 lbs. 10"—7–12 lbs.	Short
Toy	**Miniature Pinscher** BR: .80	Standard: 11–11½" 9 lbs.	Short
Toy	**Papillon** BR: .84	Standard: 8–11" 8 lbs.	Long and abundant
Toy	**Pekingese** BR: 1.50	Standard: 8" No more than 14 lbs.	Long, profuse

BR = Bulk Ratio

Color	Grooming	Function	Behavioral Description According to A.K.C.
Black and tan	2 × 20 min. Trim: Some Shed: Ordinary	Hunting, pet	Affectionate, intelligent little dog.
Red	Same	Same	Same
Red and white	Same	Same	Same
White, black and tan	Same	Same	Same
Any color	2 × 5 min. Trim: None Shed: Little	Pet	Solely a pet.
Black and white; lemon and white; red and white	1 × 1 hour Trim: None Shed: Ordinary	Once kept by nobility as gift of esteem, pet	Good companion, bright and alert. Naturally clean, makes ideal pet. Sensitive with definite likes and dislikes, but rarely forgets friend or foe.
Pure white (preferred); lemon or light tan (permissible)	7 × 15 min. Trim: None Shed: Little	Pet	Refined, faithful, healthy, spirited, clean, affectionate, eager, gentle-mannered and playful.
Black and tan	2 × 5 min. Trim: None Shed: Little	Pet	Same as Manchester Terrier except in toy size.
Solid red; black with tan; brown or chocolate with yellow	2 × 5 min. Trim: None Shed: Ordinary	Watchdog	Especially valuable watchdog, lively temperament, intelligent, fondness for home and master exceptional.
Parti-colored, white with patches of any color	2 × 10 min. Trim: Some Shed: Ordinary	Ratter, pet	Delight in country or apartment. Easy to raise, hardy, small, friendly and lively.
Red; fawn; black; black and tan; sable; brindle; white; parti- colored	2 × 1 hour Trim: None Shed: Ordinary	Sacred in China, pet	Independent, regal, calm and good-tempered. Although never aggressive, has never been known to turn tail and run. Very easy to care for. Understanding companionship and loyalty to owners.

Breed Type	Breed	Height/Weight	Coat
Toy	**Pomeranian** BR: .83	Standard: 6″ 3–7 lbs.	Long, dense
Toy	**Poodle (Toy)** BR: .60	Standard: 10″ or under 6 lbs.	Harsh, dense, long, curly
Toy	**Pug** BR: 1.35	Standard: 10–13″ 14–18 lbs.	Short
Toy	**Shih Tzu** BR: 1.38	Standard: 9– 10½″ 12–15 lbs.	Long, dense, slightly wavy
Toy	**Silky Terrier** BR: .95	Standard: 9–10″ 8–10 lbs.	Long, silky, straight
Toy	**Yorkshire Terrier** BR: .93	Standard: 7–8″ No more than 7 lbs.	Long, silky glossy
Non Sporting	**Bichon Frise** BR: 1.3	Standard: 8–12″ 11–15 lbs.	Profuse, silky, loose curl
Non Sporting	**Boston Terrier** BR: 1.67	Standard: 15″ Not over 25 lbs.	Short
Non Sporting	**Bulldog (English)** BR: Male 3.15 Female 2.86	Male: 16″ 50 lbs. Fem: 14″ 40 lbs.	Short
Non Sporting	**Chow Chow** BR: 3.5	Standard: 20″ 70 lbs.	Long, dense
Non Sporting	**Dalmatian** BR: 2.86	Standard: 19– 23″ Male: 55–65 lbs. Fem: 45–55 lbs.	Short

Color	Grooming	Function	Behavioral Description According to A.K.C.
Any solid color with lighter shadings; parti-colored; tan; sable; black	2 × 30 min. Trim: Some Shed: Ordinary	Herder, pet	Diminutive size, docile temper and vivacious spirit and sturdiness make it a great pet and companion.
Blue; gray; silver; brown; café-au-lait; apricot; cream	1 × 1 hour Trim: Profess. Shed: Little	Retriever, pet	Very active, intelligent and elegant appearance. Carries itself proudly.
Silver; apricot; fawn; black	2 × 10 min. Trim: None Shed: Ordinary		Compact, alert, clean, tractable and companionable. Requires minimum of care.
All colors	2 × 1 hour Trim: None Shed: Ordinary	House pet	Small, intelligent and extremely docile, very active, lively and alert.
Blue and tan	15 min. every other day Trim: Some Shed: Little	Pet	Friendly and forceful as a terrier can be. Agile and light-footed, designed as a pet. Quick and responsive.
Blue and tan, puppies born black	2 × 20 min. Trim: Some Shed: Little	Pet	Spirited; long hair presents problem in grooming.
White; white and apricot; cream	7 × 30 min. Trim: Profess. Shed; Little	Pet	Sturdy, lively, stable temperament, intelligent.
Brindle and white (preferred); black and white (permissible)	2 × 10 min. Trim: None Shed: Ordinary	Pet	Not a fighter but can hold its own. Gentle disposition. An eminently suitable house pet.
Red brindle; all other brindles; white; red; fawn; fallow; piebald	2 × 15 min. Trim: None Shed: Ordinary	Bull baiting, pet	Great stability, vigor and strength. Disposition equable and kind, resolute, courageous (not vicious or aggressive).
Any color with lighter shading	2 × 45 min. Trim: None Shed: Ordinary	Guarding	Massive, cobby, powerful dog. Active and alert.
White with black or liver spots	7 × 10 min. Trim: None Shed: Heavy	Coaching, firehouse mascot	Strong, muscular, active, poised and alert; free of shyness.

Breed Type	Breed	Height/Weight	Coat
Non Sporting	**Bulldog (French)** BR: 2.43	Standard: 11½" Not over 28 lbs.	Short
Non Sporting	**Keeshond** BR: Male 2.22 Female 2.06	Male: 18" 40 lbs. Fem: 17" 35 lbs.	Long, dense, harsh
Non Sporting	**Lhasa Apso** BR: 1.52	Male: 10–11" Standard: 16 lbs. Fem: Slightly smaller	Long, heavy, straight
Non Sporting	**Poodle** **(Standard)** BR: Male 2.20 Female 2.39	Male: 24–26" 45–65 lbs. Fem: 22–24" 45–65 lbs.	Harsh, dense, profuse, curly
	(Miniature) BR: 1.23	Standard: 11–15" 15–17 lbs.	Same
Non Sporting	**Schipperke** BR: 1.44	Standard: 12–13" Up to 18 lbs.	Short, dense
Non Sporting	**Tibetan Terrier** BR: 1.50 BR: 1.76	Standard: 14–16" 22–23 lbs. Some: 17" Up to 30 lbs.	Long, wavy

BR = Bulk ratio

Color	Grooming	Function	Behavioral Description According to A.K.C.
Brindle; fawn; white; brindle and white	2 × 5 min. Trim: None Shed: Ordinary		Active, intelligent and muscular.
Mixture of gray and black	2 × 45 min. Trim: None Shed: Ordinary	Pet	Alert carriage, intelligent expression, no desire to hunt, would rather stay with master. Luxurious coat.
Golden; sandy; honey; dark grizzle, slate; smoke; parti-colored; white; black; brown	2 × 2 hour Trim: None Shed: Ordinary	Guarding, pet	Gay, assertive, keen watchfulness, hardy nature. Easily trained, responsive to kindness. Obedient to those it trusts.
Blue; gray; silver; brown; café-au-lait; apricot; cream	1 × 2–5 hours (depending upon size) Trim: Profess. Shed: Little	Water retriever, pet	Very active, intelligent and elegant-appearing. Carries itself proudly.
Same	Same	Same	Same
Black	2 × 15 min. Trim: None Shed: Ordinary	Guarding	Intelligent, keen expression, not mean, rather mischievous. Very fond of children and in some cases has served as guard, taking place of human nurse, so devoted to its small charges.
Any color but chocolate	2 × 1 hour Trim: None Shed: Ordinary	Companion	Not actually a terrier, does not have terrier disposition; called terrier because of shape. Eager to protect family. Healthy.

Appendix B

General Characteristics of the Six Breed Types: Sporting Dogs, Hounds, Working Dogs, Terriers, Toy Dogs, Non-Sporting Dogs.

The Sporting Dogs as a Group

In order to facilitate comparison of all the breeds in this group, I have tabulated the temperamental characteristics of each breed in Table B-1.

On the whole, this group is moderately active indoors. Outdoors, most of the breeds are characterized as needing a lot of exercise; the rest are said to need a fair amount. All in all, this is a very active group of dogs, something to be expected from animals bred for hunting. Breeds in this group are moderately vigorous, tending to do things somewhat fast, hard and forcefully. In terms of behavioral variability, we have a 50–50 split. Half of the group tends to stay persistently with one behavior, whereas the other half are easily distractable and tend to shift rapidly from behavior to behavior. On the whole, the group tends to be submissive to people and other dogs. This group seems to vary widely in emotional stability from very stable to very vacillating. However, the majority of the breeds fall into the emotionally stable category.

The group also appears to be composed mostly of fast-learning breeds. Obedience varies from good to poor. Surprisingly, there seems to be no definite relationship between learning rate and obedience. This simply means that a fast-learning breed can be poor in obedience because it learns what it wants to learn and not necessarily what its owner desires.

TABLE B-1.
Temperamental Characteristics of the 24 Breeds That Make Up the Sporting Group

| Breed | Activity Level | | Behavioral | | | Dominance/Submission | | Emotional |
	Indoors	Outdoors	Vigor/Gentleness	Variability/Constancy	Territoriality	Strange Dogs	Familiar People	Stability/Vacillation
Pointer	very active	very active	vigorous	constant	low	intermediate to dominant	intermediate	stable
German Short-haired Pointer	very active	very active	very vigorous	constant	low	intermediate	intermediate to submissive	stable
German Wire-haired Pointer	very active	very active	very vigorous	constant	moderate to high	dominant	intermediate	stable
Chesapeake Bay Retriever	in-active	very active	vigorous to gentle	moderate	high	intermediate	intermediate	stable
Curly-coated Retriever	in-active	very active	moderate	variable	moderate	intermediate	submissive	vacillating
Flat-coated Retriever	in-active	very active	moderate	variable	low	submissive	submissive to very submissive	very stable
Golden Re-triever	active	moderate	gentle	very variable to variable	none	submissive	submissive to very submissive	stable
Labrador Retriever	active	moderate	moderate	constant	moderate	intermediate	intermediate	stable
English Setter	in-active	very active	moderate	moderate	low	intermediate	submissive	very stable

TABLE B-1.
Temperamental Characteristics of the 24 Breeds That Make Up the Sporting Group (continued)

| Breed | Activity Level | | Behavioral | | | Dominance/Submission | | Emotional Stability/Vacillation |
	Indoors	Outdoors	Vigor/Gentleness	Variability/Constancy	Territoriality	Strange Dogs	Familiar People	
Gordon Setter	moderate	very active	vigorous	constant	moderate	dominant	intermediate to submissive	normal
Irish Setter	very active	very active	very vigorous	very variable	low	submissive	submissive	vacillating
American Water Spaniel	active	very active	gentle	constant	moderate	dominant	intermediate	stable
Brittany Spaniel	active	very active	vigorous	variable	moderate	submissive	intermediate	vacillating
Clumber Spaniel	very in-active	active	gentle	very constant	low	intermediate	intermediate	very stable
Cocker Spaniel "well-bred"	active	moderate	very gentle	variable	low	submissive	submissive	normal
Cocker Spaniel "puppy-mill"	active	moderate	gentle	variable	high	dominant	dominant	very vacillating
English Cocker Spaniel	active	active	moderate	moderate to variable	low	submissive	submissive	stable
English Springer Spaniel	active	very active	moderate	moderate	low	submissive	submissive	stable

Breed							
Field Spaniel	very active	very active	vigorous	constant	low	intermediate	submissive	stable
Irish Water Spaniel	active	very active	vigorous	constant	moderate	very submissive	intermediate	vacillating
Sussex Spaniel	active	active	moderate	very constant	high	dominant	dominant	stable stable
Welsh Springer Spaniel	active	very active	moderate	constant	moderate	intermediate	submissive	normal
Vizsla	in-active	active	vigorous	constant	low	intermediate	submissive	vacillating
Weimaraner	very active	very active	very vigorous	constant	high	dominant	dominant	stable
Wirehaired Pointing Griffon	very active	active	vigorous	variable	moderate	intermediate	submissive	vacillating

TABLE B-1.
Temperamental Characteristics of the 24 Breeds That Make Up the Sporting Group (continued)

| Breed | Learning Rate | Functionality | | Watch/Guard Dog | Sociability/Solitariness | Sociability Dimension | | With Children |
		Obedience	Problem Solving			Owner/Family	With Strangers	
Pointer	slow	fair	poor	alert/unsuited; some natural	moderate	1-family	reserved	OK, if brought up with them from puppyhood.
German Short-haired Pointer	fast	fair to poor	good	very alert/natural	moderate	1-family	sociable to reserved	Too bouncy for small children.
Chesapeake Bay Retriever	slow	fair	fair	very alert/natural	moderate	1-family	reserved to aggressive	Exceptionally good.
Curly-coated Retriever	fast	good	fair	alert/unsuited	moderate	1-family	reserved	Exceptionally good.
Flat-coated Retriever	fast to very fast	good	fair	alert/unsuited	sociable	open-family	likes most everyone	Exceptionally good if brought up with them from puppyhood.
Golden Retriever	very fast	good	fair	alert/unsuited	very sociable	open-family	likes everyone	Exceptionally good if brought up with them from puppyhood.
Labrador Retriever	very fast	good	fair	alert/unsuited; some natural	sociable	1-family	likes almost everyone	Exceptionally good.
English Setter	slow	fair	fair to good	alert/unsuited	sociable	open-family	likes almost everyone	Exceptionally good.

Breed							
Gordon Setter	fast	fair	fair	alert/unsuited; some natural	moderate	1-family	reserved	Exceptionally good.
Irish Setter	fast	good	fair to good	alert/very un-suited	very socialbe	1-family	likes everyone	Exceptionally good; may be too excitable for very small children.
American Water Spaniel	fast	fair to good	good	alert/unsuited; some natural	solitary	1-person	mildly friendly	Nippy and somewhat intolerant.
Brittany Spaniel	fast	good	good	alert/unsuited	sociable	open-family	likes almost everyone	Exceptionally good.
Clumber Spaniel	slow	fair	fair to poor	sluggish/un-suited	very sociable	open-family	likes everyone	Exceptionally good.
Cocker Spaniel "well-bred"	fast	good	fair to good	alert/unsuited	sociable	open-family	likes almost everyone	Exceptionally good.
Cocker Spaniel "puppy-mill"	slow	poor	poor	alert/unsuited	very solitary	bites owners and demanding	vicious and ill-tempered	Exceptionally bad.
English Cocker Spaniel	fast	good	fair	alert/unsuited	very sociable	open-family	likes everyone	Exceptionally good.
English Springer Spaniel	fast	fair	fair	alert/unsuited	sociable	open-family	likes almost everyone	Exceptionally good.
Field Spaniel	fast	good	good	very alert/un-suited	sociable	open-family	likes almost everyone	Exceptionally good.

TABLE B-1.
Temperamental Characteristics of the 24 Breeds That Make Up the Sporting Group (continued)

Breed	Functionality			Watch/Guard Dog	Sociability/Solitariness	Sociability Dimension		With Children
	Learning Rate	Obedience	Problem Solving			Owner/Family	With Strangers	
Irish Water Spaniel	fast	poor	fair	very alert/unsuited	solitary	1-person	reserved, forbidding	Bad.
Sussex Spaniel	slow	poor	poor	alert/average	moderate	open-family	likes people	Exceptionally good.
Welsh Springer Spaniel	fast	fair	fair	alert/average	moderate	1-family	reserved	Good.
Vizsla	fast	good	fair	alert/unsuited	sociable	open-family	likes almost everyone	Exceptionally good.
Weimaraner	fast	poor	good	very alert/natural	moderate	1-family	reserved	Tolerant; too impetuous for small children.
Wirehaired Pointing Griffon	fast	good	fair	very alert/average	moderate to solitary	1-family	fearful	Good with those he knows and trusts.

In the sociability dimension, this group tends toward the sociable side, with only 2 breeds, the American and Irish Water Spaniels, being one-person dogs. All of the pointers are characterized as reserved with strangers, whereas all of the retrievers, (except puppy-mill Cocker Spaniels), the rest of the spaniels, the setters and the Vizsla are described as open and friendly with strangers. Most of the group are considered "exceptionally good with children"; the rest of the breeds have some shortcomings with kids.

Table B-2 presents the number and percentage of potential behavior problems mentioned. This group averages 2.21 problems per breed. The most common behavior problem in the sporting dogs appears to be barking; roaming and house soiling may also occur.

TABLE B-2.
Potential Behavior Problems in Sporting Dogs

Behavior Problems	# of Breeds	% of 24 Breeds	% of Total Problems in Sporting Dogs
Barking and howling	11	46	21
Roaming	8	33	15
House soiling	8	33	15
Stealing food	7	29	13
Jumping	5	21	9
Destruction	4	17	8
Fear biting	4	17	8
Picky eating	3	13	6
Snoring, wheezing, Belching	2	8	4
Restlessness	1	4	2

Behavior Problem Index 2.21

It must be kept in mind that this table represents my own opinions and those of breeders and trainers on the potential behavior problems. They, and I, will be quick to add that one can bring this potential to zero by proper handling, care and training. No breed has to be a problem if it matches the owner's life-style and personality, and if the owner knows how to prevent and/or eliminate problems.

The Hounds as a Group

Table B-3 summarizes the temperamental characteristics of all 19 breeds of hounds. Scanning this table should give you a rough picture of where each breed ranks relative to the other breeds in this group.

In terms of indoor activity, most of the breeds rate as inactive; the remaining are very active. Except for the Elkhounds, there appears to be no middle ground to this distribution. You can choose from, basically, only two categories. In general, the heavier and larger the breed, the less active. Outdoors, a majority of the breeds are ranked as very active; the rest spread between active and moderate.

In terms of behavioral vigor, a majority of the breeds are rated as gentle; the rest spread out toward the vigorous end of the dimension. Only 3 breeds are rated as very vigorous and none as very gentle. Behavioral constancy seems to form two large lumps, variable and constant; a few breeds are moderate, and only 1 falls into each of the extremes of the dimension.

As a group, the Hounds are skewed toward the low end of the territoriality dimension. The majority of the breeds are ranked as low in territoriality. None is ranked as very high; few are high; the rest exhibit no discernible territoriality.

Dominance toward strange dogs is spread almost equally between the dominant and submissive levels of the dimension. Only one breed, the Ridgeback, is rated as very dominant. None was considered very submissive.

In relation to familiar people, this group bunches on the low end of the dimension—most being rated as submissive, with only 2 breeds on each of the intermediate and dominant levels.

Most of the Hounds tend to be emotionally stable. The rest of the breeds in the Hound group fall into the emotionally vacillating level.

The learning rate for this group ranges from fast to slow, with only 1 breed, the Elkhound, being ranked as very fast. Obedience is fair to poor, with the Irish Wolfhound being ranked as good and the Greyhound being classed as very poor in obedience. The Hounds range widely in problem solving, but only 2 breeds are classed as very good problem solvers.

TABLE B-3.
Temperamental Characteristics of the 19 Breeds That Make Up the Hound Group

| Breed | Activity Level | | Behavioral | | | Dominance / Submission | | Emotional |
	Indoors	Outdoors	Vigor / Gentleness	Variability / Constancy	Territoriality	Strange Dogs	Familiar People	Stability / Vacillation
Afghan Hound	inactive	very active	gentle	constant	moderate	dominant	submissive	stable to vacillating
Basenji	very active	moderate active	gentle	variable	high	very dominant to dominant	intermediate	stable
Basset Hound	very inactive to inactive	moderate active	moderate	moderate	low	intermediate	submissive	very stable
Beagle	very active	moderate active	gentle	moderate	none	submissive	submissive	stable
Black and Tan Coonhound	inactive	active	vigorous	constant	moderate	dominant	submissive	stable
Bloodhound	inactive	active	very vigorous	very constant	moderate	dominant	submissive	very stable
Borzoi (Russian Wolfhound)	inactive	very active	gentle	constant	low	intermediate	submissive	vacillating
Dachshund	very active	very active	vigorous	very variable	moderate	intermediate	submissive	vacillating
American Foxhound	very active	very active	vigorous	variable	none	submissive	submissive	stable

TABLE B-3.
Temperamental Characteristics of the 19 Breeds That Make Up the Hound Group (continued)

| Breed | Activity Level | | Behaviorial | | | Dominance/Submission | | Emotional |
	Indoors	Outdoors	Vigor/Gentleness	Variability/Constancy	Territor-iality	Strange Dogs	Familiar People	Stability/Vacillation
English Fox-hound	very active	very active	vigorous	variable	none	submissive	submissive	stable vacillating
Greyhound	in-active	very active	gentle	variable	low	submissive	submissive	very vacillating
Harrier	very active	very active	vigorous	variable	none	submissive	submissive	stable
Irish Wolfhound	in-active	moderate	gentle	constant	moderate	intermediate to dominant	intermediate	stable
Norwegian Elkhound	active	moderate	very vigorous	constant	high	dominant	dominant	stable
Otterhound	in-active	active	gentle	moderate	low	intermediate	submissive	stable
Rhodesian Ridgeback	in-active	very active	very vigorous	constant	high	very dominant	dominant	stable
Saluki	in-active	very active	gentle	variable	low	intermediate	submissive	vacillating
Scottish Deer-hound	in-active	active	gentle	constant	low	intermediate	submissive	very stable
Whippet	in-	very	gentle	variable	low	submissive	submissive	vacillating

TABLE B-3.
Temperamental Characteristics of the 19 Breeds That Make Up the Hound Group (continued)

| Breed | Learning Rate | Functionality | | Sociability / Solitariness | Sociability Dimension | | With Children |
		Obedience	Problem Solving		Owner / Family	With Strangers	
Afghan Hound	slow	poor	good	solitary to very solitary	1-family	reserved	Tolerant, OK for considerate older children.
Basenji	fast	fair	very good	solitary	1-family	reserved	Tolerant, OK for considerate older children.
Basset Hound	slow	fair	poor	sociable	1-family	ignores or is friendly	Exceptionally good.
Beagle	fast	poor	good	very sociable	any person	likes everyone	Exceptionally good.
Black & Tan Coonhound	slow	poor	poor	moderate	1-family	reserved	Exceptionally good.
Bloodhound	slow	fair	fair	sociable	any person	likes most everyone	Exceptionally good.
Borzoi (Russian Wolfhound)	fast	fair	poor	moderate	not very demonstrative	tolerant to friendly	Bad to tolerant of considerate older children.
Dachshund	fast	poor	good	solitary	1-family	reserved	Bad to tolerant of considerate older children.

Watch/Guard Dog column:
Afghan Hound: alert/unsuited
Basenji: very alert/unsuited
Basset Hound: alert/unsuited
Beagle: alert/unsuited
Black & Tan Coonhound: alert/average
Bloodhound: alert/unsuited
Borzoi: normal/unsuited
Dachshund: very alert/unsuited

315

TABLE B-3.
Temperamental Characteristics of the 19 Breeds That Make Up the Hound Group (continued)

Breed	Learning Rate	Functionality		Watch/Guard Dog	Sociability/Solitariness	Sociability Dimension		With Children
		Obedience	Problem Solving			Owner/Family	With Strangers	
American Foxhound	slow	fair	fair	alert/unsuited	very sociable	any person	likes everyone	Exceptionally good.
English Foxhound	slow	fair	fair	alert/unsuited	very sociable	any person	likes everyone	Exceptionally good.
Greyhound	fast	very poor	poor	alert/unsuited	moderate	1-family	reserved	Bad to tolerant of considerate older children.
Harrier	fast	poor	good	very alert/unsuited	sociable	1-family	reserved	Exceptionally good.
Irish Wolfhound	fast	good	fair	sluggish/normal	sociable	1-family	tolerant to reserved	Exceptionally good, but size makes it clumsy.
Norwegian Elkhound	very fast	poor	very good	very alert/natural	sociable-solitary	1-person 1-family	likes-reserved	Some are good, some aren't.
Otterhound	slow	fair	poor	alert/unsuited	very sociable	any person	likes everyone	Exceptionally good but clumsy.
Rhodesian Ridgeback	fast	poor	good	very alert/aggressive	solitary	1-family	reserved to aggressive	Bad to tolerant with considerate older children if raised with them.

Saluki	slow	fair	poor	alert/unsuited	very solitary	standoffish with owner	reserved	Bad to tolerant with considerate older children.
Scottish Deerhound	slow	fair	poor	sluggish/unsuited	sociable	1-family	likes most everyone	Exceptionally good.
Whippet	fast	fair	fair	alert/unsuited	solitary	1-family	reserved	Bad to tolerant with considerate older children.

As watchdogs, the great majority of the Hounds are described as alert or very alert, 1 as normal and 2 as sluggish. For the most part, Hounds seem to be unsuitable as guard dogs. The Ridgeback is the only breed considered aggressive. The Elkhound is ranked as a natural guard dog, and the Irish Wolfhound varies from natural to average as a guard.

On the sociability dimension, the Hounds vary widely from very sociable to very solitary, with the majority being classed as sociable or moderate.

A majority of the Hounds are described as exceptionally good with children. However, there are several multiple-classed breeds, with many rated as tolerant and over a third rated as bad with children. Thus, parents should be careful with these breeds, testing them as puppies, socializing them early and raising them with children.

Table B-4 summarizes the problems mentioned for the Hounds. This group averages 3 problems per breed, as compared with the Sporting Dogs, which average 2.21 problems per breed. The majority of problems involve house soiling. The next-most-common problems are excessive barking, roaming and stealing food. There were four categories of problems added to this group. These were irritable snapping, phobias

TABLE B-4.
Potential Behavior Problems in Hounds

Behavior Problems	# of Breeds	% of 19 breeds	% of Total Problems in Hounds
Barking and howling	8	42	14
Roaming	8	42	14
House soiling	10	53	18
Stealing food	8	42	14
Jumping		0	0
Destruction	1	5	2
Fear biting	4	21	7
Picky eating	2	11	4
Restless indoors	3	16	5
Irritable snapping	6	32	11
Phobias and Timidity	3	16	5
Dominance	3	16	5
Pulling	1	5	2

Behavior Problem Index 3.0

and timidity, and dominance problems. Pulling was added because of the Irish Wolfhound's great strength and occasional tendency to bolt after four-legged beasts as it did in its coursing past. In general, the Hounds don't seem to be suitable apartment dogs, but some are.

The Working Dogs as a Group

Table B-5 summarizes the temperamental characteristics of the 30 breeds that constitute the Working Dogs. Not only is this the largest group of dogs, but it contains breeds with the greatest physical diversity. They vary in looks from the enormous Mastiff to the dainty Sheltie, from the long-corded-coated Komondor and Puli to the shaggy-coated Old English Sheepdog, and include the short-coated breeds like the Boxers and Dobies. It wouldn't be surprising if this group were temperamentally diverse.

Working dogs form two distinct groupings when it comes to indoor activity. Most of the breeds fall into the levels of very active and active indoors. The remaining breeds are ranked as inactive indoors. Outdoors, the entire group is ranked from moderately active to very active, with the majority of breeds being described as active outdoors.

This group of dogs is spread out over the entire behavioral vigor dimension. The Newfoundland is considered very gentle. Dobies range from very to moderately vigorous.

In terms of behavioral variability, only one breed is ranked as very variable, the Dobermans. This breed is also ranked as normal, or moderate, in variability. Apparently Dobermans, as a breed, vary in their variability. The majority of Working Dogs are classified as either variable or constant. German Shepherds are ranked in both these levels.

The group tends to be territorial, with the great majority being ranked as very high to moderate in territoriality. The rest of the Working Dogs are low in territoriality, and one breed, the well-bred Old English Sheepdog, is ranked as very low in territoriality.

Territoriality is also shown by the fact that almost all of the Working breeds are ranked as very alert or alert watchdogs.

TABLE B-5.
Temperamental Characteristics of the 30 Breeds That Make Up the Working Group

Breed	Activity Level		Behavioral		Territor-iality	Dominance/Submission		Emotional Stability/Vacillation
	Indoors	Outdoors	Vigor/Gentleness	Variability/Constancy		Strange Dogs	Familiar People	
Akita	inactive	active	vigorous	constant	high	dominant	intermediate	stable
Alaskan Malamute	very active	very active	very vigorous	variable	high	dominant	intermediate	stable
Belgians: Malinois, Sheepdog and Tervuren	active	active	gentle	variable	moderate	dominant	submissive	vacillating
Bernese Mountain Dog	inactive	active	gentle	constant	moderate	intermediate	submissive	stable
Bouvier des Flandres	inactive	active	gentle	very constant	moderate	intermediate	submissive	very stable
Boxer	active	active	vigorous	variable	moderate	dominant	submissive	stable
Briard	very active	very active	vigorous	constant	high	dominant	intermediate	normal to vacillating
Bullmastiff	inactive	active	very vigorous	constant	high	dominant	intermediate	stable
Collie, Rough-coated	inactive	active	gentle	moderate	low	submissive	submissive	stable to vacillating

Doberman Pinscher	active to very active	very active	moderate to very vigorous	normal to very variable	high	dominant	very submissive to very dominant	normal to very vacillating
German Shepherd (well-bred)	active	active	vigorous	constant to normal	high	dominant	intermediate	stable
German Shepherd (puppy-mill)	very active	active	vigorous	variable	high	very dominant to very submissive	dominant	vacillating
Giant Schnauzer	active	active	very vigorous	moderate	very high	very dominant	dominant	stable
Great Dane	inactive	moderate	gentle	very constant	moderate	intermediate	submissive	very stable
Great Pyrenees	inactive	moderate	vigorous	very constant	moderate	intermediate	intermediate	very stable
Komondor	active to very active	very active	very vigorous	variable	high	dominant	dominant	stable
Kuvasz	very active	very active	very vigorous	variable	very high	dominant	dominant	stable
Mastiff	inactive	moderate	gentle	very constant	moderate	dominant	intermediate to submissive	very stable

TABLE B-5.
Temperamental Characteristics of the 30 Breeds That Make Up the Working Group (continued)

Breed	Activity Level		Behavioral		Territor-iality	Dominance/Submission		Emotional Stability/Vacillation
	Indoors	Outdoors	Vigor/Gentleness	Variability/Constancy		Strange Dogs	Familiar People	
Newfoundland	inactive	active	very gentle	very constant	low	intermediate	intermediate to submissive	very stable
Old English Sheepdog (well-bred)	active	very active	gentle	moderate	very low	intermediate	submissive	normal
Old English Sheepdog (puppy-mill)	very active	very active	vigorous	variable	high	very dominant to very submissive	very dominant to very submissive	very vacillating
Puli	very active	very active	vigorous	variable	high	dominant	dominant	vacillating
Rottweiler	inactive	active	very vigorous	constant	very high	dominant	dominant	stable
St. Bernard (well-bred)	inactive	moderate	gentle	very constant	low	intermediate	submissive to intermediate	very stable
St. Bernard (puppy-mill)	active	active	vigorous	variable	moderate	very dominant	dominant	very vacillating
Samoyed	very active	very active	moderate	variable	moderate	intermediate	intermediate to submissive	normal

Shetland Sheepdog	active	very active	gentle	variable	low	submissive	submissive	vacillating
Siberian Husky	very active	very active	moderate	constant	low	intermediate	submissive	stable
Standard Schnauzer	very active	very active	very vigorous	very constant	very high	very dominant	dominant	stable
Welsh Corgi, Cardigan	very active	active	moderate	constant	high	dominant	submissive	stable
Welsh Corgi, Pembroke	very active	active	moderate	constant	moderate	intermediate	submissive	stable

TABLE B-5.

Temperamental Characteristics of the 30 Breeds That Make Up the Working Group (continued)

Breed	Learning Rate	Functionality		Watch/Guard Dog	Sociability/ Solitariness	Owner/ Family	With Strangers	With Children
		Obedience	Problem Solving					
Akita	fast	poor	fair	very alert/ natural	solitary	1-family	suspicious	Exceptionally good if brought up with them from puppyhood.
Alaskan Malamute	slow	poor	very good	normal/un-suited	sociable	any person	likes almost everyone	Tolerant of older dominant children.
Belgians: Malinois, Sheepdog and Tervuren	very fast	very good	good	very alert/ag-gressive	very solitary	small-family or 1-person	reserved to fearful	Exceptionally good to tolerant.
Bernese Mountain Dog	very fast	good	good	very alert/ natural	solitary	small-family or 1-person	reserved	Exceptionally good.
Bouvier des Flandres	very fast	good	good	very alert/ natural	solitary	1-family	reserved	Exceptionally good.
Boxer	fast	poor	poor	alert/natural	sociable	large-family	likes almost everyone	Exceptionally good.
Briard	slow	very poor	fair	very alert/ag-gressive	solitary	1-family	reserved	Exceptionally good if brought up with them from puppyhood.

Breed								
Bullmastiff	fast	poor	fair	very alert/aggressive	solitary	1-family	reserved	Exceptionally good if brought up with them from puppyhood.
Collie, Rough-coated	fast	very good	good	very alert/unsuited	sociable	1-family	friendly to reserved	Exceptionally good if brought up with them from puppyhood.
Doberman Pinscher	very fast to slow	very good to very poor	very good	very alert/aggressive	solitary to very solitary	1-family to 1-person	reserved to aggressive	Tolerant if raised with them from puppyhood to bad.
German Shepherd (well-bred)	very fast	very good to good	very good	very alert/natural	moderate	1-family	reserved	Usually exceptionally good.
German Shepherd (puppy-mill)	very fast	poor	fair	very alert/aggressive	solitary	no-person	very aggressive	Bad.
Giant Schnauzer	fast	fair to poor	very good	very alert/aggressive	solitary	1-family to 1-person	reserved	Unsuitable.
Great Dane	slow	fair	poor	very alert/unsuited	sociable	open-family	likes almost everyone	Exceptionally good but a bit clumsy.
Great Pyrenees	slow	fair to poor	good	very alert/natural	solitary	1-family	reserved	Exceptionally good if brought up with them from puppyhood.
Komondor	slow	poor	good	very alert/aggressive	solitary	1-family to 1-person	reserved to aggressive	Tolerant if trained early and raised with children.

TABLE B-5.
Temperamental Characteristics of the 30 Breeds That Make Up the Working Group (continued)

| Breed | Learning Rate | Functionality | | Watch/Guard Dog | Sociability/ Solitariness | Owner/ Family | With Strangers | With Children |
		Obedience	Problem Solving					
Kuvasz	fast	very poor	good	very alert/ aggressive	very solitary	no-person	very suspicious	Bad.
Mastiff	slow	fair	fair to poor	very alert/ natural	sociable	1-family	friendly to reserved	Exceptionally good.
Newfoundland	fast	good	good	alert/unsuited	very sociable	open-family	likes everyone	Exceptionally good.
Old English Sheepdog (well-bred)	slow	poor	good	alert/unsuited	very sociable	open-family	likes everyone	Exceptionally good.
Old English Sheepdog (puppy-mill)	very poor	very poor	very good	very alert/ unsuited	very solitary	1-person	suspicious	Bad to dangerous.
Puli	very fast	poor	very good	very alert/ aggressive	very solitary	1-family	reserved to suspicious	Bad.
Rottweiler	slow	poor	fair	very alert/ aggressive	solitary	1-family 1-person	reserved to aggressive	Tolerant to bad.
St. Bernard (well-bred)	fast	fair	good	very alert/ unsuited	sociable	1-family	likes everyone	Exceptionally good.

Breed							
St. Bernard (puppy-mill)	fast	fair to poor	good	very alert/ sluggish to aggressive	solitary	1-family 1-person	reserved	Dangerous.
Samoyed	fast	poor	very good	very alert/ unsuited/	solitary	1-family	reserved	Exceptionally good.
Shetland Sheepdog	very fast	very good	very good	very alert/ very unsuited	solitary	1-family	reserved to shy	Tolerant of respectful children.
Siberian Husky	fast	poor	very good	normal/un-suited	very sociable	open-family	likes everyone	Exceptionally good.
Standard Schnauzer	fast	fair to poor	good	very alert/ aggressive	solitary	1-family 1-person	reserved	Tolerant of respectful children.
Welsh Corgi, Cardigan	very fast	very good	good	very alert/ natural	solitary	1-family	reserved to mildly aggressive	Tolerant of respectful children.
Welsh Corgi, Pembroke	very fast	good	very good	very alert/ natural	sociable	1-family	friendly	Tolerant of respectful children.

Thus, the vast majority of the breeds will give an alarm when their territory is invaded. Only 2 breeds, the Malamute and Husky, are considered only normally alert, and none are considered sluggish.

The majority of the Working breeds range from very dominant to intermediately dominant toward strange dogs in their territory. This is not surprising given the fact that many were developed as guard dogs for either property or livestock. Both jobs would involve confrontation with intruders. The breeds rated as submissive are the Collie and Sheltie; both were developed for herding, but not for protecting the flock. The two breeds rated very submissive are the puppy-mill German Shepherd and puppy-mill Old English Sheepdog. These breeds are also rated very dominant—indicating that these behaviors are opposite sides of the same coin, and when mass production is used, the sacrifice in quality control causes the temperamental characteristics of a breed to become variable and unpredictable in any one specimen.

In terms of dominance toward familiar adults, a major part of this group is ranked as potentially submissive, with the remaining breeds being characterized as intermediate or potentially dominant toward familiar people. Only two breeds of Working Dogs—the Doberman and puppy-mill Old English Sheepdog—fall into the extreme of very dominant, and both also fall into the opposite extreme of very submissive.

The tendency to dominate strangers combined with moderate to high territoriality is the quality that makes a natural guard dog. Since the Working breeds are on the average dominant, overintruding and territorial, you would expect that a large number of them would be guard dogs, and this is what you find. The rest of the breeds are ranked as unsuitable for guard work. This is not only because of size, since some of the largest breeds are considered unsuitable. The Sheltie is the only breed considered very unsuitable because of its friendly nature and small size.

Emotionally, the group varies from very stable to very vacillating. The majority of the breeds are ranked as stable, but a sizable number fall into the normal and vacillating categories. Three breeds are double-classified. Dobermans can be either very vacillating or normal, Collies can be either normal or vacillating and German Shepherds can be either vacillating or stable.

The average learning rate for the majority of Working Dogs is fast or very fast. The rest are slow learners. Even so, the majority of the dogs are rated as only fair, poor or very poor in obedience. A few are double-classified as fair/poor. Not surprisingly, German Shepherds are classified in four categories from very good to poor. Dobermans are ranked as either very good or very poor.

Problem-solving abilities are skewed toward the good end of the continuum.

Problem solving and learning are related in this group, with many of the breeds being ranked similarly in both dimensions. However, these two dimensions appear to be unrelated to obedience; dogs considered either very good or very poor in obedience can wind up in all levels of the other dimensions.

The majority of the Working Dogs are ranked as solitary or very solitary on the sociability dimension. One breed, the

TABLE B-6.
Potential Behavior Problems in Working Dogs

Behavior Problems	# of Breeds	% of 30 Breeds	% of Total Problems in Working Dogs
Barking/howling	7	23	7
Roaming	5	17	5
House soiling	5	17	5
Stealing food	7	23	7
Jumping	1	3	1
Destruction	7	23	7
Fear biting	5	17	5
Picky eating	0	0	0
Restlessness indoors	10	33	10
Irritable snapping	4	13	4
Phobias and Timidity	6	20	6
Dominance: Challenging	16	53	15
Guarding objects	7	23	7
Touch shyness	3	10	3
"Shy-sharpness"	3	10	3
Willful disobedience	9	30	9
Demanding	3	10	3
Drooling, Snoring, Wheezing	6	20	6

Behavior Problem Index 3.47

well-bred German Shepherd, is ranked as moderate in sociability; the rest are sociable.

Most of the Working Dogs are ranked as exceptionally good with children. In many cases, however, this rating is qualified, and some breeds range from tolerant to dangerous with children.

Table B-6 presents a summary of behavior problems that may be encountered in members of this breed group. There have been three extra problems added to the list when compared with the list for Sporting Dogs: obedience, demanding behavior and shy-sharpness. The first is self-explanatory. Demanding behavior involves a dog's barking, growling, pushing, jumping, etc., until it gets its own way. "Shy-sharpness" means a combination of fear and dominance aggression that can lead to viciousness. The most common problem involves dominance challenges.

The average number of problems per breed in the Working Dogs is 3.47. This is higher than in either the Sporting Dogs or the Hounds. The reason for this increase is twofold. First, many of the Working breeds are natural guard dogs, with the consequent increase in dominance and territoriality, and second, most of these breeds are quite large. However, the Working Dogs show less potential for roaming and house soiling.

It has to be kept in mind that the table summarizes problems potential and not actual number of problems. It gives you an idea of how problematic a breed from this group could be if treated improperly and/or acquired by an owner/family that does not suit the breed's temperament. If the breed's temperament and the owner's personality and life-style are properly matched, there should be no or minimal problems.

The Terriers as a Group

As can be seen from Table B-7, the Terriers as a group are more homogeneous on many dimensions than the Sporting Dogs, Working Dogs or Hounds. The Terrier breeds seem to cluster together more than the other breeds. This is probably caused by the different criteria for grouping breeds in each breed group. Terriers not only share common functions but, for

TABLE B-7.
Temperamental Characteristics of the 22 Breeds That Make Up the Terrier Group

| Breed | Activity Level | | Behavioral | | | Dominance / Submission | | Emotional Stability / Vacillation |
	Indoors	Outdoors	Vigor / Gentleness	Variability / Constancy	Territor-iality	Strange Dogs	Familiar People	
Airedale Terrier	very active	very active	vigorous	constant	moderate	dominant	intermediate	stable
American Staffordshire and Staffordshire Bull Terrier	very active	active	very vigorous to gentle	very constant	very high	very dominant	intermediate to very dominant	stable
Australian Terrier	active	active	moderate	variable	moderate	intermediate	submissive	stable
Bedlington Terrier	active	active	moderate	constant	moderate	dominant	intermediate	vacillating
Border Terrier	active	active	gentle	very constant	low	intermediate	submissive	very stable
Bull Terrier	active	active	very vigorous	constant	high	dominant	intermediate	stable
Cairn Terrier	very active	moderate	moderate	moderate	moderate	intermediate	intermediate	stable
Dandie Dinmont Terrier	active	moderate	moderate	moderate	moderate	intermediate	intermediate	stable

TABLE B-7.

Temperamental Characteristics of the 22 Breeds That Make Up the Terrier Group (continued)

Breed	Activity Level		Behavioral			Dominance / Submission		Emotional Stability / Vacillation
	Indoors	Outdoors	Vigor / Gentleness	Variability / Constancy	Territoriality	Strange Dogs	Familiar People	
Fox Terrier, Shorthaired	very active	very active	vigorous	variable	very high	dominant	more dominant	stable
Fox Terrier, Wirehaired	very active	very active	vigorous	variable	high	dominant	dominant	stable
Irish Terrier	active	active	vigorous	constant	high	dominant	dominant	vacillating
Kerry Blue Terrier	active	active	vigorous	constant	high	dominant	dominant	normal
Lakeland Terrier and Welsh Terrier	very active	very active	moderate	constant	high	dominant	intermediate	stable
	very active	very active	moderate	constant	moderate	intermediate	intermediate	stable
Manchester Terrier	very active	very active	moderate	variable	moderate	intermediate	intermediate	vacillating
Miniature Schnauzer (well-bred)	very active	very active	moderate	constant	moderate	intermediate	intermediate	stable
Miniature Schnauzer (puppy-mill)	very active	very active	moderate	variable	moderate	intermediate	dominant to submissive	vacillating

Breed							
Norwich Terrier	very active	very active	moderate	constant	moderate	intermediate	intermediate	stable
Scottish Terrier	very active	very active	moderate	very variable	high	dominant	intermediate	stable
Sealyham Terrier	inactive	moderate	vigorous	constant	moderate	intermediate	intermediate	very stable
Skye Terrier	inactive	moderate	moderate	moderate	moderate	intermediate	intermediate	vacillating
West Highland White	very active	very active	moderate	constant	low	intermediate	intermediate	vacillating
Wheaten (soft-coated)	active	active	vigorous	constant	low	intermediate	intermediate	stable

TABLE B-7.
Temperamental Characteristics of the 22 Breeds That Make Up the Terrier Group (continued)

| Breed | Learning Rate | Functionality | | Watch/Guard Dog | Sociability Dimension | | | With Children |
		Obedience	Problem Solving		Sociability/ Solitariness	Owner/ Family	With Strangers	
Airedale Terrier	fast	fair to poor	good	very alert/ natural	sociable	1-family	friendly to aloof	Tolerant.
American Staffordshire and Staffordshire Bull Terrier	fast	poor	poor	very alert/ aggressive	solitary	small-family	accepting to dangerous	Exceptionally good with its own and dangerous to others.
Australian Terrier	fast	good	very good	very alert/ unsuitable	sociable to solitary	1-family	reserved	Tolerant of considerate children.
Bedlington Terrier	fast	fair	fair	very alert/ unsuitable	sociable	1-family	friendly	Tolerant of considerate children.
Border Terrier	fast	good	good	alert/un-suited	very sociable	1-family	friendly	Exceptionally good.
Bull Terrier	slow	poor	poor	very alert/ natural	solitary	1-family	reserved	Tolerant of older ones but too vigorous for young ones.
Cairn Terrier	fast	fair	very good	very alert/ unsuited	sociable	1-family	reserved	Tolerant of older considerate children.

Breed	Speed							
Dandie Dinmont Terrier	very fast	fair to poor	very good	alert/unsuited	solitary	1-family	reserved	Bad.
Fox Terrier, Shorthaired	fast	poor	very good	very alert/unsuited	sociable	open-family	likes everyone	Tolerant with older children.
Fox Terrier, Wirehaired	fast	poor	very good	very alert/unsuited	sociable	open-family	likes everyone	Tolerant with older children.
Irish Terrier	fast	poor	good	very alert/natural	solitary	1-family	reserved	Tolerant of older children; plays hard.
Kerry Blue Terrier	fast	poor	very good	very alert/natural	sociable	1-family	reserved	Tolerant of older children.
Lakeland Welsh Terriers	fast	poor	fair	very alert/unsuited	sociable	1-family	friendly	Tolerant of older children.
Manchester Terrier	fast	poor	fair	very alert/unsuited	solitary	small-family to 1-person	reserved	Tolerant to bad even with older considerate children.
Miniature Schnauzer (well-bred)	fast	fair	fair	very alert/unsuited	solitary to sociable	1-family to open-family	reserved to friendly	Tolerant of considerate children.
Miniature Schnauzer (puppy-mill)	fast	poor	fair	very alert/unsuited	solitary to sociable	1-family to open-family	suspicious	Bad.

TABLE B-7.
Temperamental Characteristics of the 22 Breeds That Make Up the Terrier Group (continued)

Breed	Learning Rate	Functionality		Watch/Guard Dog	Sociability Dimension		With Strangers	With Children
		Obedience	Problem Solving		Sociability/ Solitariness	Owner/ Family		
Norwich Terrier	fast	poor	good	very alert/ unsuited	sociable	1-person	friendly	Tolerant of consid-erate children.
Scottish Terrier	fast	poor	fair	very alert/ unsuitable	solitary	1-family to 1-person	reserved	Tolerant with older considerate children.
Sealyham Terrier	fast	poor	poor	alert/un-suited	solitary	1-family	reserved	Tolerant with consid-erate children.
Skye Terrier	fast	fair	poor	very alert/ unsuitable	very solitary	small-family to 1-person	reserved to to very suspicious	Tolerant with older considerate children.
West Highland Terrier	fast	good	very good	alert/un-suited	sociable	open-family	likes everyone	Tolerant of consid-erate children.
Wheaten (soft-coated)	fast	fair	good	alert/un-suited	very sociable	open-family	likes everyone	Exceptionally good.

the most part, look alike, whereas in the other breed groups the appearance and function of the breeds are varied.

Terriers are generally active indoors. Only two breeds, the Sealyham and Skye, are ranked as inactive indoors. Most of the Terriers are ranked as high to very high in outdoor activity. Thus, anyone getting a Terrier should be prepared for a small to medium-sized bundle of almost constantly moving energy. However, only the muscular breeds, like the Staffordshire Bulls, were described as needing a lot of outdoor exercise. The rest seemed to be able to get along with only a fair amount of exercise.

The majority of Terriers are rated as moderately vigorous. The rest are ranked as vigorous or very vigorous. The three remaining breeds, the American and English Staffordshire Bulls and Border, are classified as gentle. It's paradoxical that the two Terriers bred for pit fighting would be double-ranked as gentle and very vigorous. This is because some specimens of these breeds seem to modulate their behavior more than do the other Terriers. They are gentle at times, especially when interacting with humans, and can be very vigorous at other times. Also, some Staffordshires don't modulate and stay constantly gentle or vigorous. The Border Terrier, unlike the others, is always gentle.

Most of the Terriers are rated as constant or very constant in behavior. The next-largest category is variable, and then moderately variable. Thus, the picture of the average Terrier temperament, up to this point, is of an active, moderately vigorous, constant animal.

Territoriality in the Terriers centers around high to moderate, most of the breeds being ranked as such. The remainder are classified as low or very high in territoriality. The Staffordshires, as expected of pit fighters, are the two breeds ranked at very territorial.

One hundred percent of the Terriers are ranked as intermediate or higher in dominance toward strange dogs. The majority are classed as intermediate, next most frequent is dominant and finally the two Staffordshire are the only breeds ranked as very dominant.

In terms of dominance toward familiar adults, most of the Terriers are rated intermediate in this category. Some are

ranked as potentially dominant or very dominant (the Staffordshires again) toward people. Only two breeds, the Australian and Border Terriers, are rated as potentially submissive.

The picture one gets is of a moderately territorial animal
that is likely to try to assert dominance over dogs and people
that show signs of fear and/or submission. These breeds are
likely to test their owner's dominance periodically by willful
disobedience and demanding behavior. Direct dominance
challenges are likely only with the potentially dominant breeds
and those which perceive their owner's timidity toward them.
The Terriers' fighting tenacity, idealized in the Staffordshires,
makes them small but formidable opponents. One should treat
most of the breeds with a firm command, based upon a secure
feeling of dominance and mastery, but not with prolonged or
intense physical force or punishment. Pain will make many
Terrier breeds counterattack. If you then lose the dogfight, your
dominance will be harder to win back.

The Terriers' territoriality makes them excellent watchdogs,
with 100 percent being rated as alert to very alert in watchfulness. Many Terriers, because of their watchfulness, may work
up a racket when they feel their territory invaded by strangers.
Despite their watchfulness, most of the Terrier breeds are
unsuitable as guard dogs, primarily because of their small size.
A small proportion of the Terriers bred are natural guards, and
these are the larger and more assertive animals. Of course, the
Staffordshires are considered, despite their size, to be aggressive guards. I would hate to be confronted by a large American
Staffordshire when it feels its territory is being invaded by me.

In terms of learning rate, almost all the Terriers are ranked
as fast, with one breed, the Dandie Dinmont, classed as very
fast; only one, the Bull Terrier, is classed as slow. Despite their
generally rapid learning, most Terrier breeds are considered
only fair to poor in obedience, with the remaining three breeds
(the Australian, Border and Westie) being ranked as good in
obedience. The middling to poor obedience of most Terriers is a
function of their potential dominant position.

The Terrier breeds vary greatly in problem-solving ability. A
small majority are rated as good, and the next-largest
grouping is rated very good. Then come the poor problem

solvers, and finally the fair problem solvers. There seems to be no powerful relationship between problem solving, obedience and learning rate; most of the poor problem solvers are rated as fast learners, and so on.

The Terriers form two distinct groupings on the sociability dimension. There is a split between sociable and solitary, with two breeds, the Border and Wheaten terriers, ranked as very sociable.

Only two breeds, again the Border and the soft-coated Wheaten, are described as exceptionally good with children, and I feel the Wheaten is questionable in this regard, since I have encountered a number of Wheatens whose main problem involved the biting of children. The rating means only that they are not likely to bite considerate older children. The rest of the Terriers are considered only tolerant with children. The Staffordshires are classed as dangerous because of a potential for tenacious and ferocious attack if they feel threatened.

Table B-8 summarizes the potential behavior problems mentioned for the Terriers. The average number of behavior problems per breed for the Terriers is 2.77. This is a bit more than

TABLE B-8.
Potential Behavior Problems in Terriers

Behavior Problems	# of Breeds	% of 22 Breeds	% of Total Problems in Terriers
Barking	7	32	11
House soiling	6	27	10
Stealing food	2	9	3
Jumping	1	5	2
Fear biting	2	9	3
Picky eating	2	9	3
Restlessness indoors	4	18	7
Irritable snapping	5	23	8
Phobias and Timidity	3	14	5
Dominance: Challenging	15	68	25
Guarding	8	36	13
Touch Skyness	1	5	2
Willful Disobedience	2	9	3
Snoring, Drooling and Wheezing	1	5	2
Overprotectiveness	3	14	5

Behavior problem index 2.77

for the Sporting Dogs (2.21), but less than for the Hounds (3) and the Working Dogs (3.47). Terriers don't seem to show problems with roaming, household destruction, demanding behavior and shy-sharpness as much as the other breeds. In fact, these behaviors were not mentioned at all. Thus they were dropped from the Terrier table. The most common behavior problem in Terriers is dominance challenges. The second-most-common problem is guarding objects or food from their owners. The third-most-common problem is excessive barking (Note: Terriers don't usually howl). This goes along with the general conception of Terriers as an aggressive and yappy group. However, they are less potentially yappy than is commonly believed.

It must be kept in mind that these potential problems are just that: potential. They do not have to occur. For instance, Miniature Schnauzers are noted for their yappiness. I live with a Miniature Schnauzer, named Smokey. Smokey is very alert and yaps at people who approach the house, especially when he is teathered outside, but becomes quiet on command and is reasonably silent indoors. The reason he doesn't carry on like some of his breed is that I anticipated the problem and worked on it from puppyhood. I didn't discourage it outdoors, since I value an alert barker as a watchdog. However, I made sure never to reward the behavior with attention and did discourage it indoors. In fact, I intentionally rewarded quieted behavior indoors. Thus Smokey, atypical for his breed, is a quiet and somewhat inactive dog indoors. The point being that forewarned is forearmed.

The Toys as a Group

Table B-9 summarizes the temperamental characteristics of the Toys. Perhaps because of their similarity in size, the Toys are homogeneous in temperament on many dimensions. A few generalizations can be made. Within and between breeds, the smaller the specimen, the more high-strung, behaviorally variable, emotionally vacillating and gentle you can expect the animal to be. Puppy-mill varieties are also prone to be similar to the smaller specimens.

On the activity dimension, a large majority of the Toy breeds tend to be very active to active indoors. The remaining three breeds, the English Toy Spaniel, Pekingese and Pug, are ranked as inactive indoors. The active breeds are not referred to as restless indoors, since their smaller size makes indoor hyperactivity tolerable or even amusing to their keepers instead of a pain in the posterior as the same behavior in the larger breeds can be. All Toy breeds are described as needing little outdoor exercise, primarily because they can get all the exercise they need running around the house or apartment. However, most of them are described as potentially active to very active outdoors.

On the vigor dimension, only one breed, the puppy-mill Poodle, is characterized as vigorous. The majority are ranked as moderately vigorous or less so. You would expect this, given their diminutive size.

These breeds form two clusters in terms of their ranking in variability. Over half are classed as variable to very variable (puppy-mill Toy Poodles). There are two moderately variable breeds, the Italian Greyhound and the Japanese Spaniel. The remaining breeds are ranked as constant.

Toys cluster in territoriality at high and low; the rest are described as moderate on this dimension. One hundred percent are ranked as very alert to alert as watchdogs. The very alert ones make a racket when intruders are perceived, owing to their size, all are considered unsuitable for guard work.

Their behavior toward strange dogs varies equally from attempts at domination to modulating their behavior in accordance with the behavior, but not the size, of the dog with which they are interacting. These animals will challenge even enormous dogs that back down to them, but will back down from dogs that act dominant. A few of the Toys are generally submissive in canine interactions.

With familiar adults, the majority of the Toys will act submissive. However, some Toys consistently try to dominate their human caretakers and will be intermediate in dominance, challenging those people they perceive as submissive and being submissive to those they perceive as dominant.

The majority of the Toys are described as emotionally vacil-

TABLE B-9.
Temperamental Characteristics of the 17 Breeds That Make Up the Toy Group

Breed	Activity Level		Behavioral		Territoriality	Dominance/Submission		Emotional Stability/Vacillation
	Indoors	Outdoors	Vigor/Gentleness	Variability/Constancy		Strange Dogs	Familiar People	
Affenpinscher	very active	very active	gentle	variable	moderate	intermediate	intermediate	vacillating
Brussels Griffon	very active	very active	moderate	variable	moderate	intermediate	dominant	vacillating
Chihuahua	very active	very active	gentle	variable	high	intermediate	submissive	vacillating
English Toy Spaniel	inactive	moderate	gentle	constant	low	submissive	submissive	normal
Japanese Spaniel	active	inactive	very gentle	moderate	low	submissive	submissive	stable
Maltese	very active	moderate	very gentle	variable	moderate	intermediate	very submissive	normal
Manchester, Toy	very active	very active	moderate	variable	high	dominant	intermediate	vacillating
Miniature Pinscher	very active	very active	moderate	variable	high	dominant	dominant	vacillating
Papillon	active	moderate	very gentle	variable	low	submissive	submissive	vacillating

Pekingese	inactive	inactive	moderate	constant	moderate	intermediate	intermediate	normal
Pomeranian	very active	moderate	moderate	variable	high	dominant	intermediate	stable
Poodle, Toy (well-bred)	very active	very active	gentle	variable	low	submissive to dominant	submissive	vacillating
Poodle, Toy (puppy-mill)	very active	very active	vigorous	very variable	high	submissive to dominant	dominant	very vacillating
Pug	inactive	inactive	gentle	constant	moderate	intermediate	submissive	stable
Shih Tzu	active	inactive	moderate	constant	low	dominant	dominant	stable
Silky Terrier	active	active	moderate	constant	low	submissive	submissive	stable
Yorkshire Terrier	very active	very active	moderate	constant to variable	high	dominant	intermediate	vacillating

TABLE B-9.
Temperamental Characteristics of the 17 Breeds That Make Up the Toy Group (continued)

Breed	Learning Rate	Functionality				Sociability Dimension		
		Obedience	Problem Solving	Watch/Guard Dog	Sociability/ Solitariness	Owner/ Family	With Strangers	With Children
Affenpinscher	fast	fair	good	very alert/ unsuited	sociable	open-family	likes everyone	Bad
Brussels Griffon	fast	poor	very good	very alert/ unsuited	sociable	open-family	friendly	Tolerant of careful children
Chihuahua	fast	very good to poor	very good	very alert/ unsuited	very solitary	1-person	reserved to suspicious	Bad
English Toy Spaniel	fast	fair	poor	alert/un-suited	solitary	1-family	reserved	Tolerant with considerate children
Italian Greyhound	fast	good	poor	alert/un-suited	solitary	1-family	reserved	Unsuitable and bad
Japanese Spaniel	fast	very good	very good	very alert/ unsuited	very sociable	open-family	likes everyone	Tolerant but fragile
Maltese	fast	good	good	very alert/ unsuited	solitary	1-family	reserved	Tolerant of careful children
Manchester, Toy	fast	poor	good	very alert/ unsuited	solitary	1-family 1-person	reserved	Bad

Breed							
Miniature Pinscher	fast	very poor	good	very alert/unsuited	very solitary	1-family to aloof	suspicious	Tolerant if raised with them
Papillon	fast	very good	good	alert/unsuited	sociable	open family	friendly	Tolerant of very careful children only
Pekingese	fast	very poor	poor	very alert/unsuited	very solitary	small-family to 1-person	reserved to aloof	Bad
Pomeranian	fast	very poor	good	very alert/unsuited	very solitary	small family to 1-person	reserved to aggressive	Bad
Poodle, Toy (well-bred)	very fast	very good	very good	very alert/unsuited	solitary	1-family	reserved	Bad
Poodle, Toy (puppy-mill)	very fast	poor	very good	very alert/unsuited	very solitary	1-person to no-person	aggressive to submissive	Dangerous
Pug	fast	fair	poor	alert/unsuited	solitary	1-family 1-person	reserved	Exceptionally good
Shih Tzu	fast	fair	poor	very alert/unsuited	sociable	open-family	friendly	Tolerant of considerate children
Silky Terrier	fast	fair	good	very alert/unsuited	sociable	1-family	friendly	Tolerant of considerate children
Yorkshire	fast	fair to poor	good	very alert/unsuited	sociable	1-family	friendly	Tolerant of considerate children

lating and high-strung to very vacillating. The remainer are ranked as normal and stable.

One hundred percent of the Toys are fast or very fast learners. A majority are good to very good problem solvers, with the remainder ranked as poor problem solvers. However, obedience varies across the entire dimension, some being very good, with the well-bred Toy Poodle ranked as the best.

On the sociability dimension the Toys form two clusters. In the largest one, the breeds rank as solitary or very solitary. The other cluster comprises sociable dogs, and one, the Japanese Spaniel, is ranked very sociable. Only one breed, the Pug, is classed as exceptionally good with children. About half are described as only tolerant with gentle, considerate children. Most of the rest are described as bad with children because of their potential for irritable snapping. One breed, the puppy-mill Poodle, is considered to be potentially dangerous. Italian Greyhounds are ranked as unsuitable, primarily because they are very fragile and high-strung.

Table B-10 summarizes the potential behavior problems mentioned for the Toy breeds. This group has the highest

TABLE B-10.
Potential Behavior Problems in Toy Dogs

Behavior Problems	# of Breeds	% of 17 Breeds	% of Total Problems in Toy Dogs
Barking	10	59	12
House soiling	9	53	11
Stealing	2	12	2
Fear biting	5	29	6
Picky eating	2	12	2
Irritable snapping	11	65	14
Phobias and Timidity	3	18	4
Dominance: Challenges	3	18	4
Guarding	8	47	10
Touch shyness	2	12	2
Willful disobedience	4	24	5
Demanding	9	53	11
Drooling, snoring and wheezing	5	29	6
Trembling	6	35	7
Pulling	2	12	2

Behavior problem index 4.76

average rate of behavior problems per breed so far encountered, the behavior-problem index being 4.76. Thus, Toys are a problematic class of tiny beast. However, their small size allows their owners to overlook their faults. In fact, the tininess may encourage owners to pamper them and give in to their demands. This would inflate the behavior-problem index by rewarding problem behaviors with attention.

The data indicate that the Toys, as a group, match their stereotype. Many of the breeds are prone to irritable snapping and may become excessive yappy barkers. More than half can show housebreaking problems, the same number act aggressively demanding of their owner's attention, and so on.

On the bright side, this group typically is not described as prone to roaming, jumping on people entering the house, destroying property, acting restless indoors or being viciously "shy-sharp." Obviously, they are too small for these types of behavior to be considered as problems. They may jump on people, but their impact is slight; they can't roam because they are rarely given the freedom. Destruction is minimized because of their small size. Restlessness may be interpreted as indoor playfulness, and even vicious Toys are relatively innocuous and can be controlled by most owners, some people thinking this behavior is cute and spunky.

In short, all Toys were bred to be pampered and protected by their owners. They are only a companion dog. Their only purpose is to suit the fancies and whims of their doting protectors.

The Non-Sporting Dogs as a Group

Table B-11 summarizes the temperamental characteristics of the Non-Sporting Dogs. This is done to facilitate comparison; however, it is not as meaningful for the Non-Sporting dogs as a group as it was for the other groups of dogs, since this group is basically a hodgepodge of breeds varying widely in size, shape and function.

One would expect the temperamental characteristics to vary as well as the physical characteristics, and this is exactly what is found. Indoor activity level forms two clusters, one that is ranked as active to very active and the other ranked as inactive

TABLE B-11.
Temperamental Characteristics of the 11 Breeds That Make Up the Non-Sporting Group

Breed	Activity Level		Behavioral			Dominance / Submission		Emotional Stability / Vacillation
	Indoors	Outdoors	Vigor / Gentleness	Variability / Constancy	Territor-iality	Strange Dogs	Familiar People	
Bichon Frise	very active	moderate	gentle	moderate	low	submissive	submissive	stable
Boston Terrier	inactive	moderate	gentle	moderate	low	intermediate	submissive	vacillating
Bulldog (English)	very inactive	inactive	gentle	very constant	high	dominant	intermediate	very stable
Chow Chow	inactive	active	very vigorous	very constant	very high	dominant	dominant	stable
Dalmatian	very active	very active	very vigorous	variable	moderate	intermediate	intermediate	vacillating
French Bulldog	very active	moderate	moderate	constant	moderate	intermediate	submissive	stable
Keeshond	active	active	gentle	variable	low	submissive	submissive	stable
Lhasa Apso	very active	moderate	vigorous	variable	moderate	intermediate	intermediate	vacillating
Poodle, Standard	inactive	active	vigorous	moderate	moderate	intermediate	intermediate	stable

Breed							
Poodle, Miniature	very	very active	moderate active	variable	high	intermediate	submissive	vacillating
Schipperke	very active	very active	vigorous	variable	high	intermediate	intermediate	vacillating
Tibetan Terrier	inactive to very active	moderate	vigorous	variable to constant	moderate to high	intermediate	intermediate	stable to vacillating

TABLE B-11.
Temperamental Characteristics of the 11 Breeds That Make Up the Non-Sporting Group (continued)

Breed	Functionality				Sociability Dimension			
	Learning Rate	Obedience	Problem Solving	Watch/Guard Dog	Sociability Solitariness	Owner/Family	With Strangers	With Children
Bichon Frise	fast to very fast	very good	very good	alert/un-suited	very sociable	open-family	very friendly	Exceptionally good
Boston Terrier	fast to very slow	fair to very poor	good to very poor	very alert/unsuited	sociable	1-family	friendly	Exceptionally good
Bulldog (English)	slow to very slow	poor	poor to very poor	very sluggish/aggressive	moderate	open-family	oblivious to friendly	Exceptionally good
Chow Chow	fast	very poor	good	very alert/naturally aggressive	very solitary	1-person to no-person	suspicious	Bad
Dalmatian	fast	good	good	alert/natur-al to unsuited	solitary	1-family	reserved	Unsuitable
French Bulldog	fast	poor	poor	alert/un-suited	solitary	1-family	reserved	Bad
Keeshond	fast	fair	fair	very alert/unsuited	sociable	open-family	friendly	Exceptionally good

Breed								
Lhasa Apso	fast	poor	fair	very alert/unsuited	solitary	1-family	reserved	Bad
Poodle, Standard	very fast	very good	very good	very alert/some natural	moderate	1-family	friendly to reserved	Exceptionally good
Poodle, Miniature	very, very fast	very good	very good	very alert/unsuited	solitary	1-family	reserved	Tolerant of considerate children
Schipperke	fast	poor	very good	very alert/natural	very solitary	1-family	reserved to suspicious	Bad
Tibetan Terrier	fast to slow	poor	fair	alert to very alert/unsuited to natural	solitary to very solitary	1-family	reserved to suspicious	Tolerant to bad

351

to very inactive. It seems that indoor activity varies inversely with the size and weight of the breed, with the Tibetan being doubly ranked. Outdoor activity varies widely from very active to moderate; the Bulldog is the only breed ranked as inactive.

Vigorousness varies from very vigorous to gentle. Behavioral variability varies from variable to very constant.

Territoriality clusters around moderate, with an equal number ranked high and ranked low in this dimension. Almost all these breeds are described as alert or very alert watchdogs, with only the bulldog ranked as very sluggish. For guard work the group forms two clusters, a slight majority being ranked as natural to aggressive in this work. The remainder are classed as unsuitable for guard work on the basis of temperament and/or size.

The Non-Sporting dogs are generally intermediate in dominance toward strange dogs. Most of these breeds are considered to be intermediate or submissive toward familiar adults, with only the chow ranked as dominant in this dimension.

In terms of emotional stability, there are two clusters—some

TABLE B-12.
Potential Behavior Problems in Non-Sporting Dogs

Behavior Problem	# of Breeds	% of 11 Breeds	% of Total Problems in Non-Sporting Dogs
Barking	1	9	2
House soiling	5	45	11
Destruction	1	9	2
Fear biting	2	18	5
Restlessness	1	9	2
Irritable snapping	5	45	11
Phobias and Timidity	1	9	2
Dominance: Challenging	4	36	9
Guarding	5	45	11
Touch shyness	5	45	11
Shy-sharpness	3	27	7
Willful disobedience	4	36	9
Drooling, snoring and wheezing	3	27	7
Hair Chewing	2	18	5
Trembling	2	18	5

Behavior Problem Index 4.00

breeds being ranked as stable and the Bulldog as very stable, with the remainder classed as vacillating.

Learning rate in this group is generally good to very good, with a few breeds described as slow or very slow. Problem solving varies from very good to very poor. Obedience also varies from very good to very poor.

In terms of sociability, the Non-Sporting breeds are skewed toward the solitary end of the dimension. Most are ranked as very solitary or solitary; one breed, the Bichon Frise, is ranked as very sociable. A cluster of breeds are described as exceptionally good and another cluster as bad with children. The Dalmatian is classed unsuitable.

Potential behavior problems are summarized in Table B-12. The behavior-problem index for the Non-Sporting Dogs is 4, but this doesn't mean very much given the range of breeds in the group. The highest potential is for house soiling, irritable snapping, guarding objects or being touch-shy. Some breeds may become dominant and challenging and/or show willful disobedience.

This breed group should probably be eliminated and the breeds reclassed in the other breed categories.

Appendix C

Considerations Based on Combinations of Temperamental and Behavioral Traits of Dogs: Implications for the Personality and Life-style of the Owner

Up to this point we have looked at each dimension of temperament separately. However, this is somewhat of an oversimplification. Each dimension of temperament interacts with the other dimensions to form a unique combination. The combination, like a chemical compound, may be different from the sum of the ingredients that go into making it. For example, table salt, or sodium chloride, is a chemical compound made by the seemingly explosive combination of sodium, a soft metal that burns on contact with water, and chlorine, a greenish gas that is poisonous when inhaled. Table salt is a crystal that dissolves in water and in any normal quantity is not at all poisonous.

So too do the dimensions of temperament combine, forming a psychological compound. Each dimension modifies or magnifies the other dimensions. Thus, it would make a considerable difference whether a very active breed was vigorous or gentle. A very active and vigorous breed would be producing a lot of forceful behavior per unit time; this would be intolerable to some people. Conversely, the high activity level of a gentle breed may be more tolerable.

What follow are five matrices that combine the dimensions I have deemed important to combine. The *movement matrix* combines indoor and outdoor activity dimensions with behavioral vigor and constancy plus the breeds' grooming needs. Grooming, of course, requires movement on the part of a dog's owner. The *dominance matrix* combines the dimensions of dominance toward familiar people and toward strange dogs with emotional stability. The *family sociability matrix* combines the dimensions of sociability toward the owner/family

354

with those of sociability toward children, dominance toward familiar people and emotional stability. Finally, the *watch / guard matrix* combines the dimension of watch- and guard-dog ability with territoriality and emotional stability.

Table C-1, the movement matrix, compares all breeds on the temperamental dimensions just outlined. To facilitate this, the dimension of indoor and outdoor activity was collapsed into two levels. The vigorous and constancy were collapsed down to three levels. Not all the cells of the matrix are filled, and the most frequent combination is breeds considered active indoors and outdoors as well as behaviorally vigorous and variable, with 20 breeds in that cell.

When there was more than one breed listed in a cell, they were organized in terms of increasing stockiness (bulk ratio) There is an asterisk, a plus or a check after some breeds. These codes show how much grooming is necessary. No symbol means a minimal amount of grooming, no more than twice a week for 20 minutes each time. An asterisk means a moderate amount of grooming, a plus means a good deal of brushing and grooming, a check means you should enjoy brushing and grooming because you are going to be doing a lot of it.

The following is a description of the people best suited for the breeds in each cell:

Description of People Best Suited for Each Occupied Cell in the Movement Matrix

Cell No.	Description
1	People best suited for these breeds should have a lot of energy, usually feel full of pep and like to keep busy during their leisure time. They should be the type that gets more done in a day than most people. They should like to work fast and keep busy, but may not like getting dirty. However, they shouldn't get restless or fidgety or impatient with stragglers. They should like sports like tennis and badminton and other outdoor activities that involve a mild amount of physical exertion. They could enjoy window-shopping, could be sentimental and may not like off-color stories or hearing "four-letter words". They should be efficient, rarely forgetting appointments, working hard, feeling uncomfortable when work piles up or in unclean and sloppy surroundings. They usually can be relied upon fully.
2	People best suited for these breeds would be identical to the previous group except that they should be more casual, taking their responsibility a bit more lightly. They should be the type that occasionally lets things slide, sometimes wishing they could be more organized. People suited

TABLE C-1.
Movement Matrix

Indoor and Outdoor Activity Level			(Variable)	(Moderate)	(Constant)	(Variable)
INDOORS ACTIVE - VERY ACTIVE	Outdoors Active - Very Active		*Keeshond *Shet. Sheep. Chihuahua *Affenpinscher *Ter. Poodle (wb) **(1)**	✓O. E. Shp. (wb) It. Greyhnd **(2)**	Am. Staff. +St. Schnauz *Am. Water Sp. Border Ter. **(3)**	*Samoyed W. Spr. Sp. *Scot. Ter. ✓Mini. Poodle +M. Schnz (pm) Australian Manchest. Ter. Toy Manch. Ter. *Yorkshire Ter. Brus. Griff. Min. Pin. **(4)**
	Outdoors Inact. - Mod.		*Golden Ret. *Cocker Sp. (wb) Basenji Papillon +Maltese **(10)**	Beagle ✓Bich. Fris. +Japan. Sp. **(11)**		*Pomeranian **(12)**
INDOORS VERY INACTIVE - MODERATE	Outdoors Active - Very Act.		Greyhound Saluki Whippet **(17)**	Ches. Bay R. *Otterhound *Rgh. Collie Sm. Collie **(18)**	*Newfound. *Bouv. des Fl Ber. Mt. Dog Clumber Sp. Sc. Deerhnd +Fem. Borzoi *Male Borzoi +The Belgian *Afghan Hnd. **(19)**	
	Outdoors Inact. - Moderate			Boston Ter. **(24)**	+St. Bern. (wb) Mastiff Gr. Dane +Ir. Wolfhnd Eng. Bulldog Pug *Eng. Toy Sp. **(25)**	C. Coat Ret. **(26)**
			Variable	Moderate	Constant	Variable
			VERY GENTLE — GENTLE			MODERATE —
			Behaviorial Constancy and Vigor			

*Eng. Cocker	Car. W. Corgi Pem. W. Corgi Eng. Spr. Sp. Sussex Sp. Sib. Husky *Eng. Cocker West High. Ter. *Welsh Ter. *Bedlington +M. Schnz (pm) +M. Schnz (wb) *Lakeland Ter. *Norwich Ter. *Yorkshire Ter.	+St. Bern (pm) ✓O. E. Shp (pm) *Komondor *Kuvasz *Al. Malamute +Ger. Shep (pm) Eng. Foxhound Boxer Am. Foxhound +Dalmatian Dob. Pinscher WH Pt. Grif. *Ir. Setter Harrier Sm. Dachshund +WH Dachshund Brit. Span. *Puli Schipperke Sm. Fox Ter. +WH Fox Ter. *T. Poodle (pm)	+Gi. Schnauz.	+Briard Am. Staff. +Ger. Shep (wb) Weimaraner Ir. Water Sp. G. SH Point. Pointer +Airedale Ter. Field Sp. +Wheaten Ter. +Kerry Blue Irish Ter.
(5)	**(6)**	**(7)**	**(8)**	**(9)**
*Dand. Dinmont Cairn Ter.	Labrador Ret. Fr. Bulldog +Shih Tzu +Silky Ter.	+Lhasa Apso		*Nor. Elkhnd
(13)	**(14)**	**(15)**		**(16)**
*Eng. Setter		*Gordon Str.	Ches. Bay R. ✓St. Poodle	Bullmastiff Bloodhound B&T Coonhnd Rh. Rdgback Vizsla
(20)		**(21)**	**(22)**	**(23)**
Basset Hnd. Fl. Coat Ret. *Skye Ter.	+Pekingese	+Tibetan Ter.		*Gr. Pyrenees *Chow Chow *Sealyham Ter. +Tibetan Ter.
(27)	**(28)**	**(29)**		**(30)**
Moderate	Constant	Variable	Moderate	Constant
VIGOROUS			**VERY VIGOROUS**	

Behaviorial Constancy and Vigor

= NEEDS MINIMAL GROOMING
* = SOME GROOMING
+ = NEEDS A LOT OF GROOMING
✓ = REQUIRES PROFESSIONAL SKILL

for the Old English Sheepdog should be tolerant for a great deal of indoor activity and enjoy brushing and grooming, but they don't have to be highly protective of their dog. People suited for the Italian Greyhound should be highly protective of the frailest of all dogs.

3   People best suited for these breeds would be identical to group 1 except that it would be best if they were even more responsible. They should be less likely to jump to a conclusion, figuring a problem out step by step.

4   People best suited for these breeds are similar to group 1 except that they should be a bit more tough-minded, logical, occasionally enjoying rough play. Miniature Poodle people should enjoy grooming and combing.

5   People best suited for the English Cocker Spaniel are similar to group 2 except that they should be a bit more tough-minded and logical, and able to stand a modicum of rough play.

6   People best suited for these breeds are similar to group 3, except that they should be a bit more tough-minded, logical and able to stand some roughhousing.

7   People best suited for these breeds should be as athletic, peppy and active as group 1. They should like to have a lot to do, setting themselves a fast pace. They should be as athletic as group 1 or more, being able to participate in the more vigorous sports like wrestling, boxing, football, etc. They should be more responsible and hardworking than group 1, using time to its best advantage and always planning ahead. However, they should be very tough-minded, enjoying working with tools, not minding work that gets their hands dirty or grimy. They should be the type that would enjoy a race or game better if they bet on it and the type that could be or once was the captain of a team. They should be very responsible and careful planners, people who would think ahead and consider the future consequences of their own or their dog's actions, being able to accurately foresee a potential behavior problem and start doing something about it right away. Most of the breeds in this group are sturdy to very strong in bulk and need a physically strong owner to control them. Potential owners of German Shepherds, Dalmatians and St. Bernards should be able to tolerate a lot of shedding and/or be willing to provide a lot of brushing. Old English Sheepdog owners should enjoy brushing.

8   People best suited for this breed are identical to group 7 except that they are only slightly less rigid, without imposing the rules through force.

9   People best suited for this group are similar to group 7 except that they should be prepared to exert more command over their dog, especially if they want to distract it from an ongoing behavior. Potential Airedale, Wheaten, Kerry Blue and Irish Terrier owners should be as tenacious as these terriers.

10   People best suited for this group should be similar to group 1, but they wouldn't have to be as athletic or involved in outdoor sports. Maltese owners must enjoy brushing and grooming.

11   People best suited for this group should be similar to group 1, but they would not have to be at all athletic. Potential Japanese Spaniel owners

must enjoy brushing and grooming, and Bichon Frise owners must be in love with these activities.

12   People best suited for the Pomeranian should be similar to group 4 minus the desire for vigorous outdoor exercise.

13   People best suited for these Terriers should be similar to group 5 minus the desire for athletics.

14   People best suited for this group should be similar to group 6 minus the desire for athletics. Shih Tzu owners should enjoy brushing and grooming.

15   The people best suited for Lhasa Apsos should be similar to group 7 minus the desire for athletics and the need to be very strong. They should enjoy grooming and combing.

16   The people best suited to a Norwegian Elkhound are similar to group 7 minus the desire for outdoor athletic activities.

17   People best suited for these breeds are similar to group 2, but they are more likely to be impatient with stragglers and irritated by a dog that would be active indoors.

18 & 24   People best suited for these breeds are similar to group 1 except that they are likely to get irritated by a dog that is active indoors. Most Terrier people don't need to be athletes and can be lethargic.

19 & 25   People suitable for these breeds are like group 3 people except for their intolerance of indoor activity. People suited for group 25 have to be willing to spend time exercising the larger breeds outdoors even though these dogs may not want to be exercised. They can be lethargic and quiet indoors. The Pug and English Toy Spaniel don't need much exercising.

26   People suited for the Curly-coated Retriever are like those in group 4 except that they should be willing to give it a bit more exercise and they are intolerant of indoor activity and restlessness.

20 & 27   These people are similar to the ones suited to the English Cocker Spaniels (group 5) except that they are intolerant of dogs that are active indoors. Also, they would have to be willing to exercise the Flat-coated Retriever moderately and provide extensive exercise for the English Setter.

28   Pekingese people are a very special breed. They don't have to be athletic, and they are generally intolerant of a dog that is active indoors. Otherwise they are like group 5. They also have to enjoy grooming and brushing their dog.

21 & 29   Tibetan Terrier people should be like group 7 but should have a desire for a quiet indoor dog, lack athletic desires and enjoy brushing and grooming. Gordon Setter people are also like group 7. In addition, they should enjoy a quiet evening at home, but be willing to give the dog a vigorous outdoor workout. Thus they should enjoy the outdoors. They don't have to do as much grooming as the Tibetan Terrier people.

22   People best suited for the Standard Poodle and Chesapeake Bay Retriever can be similar to group 8 people, but they can be intolerant of indoor activity or desirous of spending quiet evenings at home. How-

ever, they should be prepared to give their dogs sufficient exercise. Standard Poodle people should enjoy grooming.

23 & 30 People suited for these breeds should be like group 9 plus having an intolerance for indoor activity; such people are not athletic. The Chow and Pyrenees necessitate strength as well. The breeds in Cell 23 necessitate more of a willingness or desire on the owner's part to be athletic than the owners in Cell 30. Save the Vizsla, all the breeds in Cell 23 need very powerful owners. Tibetan Terrier owners should enjoy grooming.

The Dominance Dimensions Summarized

Table C-2, the Dominance Matrix, compares all breeds in dominance toward familiar adults and strange dogs (horizontally) as well as their emotional stability (vertically). The dogs are arranged in order of stockiness, the breeds with the highest bulk rate being placed at the top of each cell. In order to read the matrix, all one has to realize is that the dog's emotional stability, or lack of it, modifies whether it is dominant and bold or submissive and timid. Thus dogs in the cells labeled 1, 2 & 3 are very stable about their submissiveness toward familiar people; in addition, some are very stably submissive and some are very stably dominant toward strange dogs. The breeds in cell No. 11 show stable dominance toward man and beast alike. In No. 26, Italian Greyhounds, Old English Sheepdogs and Greyhounds are submissive to timid toward man and beast alike, but they vacillate in this, sometimes being very timid, nervous and high-strung. Cells No. 24 and 25 contain breeds that are emotionally very vacillating but dominant toward people. This is what breeders have called "shy-sharp." These breeds may be very dangerous to people, but may or may not present a threat to other dogs; it depends upon whether they are classed as dominant or submissive toward other dogs and, of course, their size.

The following provides a description of the personality of people most suited for the breeds in each cell.

People's Personality Suitable for Combinations of Emotional Stability and Dominance

| Cell No. | Description |

Cell No. — *Description*

1—3 These breeds are generally submissive toward people and could be suitable for both dominant (3) and submissive (1) people. Irritable people would not find 1 & 2 to be a problem. Note that St. Bernards and Newfs are listed in 2 & 4, so that submissive people should be careful to get the more submissive (or females) of these breeds.

4 & 5 These breeds are suitable for dominant people who have the power to control the dogs, especially in Cell 5. These people can be irritable with little adverse effect on the dog.

6—8 These breeds are suitable to submissive people. These people must be a bit more placid emotionally than those in Cells 1—3. Note that the Collie, German Shorthair and Afghan are multiple-classified.

9 & 10 These breeds are suited to emotionally stable people who are dominant to very dominant.
Note: 1. Three breeds are checked, meaning they are dangerous and aggressive toward strange dogs. People owning these breeds should be capable of exerting considerable control over their dogs to prevent serious dogfights.
2. Six breeds are multiple-classified.

11 The larger of these breeds can be owned only by superdominant, highly skilled, emotionally stable, fearless people—who should have their heads examined if they get one.

12—14 Except for the Dobermans, which are multiple-classified, these breeds are suitable for somewhat placid but submissive people.

15—16 These breeds are suitable to somewhat placid people who can be dominant (15) or very dominant (16) over their dogs. Note that the Samoyed is multiple-classified.

17 The Doberman in this cell should be owned only by very dominant, powerful, knowledgeable people who don't mind taking a risk.

18—20 These are high-spirited breeds which are suited for placid people who vary from submissive (18 & 19) toward to dominant (20) over their dogs. Note that the Toy Poodle, Collie and Afghan are multiple-classified.

21—23 These breeds are suitable for people who can be dominant (21 & 22) or very dominant (23) over their dogs. German Shepherd owners should be ready to exert powerful control over their dogs when other dogs are near.

24—25 Since all of these breeds are relatively small, their dominance can be controlled by people who are potentially dominant (25) to very dominant over their animals. Note that the Miniature Schnauzer (puppy-mill) is multiple-classified.

26—27 These breeds can be very timid, nervous, high-strung and snappy. The people suited for the Italian Greyhound and Greyhound can be submissive and should be very placid to put up with their dog's nervousness. Intermediately dominant people (27) who have little tendency toward physical aggression can live without fear with a submissive Dobie or Sheepdog, but remember, if these dogs are beaten or treated harshly

TABLE C-2.
Dominance Matrix

Emotional Stability					
Very Stable	FC Ret. **(1)**	+St. Bern. (wb) +Newfound. Gr. Dane Basset Hnd. Bouv. des Fl. Eng. Setter Border Ter. **(2)**	+Mastiff Bloodhound **(3)**		
Stable	Eng. Foxhound Golden Ret. Am. Foxhound +Collie Eng. Spr. Sp. Harrier Keeshond Eng. Cocker Beagle Bichon Fr. Silky Ter. Japan. Span. **(6)**	Otterhound CC Ret. Pem. W. Corgi +G. SH Point. Fr. Bulldog Field Span. Sib. Husky Pug Australian **(7)**	B&T Coonh. Boxer Car. W. Corgi +Afghan **(8)**		
Normal	C. Span. (wb) **(12)**	O.E. SHP. (wb) +Samoyed W. Spr. Sp. *Maltese **(13)**	+Doberman* **(14)**		
Vacillating	+Collie Ir. Setter Whippet Sheltie Papillon +Poodle, Ter.(wb) **(18)**	Borzoi Belgians WH Pt. Grif Vizsla Saluki Dachshund Boston Ter. Poodle, M. *Schnz. M. (pm) Chihuahua **(19)**	+Afghan +Poodle, Ter.(wb) **(20)**	+G. Shep. (wb) Ir. Water Sp. Britt. Span. **(21)**	
Very Vacillating	+O.E. Shp. (pm)♪ Greyhound It. Greyhnd. **(26)**		+O.E. Shp. (pm)♪ +Doberman (pm)* **(27)**		
	Submissive	Intermediate	Dominant	Submissive	
	DOMINANCE TOWARD STRANGE DOGS			DOMINANCE	
	SUBMISSIVE			INTERMEDIATE	
				Dominance Toward	

+ MULTIPLE-CLASSED
✓ VERY TOWARD DOGS
* VERY TOWARD PEOPLE

+St. Bern. (wb) +NewfoundInd. Gr. Pyrenees Clumber Sp. Sealyham Ter. **(4)**	+Mastiff Eng. Bulldog **(5)**			
+Ir. Wolfhound Sc. Deerhound Labrador Ret. Ches. Bay Ret. +G. SH Pointer +Pointer Dandi Dinmont St. Poodle Wheaten Ter. +Tibetan Ter. Cairn Ter. Welsh Ter. Schn. M (wb) Norwich Ter. **(9)**	Bullmastiff +Ir. Wolfhound Akita ✓Am. Staff. Ter. G. Shep. (wb) G. WH Pointer ✓Staff. Bull Bull Ter. +Pointer Airedale Ter. Am. Water Sp. Scottish Ter. ✓Basenji Lakeland Ter. Yorkshire Ter. Pomeranian **(10)**			Rottweiler Komondor Kuvasz Chow Chow Kuvasz ✓Gi. Schnz. Weimaraner ✓Rh. Ridgebk. Nor. Elkhnd. ✓St. Schnz. Shih Tzu WH Fox Ter. SH Fox Ter **(11)**
+Samoyed Pekingese **(15)**	Briard Gordon Set. Kerry Blue Ter. **(16)**			+Doberman* **(17)**
Dalmatian Skye Ter. +Tibetan Ter. Lhasa Apso Westie Schipperke Manchest. Ter. Affenpinscher **(22)**	+G. Shepherd ✓ Bedlington Ter. Manch., Toy **(23)**		+Schnz., M. (pm) Brus. Griff **(24)**	Sussex Sp. Puli Irish Ter. Min. Pinscher **(25)**
		+Poodle, Ter. (pm) +O.E. Shp.✓ **(28)**		*St. Bernard +O.E. Shp. (pm)* +Doberman** Cocker Sp. (pm) +Poodle, T. (pm) **(29)**
Intermediate	Dominant	Submissive	Intermediate	Dominant
TOWARD STRANGE DOGS		DOMINANCE TOWARD STRANGE DOGS		
INTERMEDIATE		DOMINANT		

Familiar People

they can become serious biters, especially the Dobies. Both breeds in Cell 27 may be prone to intense dog fighting and are sometimes very protective toward their masters. Specimens of either breed may attack another person or dog if the specimen misinterprets behavior toward its master as aggressive. Or they may be so timid and shy that they will hide from strangers, man and beast alike.

28   You can live with these breeds, but note their multiple classification.

29   Anybody intentionally getting one of the breeds classified in this cell is a self-abusive masochist. See your nearest psychologist if you have a strong desire to own a specimen of any of these breeds. However, some people get stuck with specimens falling into this category, since all are classified in more than one cell. For these people I feel truly sorry. Your dog's temperament can be altered, but it takes a very stable and placid, very dominant and assertive, and highly trained individual to pull it off without danger to himself (or herself) or others.

The Sociability Dimensions Combined

Sociability also can vary with the type of dog. It can mean the speed and number of people with whom a dog is able to permanently bond. It can mean playfulness even if no bond is formed. A dog can be considered sociable if it is friendly to strangers, and a dog can be friendly in a dominant or submissive way.

Family Sociability, Emotionality and Dominance

Table C-3 combines sociability with owner and family on the vertical axis, with the dominance toward familiar people and goodness with children on the horizontal axis, while emotional stability is indicated with asterisks. The breeds in each cell are listed in order of stockiness, the breed with the highest bulk ratio at the top of the cell. This combination can give you some idea of the ideal breeds for your family situation.

Within one cell, the dominance or submissiveness of a breed is shown by the typeface of the breed name. If the name is written in boldface type, the breed is considered dominant with familiar people. If the breed name is written in italic type, it should be considered submissive with familiar people. If written in standard type, consider the breed to be intermediate, modulating its displays of dominance and submission according to its perceived position of the person with whom it is interacting and the interpretation of that person's social signals. The families best suited for the breeds listed in each cell of the matrix are described below.

Description of Families Most Suitable to Breeds Grouped in Each Cell

Cell No.	Family Description
1	Families most suitable to the big Bernese Mountain dog or miniature Pug would be small and insular, not readily accepting others into the family structure and preferring to stay mostly by themselves. Bernese Mountain Dogs and Pugs tend to be shy with strangers and should be socialized early. The family would consist of a couple with no more than one child. These breeds will tend to be protective of the child, but obedient only to their adult master.
2	Families most suitable to these breeds can have or plan to have no more than two children. They can be relatively insular, but less so than group No. 1. The breeds intermediate in dominance will tend to listen more readily to dominant adult family members and be playful with, but not heed the commands of, the younger children. These breeds would be suitable for and could be protective of small children in the family. The children should have a limited number of friends coming and going.
3	The family best suited for these breeds is an open family with a fluid family structure. The family can be large, with many kids going into and out of the house. Except for the Sussex and Brittany, the breeds can stand the chaos caused by many children, running around, making noise and always being on the move. Note that the Sussex Spaniel is dominant and may heed only its master, ignoring even older children. The Clumber and Brittany spaniels may ignore the commands of younger ones. Some breeders feel that the Clumber Spaniel is ideal for an older couple who like a bit of outdoor exercise like a stroll, but want a quiet inside dog that can stand the comings and goings of grandchildren. The other less active breeds in this cell would fit this bill as well.
4	The family best suited for these breeds is a chaotic family with no definite hierarchy, either egalitarian or mixed. The family can be very large without causing trouble. Family members should be open and accepting of most people and not expect their dog to protect them. The dog would serve only as a playmate.
5	The Belgian Sheepdogs, Tervurens and Malinois would be suitable to the same family type as group No. 1 except that some Belgians are merely tolerant of children and should be socialized early. Also, the Belgians tend to be more emotionally vacillating, calling for a calmer family situation.
6	The families most suitable for these breeds would be as insular as those in group No. 2, but the family structure should be more packed. Most, if not all, of the members should be dominant over the dog. Children in

TABLE C-3.
Family Sociability Matrix

	NO PERSON		
	ONE PERSON	*Bern. Mt. Dog* Pug **(1)**	*The Belgians* **(5)**
Sociability with Owner/Family / **ONE FAMILY**		Mastiff *Basset Hound* *Bouv. des Fl.* *Bern. Mt. Dog* *B & T Coonhnd.* *Sc. Deerhound* Eng. Bulldog Boxer (L) Samoyed Labrador Retriever Ches. Bay Retriever Gordon Setter Harrier St. Poodle *Boston Terrier Pug Border Terrier **(2)**	Bullmastiff Gr. Pyrenees Irish Wolfhound Akita Briard Am. Staff. Bull Terrier (S) German Shepherd (wb) *The Belgians (S) *Curly Coat Retriever* *Collie *Irish Setter* **(6)**
	OPEN FAMILY	Newfoundland Clumber Spaniel Samoyed *English Setter* *Eng. Spr. Spaniel* *Sussex Spaniel *Vizsla *Field Spaniel* Keeshond Eng. Cocker Spaniel *Brittany Spaniel Bichon Frise **(3)**	St. Bernard (wb) Great Dane *Old English Sheepdog (wb)* *Golden Retriever* *Fl. Coat Retriever* *Wheaten Terrier Cocker Spaniel (wb)* **(7)**
	ANY PERSON	Bloodhound Eng. Foxhound Am. Foxhound Beagle **(4)**	Otterhound **(8)**
		EXCEPTIONALLY GOOD	**EXCEPTIONALLY GOOD + PROVISO**

(S) = SMALL FAMILY
(L) = LARGE FAMILY
** = VERY VACILLATING EMOTIONALLY
* = VACILLATING EMOTIONALLY

BEHAVIOR

TOLERANT		UNSUITABLE OR WORSE
*Borzoi *Saluki **(9)**		Kuvasz Chow Chow *G. Shep. (pm) Kuvasz *Borzoi *Ir. Water Spaniel **Greyhound *Saluki **Cocker Spaniel (pm) **Toy Poodle **(14)**
Komondor *The Belgians *Skye Terrier *Nor. Elkhound St. Schnauzer Scottish Terrier Norwich Terrier **(10)**		Chow Chow Giant Schnauzer Nor. Elkhound Am. Water Spaniel Pekingese *Manchester Terrier Manchester Toy Terrier *Chihuahua Pomeranian **Toy Poodle **(15)**
Rottweiler Komondor Weimaraner Rhod. Ridgeback *The Belgians Card. W. Corgi Pem. W. Corgi **Dobermans **Dobermans **Dobermans WH Point. Griffon Nor. Elkhound Pointer **Greyhound Bull Terrier Airedale Terrier St. Schnauzer *Afghan Hound	Welsh Spr. Spaniel Sealyham Terrier *Dachshund Kerry Blue Terrier Irish Terrier Cairn Terrier Basenji *Shet. Sheepdog *Whippet Welsh Terrier *Mini Poodle Mini Schnauzer (wb) *Bedlington Terrier Lakeland Terrier Australian Terrier Silky Terrier *Yorkshire Terrier Eng. Toy Spaniel *Miniature Pinscher *Manchester Toy Terrier **(11)**	*St. Bernard (pm) Rottweiler **Old English Sheepdog (pm) **Old English Sheepdog (pm) **Old English Sheepdog (pm) Am. Staff. Bull Terrier Giant Schnauzer Rhod. Ridgeback *Dalmatian **Doberman **Doberman **Doberman Nor. Elkhound Ger. WH Pointer Ger. SH Pointer Fr. Bulldog Dandie Dinmont *Puli *Lhasa Apso *Tibetan Terrier *Schipperke *Whippet *Manchester Toy Terrier *Toy Poodle (wb) **It. Greyhound **(16)**
West Highland White Shih Tzu Fox Terrier *Brussels Griffon *Papillon Maltese **(12)**		*Mini. Schnauzer (pm) *Mini. Schnauzer (pm) *Mini. Schnauzer (pm) *Affenpinscher **(17)**
Alaskan Malamute **(13)**		*Mini. Schnauzer (pm) *Mini. Schnauzer (pm) *Mini. Schnauzer (pm) **(18)**
TOLERANT		**UNSUITABLE OR WORSE**

WITH CHILDREN

Bold Face Type = Dominant or Above
Standard Type = Intermediate
Italic Type = Submissive or Below

these families should be older and able to exert control of the more dominant or intermediately dominant breeds and be able to take the rambunctiousness of the active breeds. Also, most of these breeds should be gotten young and raised as a puppy with the older children.

7   The families most suitable for these breeds would be as open as those suitable to cell 3. However, it would be best for the children to be older.

8   The families most suitable for the Otterhound are similar to those suitable to cell 4, but the children should be older to withstand this breed's clumsiness.

9   It is very hard for me to figure out what family would want the Borzoi or Saluki. These are antisocial, aloof dogs that are only tolerant to bad with children, not playful, and don't show much affection to their owners. Whoever gets one of these dogs should not have children. It seems to me that these breeds would be most suitable to a single person or couple, people not very accepting of outsiders or very demonstrative with themselves, and who like to show off.

10   These breeds would be best suited to singles or childless couples who have no intention of having children. They would be insular, critical of outsiders and, if accepting, only of very close friends and each other. Potential owners of the larger dominant breeds probably feel threatened by social forces and need the security of a powerful one-person guard dog. These people should not desire or need many visitors or friends. Owners of the smaller breeds probably don't feel as threatened by malevolent social forces, but they still would like to be warned.

11   Families most suitable for these breeds would be similar to group No. 2 except that they would be a little more threatened by societal forces. They shouldn't have any young children or have the possibility of being visited by young children. These breeds are suitable to self-contained families with older, mature, considerate, mostly assertive children. For the dominant breeds, the family hierarchy should be tightly packed, with all members capable of being dominant over the dog and controlling it. It would be best if families considering these breeds were emotionally placid and never given to arguments or excitation. All family members should be prepared to do some work training, socializing and dominating these breeds. The bigger and bulkier the breed, the older and more expert at dog control the family members should be.

12   These breeds are good for a single person, childless couple or older couple who have teen-age or older children. They can have a more open structure than group No. 11, and they can feel comfortable inviting people over. The families suitable to the dominant breeds should be dominant themselves, with all members being able to exert control over them.

13   The Alaskan Malamute is considered an any-person dog because it will try to dominate any person. The families best suited for this breed are Eskimos, and this is debatable.

14   There are no families suitable to these breeds, especially the dominant ones that are very vacillating.

15   These dogs are best suited to a single person or childless couple who have no intention of having children and have little or no interaction with children. They may not even like children. They are insular, having few

close friends. Owners of the toy dogs may want a dog as a child substitute.

16   Families suited to these breeds are similar to group 15, but a bit less insular. Owners of the larger dominant dogs probably feel threatened by outside societal forces. They should be very secure in their own dominance and ability to control animals. Owners of the smaller ones probably feel less threatened. Owners of the miniatures or toys may want a child substitute.

17   I haven't the foggiest notion of what families would be suited to a puppy-mill Mini Schnauzer. The Affenpinscher would be best for a single person or childless couple who don't interact much with kids but have many friends over.

Watchfulness and Guardian Capabilities Summarized

Table C-4 combines the watchdog and guard-dog dimensions with territoriality and emotional stability. The breeds are listed in each cell in order of sturdiness, which can be translated into the level of danger for intruders when they encounter natural or better guard dogs.

Cell 1: because these breeds are emotionally vacillating, low in territoriality, submissive to timid with strangers, and very alert watchdogs, they tend to be a nuisance. They will bark incessantly, usually from under a table or behind a chair, when any visitor enters or at the slightest noise, frazzling their owner's probably already shattered nerves. Most are small to tiny dogs, save the interesting addition of the puppy-mill St. Bernard. These breeds may be too noisy for an apartment, barking up a storm whenever someone walks past the door.

Cell 2 also contains incessant barkers. These are less likely to hide and more likely to shut up eventually than the breeds listed in Cell 1, especially if not threatened by the so-called "intruder."

Cell 3 may also be incessant barkers, but they are less alert and thus more discriminating than those in Cell 1 while they also bark from the safety of hiding places, they don't usually bark at the slightest hall noise outside an apartment.

Cell 4 may contain the best watchdogs. They will bark at noises, but are more discriminating than their comrades in Cells 1, 2 and 3. They will learn to adapt to repetitive hall

TABLE C-4.
Watch/Guard Matrix

Watchdog Capability

VERY ALERT

EMOTIONALITY: Vacillating

(1)
- St. Bernard (pm)
- Dalmatian
- Skye Ter.
- Collie
- WH Pnt. Griffon
- Ir. Water Span.
- Dachshund
- Boston Ter.
- Lhasa Apso
- Tibetan Ter.
- Bedlington Ter.
- Schnz. Min. (pm)
- Manchester Ter.
- Brussels Griff.
- Papillon
- Affenpinscher
- Poodle, Toy (wb)

(6)
- O.E. Sheep. (pm)
- Sussex Span.
- Tibetan Ter.
- Poodle, Mini.
- Manch. Toy Ter.
- Yorkshire Ter.
- Chihuahua
- Mini. Pinscher
- Poodle, Toy (pm)

EMOTIONALITY: Stable

(2)
- St. Bernard (wb)
- Great Dane
- Collie
- Ger. SH Pointer
- Harrier
- Field Span.
- Sealyham Ter.
- Keeshond
- Tibetan Ter.
- Cairn Ter.
- Shih Tzu
- Pug
- Welsh Ter.
- Schnz., Min. (wb)
- Norwich Ter.
- Australian Ter.
- Silky Ter.

(7)
- Chow Chow
- Pem. W. Corgi
- Scottish Ter.
- Tibetan Ter.
- Basenji
- Lakeland Ter.
- Fox Ter.
- Pomeranian

ALERT

EMOTIONALITY: Vacillating

(3)
- Irish Setter
- Greyhound
- Vizsla
- Saluki
- Afghan Hound
- Britt. Spaniel
- Tibetan Ter.
- West High. White
- Shet. Sheepdog
- Whippet
- It. Greyhound

(8)
- Cocker Span. (pm)
- Tibetan Ter.

EMOTIONALITY: Stable

(4)
- Newfoundland
- O.E. Sheep. (wb)
- Basset Hound
- Bloodhound
- Otterhound
- B&T Coonhound
- Eng. Foxhound
- Golden Ret.
- Samoyed
- Labrador Ret.
- Flat-coat Ret.
- Am. Foxhound
- Curly-coat Ret.
- Gordon Setter
- Ir. Water Span.
- Eng. Setter
- Eng. Spr. Span.
- Pointer
- Fr. Bulldog
- Welsh Spr. Span.
- Dandie Dinmont
- Wheaten Ter.
- Eng. Cocker Sp.
- Beagle
- Cocker Sp. (wb)
- Pekingese
- Tibetan Ter.
- Bichon Frise
- Border Ter.
- Eng. Toy Span.
- Japanese Span.
- Maltese

(8)
- Tibetan Ter.

VERY SLUGGISH-ATTENTIVE

EMOTIONALITY: Vacillating

(5)
- Borzoi

EMOTIONALITY: Stable

(5)
- Ir. Wolfhound
- Clumber Span.
- Scot. Deerhound
- Sib. Husky

(9)
- Alaskan Malamute

Low - Moderate	High - Very High
TERRITORIALITY	
VERY UNSUITABLE TO MODERATE	

Guard-Dog Capability

Tibetan Ter.	Tibetan Ter. Irish Ter. Schipperke	Ger. Shep. (pm) Bel. Malinois Bel. Sheepdog Bel. Tervuren	St. Bernard (pm) Rottweiler Ger. Shep. (pm) Doberman Pinscher Puli
(10)	**(14)**	**(17)**	**(18)**
Mastiff Bouv. des Fl. Gr. Pyrenees Bernese Mt. Dog Card. W. Corgi Airedale Ter. Poodle, Std. Tibetan Ter.	Akita Ger. Shep. (wb) Weimaraner Ches. Bay Ret. Nor. Elkhound Ger. WH Pointer Bull Ter. Kerry Blue Ter. Tibetan Ter.		Bullmastiff Komondor Kuvasz Briard Am. Staff. Bull Ter. Schnauzer, Std. Kuvasz Giant Schnauzer Rhod. Ridgeback Doberman Pinscher
(11)	**(15)**		**(19)**
Dalmatian Tibetan Ter.	Tibetan Ter.		
(12)	**(16)**		
Boxer Labrador Ret. Gordon Setter Ir. Water Span. Pointer Tibetan Ter.	Tibetan Ter.		
(13)	**(16)**		
			Eng. Bulldog
			(20)
Low - Moderate	High - Very High	Low - Moderate	High - Very High
TERRITORIALITY		**TERRITORIALITY**	
NATURAL		**AGGRESSIVE**	
Guard-Dog Capability			

noises in an apartment and select for attention only those noises and people they find novel or peculiar. With reassurance they can be induced to be quiet. In essence, they give alarm and then, if everything turns out to be Kosher, they will quiet down.

In Cell 5, we have the breeds that may sleep through an intrusion into their owner's household. The Borzoi may snap at an intruder if disturbed. The Husky may greet intruders with friendship. The size of the two gigantic hounds may be enough to scare wrongdoers away, even though their placid temperament precludes attack. Some Irish Wolfhounds may be natural guard dogs; then heaven help the intruder.

In Cell 6 we are back to the incessant barkers. Like those in Cell 1 they may continuously bark with uninterrupted ardor. However, these breeds are more likely to put on a brave show, lunging out from their hiding places, the smaller ones snapping at the heels of passersby. Old English Sheepdogs may become formidable but fearful attackers, easily scared off by an aggressive approach. These are the breeds that will bark continuously at an intruder from a distance. They may become brave if the intruder turns his or her back to them, which may result in some nipping at heels, but they will immediately retreat to a defensive distance when the intruder turns and faces them. They are intimidated by a direct frontal approach and encouraged by a retreat. They are also hard to shut up and don't readily habituate to innocuous noises they have heard repeatedly.

The Cell 7 breeds are not as "cowardly" as their comrades in Cell 6. They may be incessant barkers and may react to a frontal approach aggressively. The small ones may nip at the intruder's trousers from the front as well as the back. The owners call them brave. The Tibetan and Lakeland terriers, the Corgi and the Basenji may be able to back up their threats by a formidable bite. The Chow can be quite ferocious, but usually isn't.

The Cocker Spaniel and Tibetan Terrier in Cell 8 may bark at intruders. The puppy-mill Cockers are usually smaller than their well-bred cousins and don't have the physique to back up their threats, but they may bark incessantly. Tibetan Terriers are peculiar, since they can be found in Cells 1, 2, 3, 4, 6, 7, 8,

10, 11, 12, 13, 14, 15 and 16. This is because they are a relatively new breed in the United States whose type has not as yet been established.

Cell 9 contains the Alaskan Malamute, which is attentive to noises, may bark, but despite its size is not considered a good guard. However, some Malamutes can be ferocious.

In Cell 10, we have the Tibetan Terrier again. In 11 we have some of the better guard dogs, since they are very alert when on the lookout, but don't bark incessantly because they become habituated to common noises. Their protectiveness toward home and family are readily controllable by most owners. The great size of some naturally scares away intruders. They tend to hold intruders at bay rather than attacking. The Airedale can be a tenacious fighter. The Cardigan will drive intruders away. Surprisingly, the Standard Poodle falls into this category.

Cell 14 contains some very alert natural guard dogs that are high in territoriality, but are emotionally vacillating. This means that they may fearfully attack and/or challenge would-be intruders. The Terriers would not be dissuaded by a counterattack. They may be incessant barkers. Counter threats may increase both their fear and their ferocity.

Cell 15 contains barkers and good guard dogs. They will bark at strange noises, most may challenge intruders and they can be taught to attack. However, they can usually be controlled by their owners.

In Cell 17 the breeds are starting to get dangerous. The ones in this cell may be dangerous because of their vacillating fearfulness. However, they are outclassed by those in Cell 18. Breeds in this cell can be the most viciously dangerous breeds known. They are what breeders call "shy-sharp." They attack both out of fear and for territorial defense. Their great size can make them very formidable to intruders and very protective of home and loved ones. But watch out—they may be uncontrollably aggressive even toward visitors. They don't make ideal pets.

Cell 19 contains the potentially dangerous breeds. They may attack out of sheer dominance and territoriality. These breeds, especially the larger ones, should be owned only by experts in controlling aggressive dogs. Their potential for harm is too great for anyone else to own them. Even then, they should receive extensive training and socialization. With that, they may be passable as pets.

The English Bulldog is all by itself in Cell 20. It is the only breed that is a very sluggish watchdog but a formidable guard dog. In essence, you have to wake it up and point it toward the intruder, whom it may attack if sufficiently annoyed and if it has the energy.

Index